LAID

YOUNG PEOPLE'S EXPERIENCES *with* SEX *in* *an* EASY-ACCESS CULTURE

Edited by Shannon T. Boodram

SEAL PRESS

Laid
Young People's Experiences with Sex in an Easy-Access Culture

Published by
Seal Press
A Member of the Perseus Books Group
1700 Fourth Street
Berkeley, California

Library of Congress Cataloging-in-Publication Data

Laid : young people's experiences with sex in an easy-access culture / edited by Shannon T. Boodram.
p. cm.
ISBN 978-1-58005-295-5
1. Young adults—Social conditions. 2. Young adults—Sexual behavior. 3. Sex in popular culture. I. Boodram, Shannon T.
HQ799.5.L325 2009
306.7084'2—dc22
2009010281

Cover design by Silverander Communications, Santa Barbara, CA
Interior design by Tabitha Lahr
Printed in the United States of America
Distributed by Publishers Group West

CONTENTS

CHAPTER 5
SAVE YOUR CHERRY . . . OR BANANA

LAID

THE BASEMENT SMELLED LIKE SEX—THAT THICK, MUSTY scent that sits in the air and clings to everything it touches.

I inhaled deep and hard, thinking about the heated moments that had just passed. The moments when I was too busy creating the odor to even notice its sticky presence. And now that it was all over, I could feel it in the back of my throat, see it rising from the indecent sheets, and taste it in my tears.

I adored him, but he and I had somehow worked ourselves into some kind of arrangement where it was okay for him to get off and get out. My generous moans and sex-kitten expressions would give him the impression that I was in fact getting mine as well. And on some nights I would work my mind up so feverishly that I believed this was in fact what I wanted from him and for myself.

At age seventeen, I fancied myself a kind of a sexual vixen. It was not that I particularly loved the feeling of another body inside of mine; sex was like a part of life that I had become accustomed to. More accurately, it was something that the males in my life had grown accustomed to—quite fondly accustomed to. It had gotten to the point where I sincerely wondered if I was even interesting without it.

I inhaled again, in an attempt to absorb the air's heavy stench that was weighing down my shoulders. I closed my eyes and tried to forget the heartbreaking words he'd shared just before he left: "You're the coolest, Shannon—you're just like a guy." He'd given me an appreciative glance, then turned and left.

I understood his words more than I cared to: I was cool enough to make him come, but apparently not enough of a woman to make him stay.

Seventeen years old, three sexual partners, and zero pleasant experiences or relationships to justify any of them. I realized that if this was getting laid, maybe I should try standing up instead.

INTRODUCTION

LAID IS NOT YOUR TYPICAL SEXUAL EDUCATION BOOK. It's raw, honest, steamy, scary, inspiring, and exciting stories from young people ages eighteen to twenty-five, across North America, on their experiences with sex as teenagers. The book is separated into five chapters based on five common young-adult sexual scenarios: hookups, positive experiences, physical consequences, date rape, and abstinence. No two stories are alike, but in each chapter you will find the following components:

THE CHAPTER INTRODUCTIONS

I have read every story in each chapter—and the ones that were not included—more times than I could possibly count! So I have a good idea of what you're about to get into and some of the things you should keep in mind before you dive in. These intros will brief you on the content and give you an inside look at how the chapters were created and inspired.

THE STORIES

Each chapter includes anywhere from seven to ten different submissions. Some people chose to share their monumental sexual experience in story form; others opted for poetry or letters. No matter what the medium, I had a stringent requirement that everyone's delivery remain consistent. This is exactly what I told all the authors before they wrote their stories: Write as though you are talking to your best friend. Your piece should show and *not* tell. Include as much detail as possible, and avoid lecturing at all costs! Give each component of the story equal attention: Set the scene for the reader, give an in-depth description of the sexual encounter, and illustrate how that experience shaped you after the fact. Show us who you are, describe to us how you felt, but please trust us (the reader) to draw our own conclusions.

You will notice that the stories tend to end slightly abruptly, without a "what I learned" conclusion—this was done purposely.

GOT QUESTIONS?

Remember sex ed in school, where you had the most inappropriate questions that you would never dare ask, for fear of coming across as a nosy weirdo? I found while reading people's stories, I had a lot of questions like that. To be honest, I had never heard of HPV, I wasn't clear on what date rape was, exactly, and I sure as heck didn't know much about the G-spot until I read certain submissions. So I thought, *Okay, if I don't know this stuff, chances are some readers won't either.* The Q&A section is a place where those stupid/bold/crude/insensitive/nosy and incredibly valuable questions get answered. Unless stated otherwise, I wrote the responses. In addition, contributors to the book, anonymous donors, and experts took a crack at shedding light on some of the gray areas you may run into while reading each chapter.

CHECKPOINTS: THE READER ACTIVITIES

This book is 100 percent about you. Every single story was written so you could learn from it, but I know better than to assume that listening and absorbing are all the sexual education you'll need. The best lessons come from self-discoveries. The activities are a way for you to relate each chapter's information to yourself and your own experiences. You'll find Checkpoints at the end of each chapter that will help you draw conclusions while it's still fresh in your mind. These are extremely important, so if I come to your house and see *Laid* on your coffee table with the Checkpoint pages left blank . . . you better start running.

So, that's *Laid* in a nutshell. Although all of you will interpret this book in your own way, I (and the other *Laid* contributors) have tried to make it as straightforward as possible. Here are some more things that I think you should know before you begin:

THE GOAL

The purpose of this book is to arm you with the information, hindsight, and confidence to pursue an amazing sex life. What that amazing sex life entails is up to you. Sexuality is an extremely personal aspect of every individual's life. There is no one-size-fits-all format. As long as you adopt a sexual mindset that makes you happy, keeps you healthy, and does not impinge on the health or happiness of your chosen partners, it's right. We truly live in an easy-access culture, which, as I'm sure you've learned, is both a blessing and a curse. Although multiple forms of expression like text-messaging, downloading, googling, and net chatting may appear to make monitoring youth's activities simpler, in actuality these tools give youth independence, personal identity, and privacy from adults much sooner than in previous generations, which means that we should be savvy about adult behavior a lot sooner as well. Personally, I don't think it matters how old you are—I want you to read this book and in the end feel like a proud, confident, sexual being. I want you to hear each story out, then form an enhanced understanding of the experiences you want, and the ones you want to avoid.

THE INSPIRATION

At around the age of fourteen, I became very curious about sex. I wanted to know everything, and I snatched any medium at my fingertips that could answer my questions without arousing any suspicion from anyone I knew. Sadly, online porn is more accessible and private than credible sources. I now consider this a huge reason why I threw myself into a sexually unsatisfying lifestyle. Young adults need to be taught about pornographic content the same way they are warned about WWE wrestling: It's not real.

There were other reasons why I became a pleaser: My understanding of my own sexual anatomy was grossly underdeveloped; I learned early that sex was the easiest way to approach a guy; I found it very hard to say stop, even harder to express what I actually wanted; and at least by limiting myself to hookups, no one could break up with me, since the guys never seemed to want to be my boyfriend anyway.

By the age of eighteen, I felt trapped by my own sexuality. I was in a lot of emotional pain, and I didn't find that I was experiencing the physical gain to justify it.

I lacked truth—or, more accurately, I lacked enticing truth. The numbers, facts, and "sex should wait for love" school curriculum did not fit in with what I understood as my friends and role models or my own reality.

By nineteen, I began to realize how phony that "reality" was. Friends were getting abortions; some had children; others finally admitted to the lack of physical pleasure in their sexual experiences. Stories of STIs were creeping out of the woodwork, and testimonies of emotional emptiness trailed behind broken sexual relations. It seemed everyone was getting tired of lying.

After being exposed to so much honesty, I became as sexually curious as I had been at fourteen, but this time I knew where to look for the real answers. I feverishly sought out facts, numbers, and my peers' stories because they now held relevance. I avoided the media and its orgasmic tales and I read up on female sexual anatomy, but I still felt there was more I needed to learn. I had gotten so much information from my small circle that I decided to branch out and see what others around North America had experienced.

On what seemed like an overnight whim, I launched a website called Save Your Cherry (www.saveyourcherry.com), a small, poorly designed site that shared my own experiences and encouraged others to write in and tell theirs. It initially broke my mother's heart, but it went on to help hundreds of thousands of curious and perhaps a little fed-up young people like me. Based on the site's success, I decided to try to turn the collection into a book. I obsessively recruited writers using youth-networking services like MySpace, Facebook, and Urbis. There is no way to calculate just how many hours I spent telling others about a book that needed their voice.

Laid is a labor of my love and a testament to the power of peer mediation. At times it is shocking, tear-jerking, and beautiful, but most important, it is always honest.

THE QUESTION

Reader, if your sexuality was a canvas and every partner you've ever had painted something on it, what would it look like? Is your canvas crowded? Is it a masterpiece? Or is it straight graffiti?

Right now I'm going to ask you to turn to page one so that you can begin to analyze and learn from canvases that belong to about forty different young people who have chosen to share their experiences with sex in an easy-access culture.

CHAPTER 1

HOOKUPS THAT FELL DOWN

INTRODUCTION

"So why do people hook up with strangers?" I was being interviewed, along with two other young women, for an annual article on teen sex in a Toronto paper.

The three of us immediately began throwing out different rationalizations: to make people like them; because the media says it's cool; to be popular; because they're afraid to say no; to feel good. All of our responses had truth to them, but we all knew that not one of us had the exact right answer.

People hook up with people they "don't have feelings for" (chances are, at least one of them has genuine feelings for the other) for a lot of different reasons. Obviously—there are tons of books and movies out there on the subject, because no one has cornered the market on the full range of experiences. But I'm going to go ahead and take a stab at an all-encompassing answer: Hooking up is nothing more than settling; it is the microwavable burrito of sex.

It's the fast-food version of getting what you really want, be that love, attention, rebellion, an orgasm, or just something to talk about. You buy into it because it seems like a good, quick meal idea, but shortly after the few first bites you realize that the momentary hunger relief is not going to make up for the crappy feeling you're probably going to have later.

For a while on Facebook, when you added a new friend to your buddy list you were prompted to explain how you met that person. On a list of twelve possible introduction scenarios, right under "We met randomly" and right before "We dated," was the box "We hooked up."

It's no wonder that I received the most submissions for "Hookups That Fell Down." There are over fifty more testimonies from young people that I could not include in this chapter because I simply didn't have enough space, and I wanted to make each submission as distinct as possible.

Laura Sessions Stepp, Pulitzer Prize–winning journalist and *Washington Post* columnist, wrote a book on the new generation's phenomena titled *Unhooked: How Young Women Pursue Sex, Delay Love, and Lose at Both.* The book is an in-depth exploration of why many young women are pursuing empty sexual encounters, even though doing so drives them further from what Stepp gathers are women's ultimate goals: requited love and self-empowerment. She found that most people use the hookup option as an excuse to approach a person they are attracted to.

"There are a couple of other possible goals," Stepp told me in an interview. "One may be sexual pleasure. Another is the feeling of being really close to another person, if only for a short while. And some hook up hoping to get a boyfriend."

But what about the scream at the top of your lungs, throw caution to the wind, no emotional strings, and freedom aspects of hooking up? For the too-busy-for-romance-woman or the jaded lover, a hookup buddy could surely be an ideal situation, providing her with sexual release without her having to risk a soured relationship. However, when I asked Stepp, who researched for her book by shadowing college and high school women, if this may indeed be the case, she responded, "Not really.

"The best sex is in a loving relationship," she continued. "I'm not saying have less sex; I'm saying have more romance."

I recall the times when I was involved in a "friends with benefits" relationship. I modeled my sexuality after make-believe media stars while desperately trying to find someone who didn't want my body solely for his own satisfaction.

I recall a conversation I had when I was seventeen with a boy I had just met at the mall: "So, how often do you like to have sex?" Looking back now, I realize that I sounded more like a prostitute than I did the secure, confident vixen I was trying to play. Needless to say, after that conversation this individual was never interested in finding out what my hobbies were or what my favorite color was. He wasn't necessarily a dog, but I certainly was a dipstick for not realizing that people will want what you've told them they can expect—so use your body as a way to market yourself only if that's what you intend to sell.

The chapter you are about to read is more than likely a summation of the most common North American teenage sexual experiences. This is the chapter for which I received the most poems, stories, and letters by far. This is the chapter that I could categorize four-fifths of my friends' experiences under, and it's the subject matter you'll delve into here that inspired me to begin compiling this book.

A report published by psychologist Elizabeth Paul, of the College of New Jersey, based on surveys of about five hundred students from 2002 to 2004, found that three-quarters of those surveyed had hooked up. Of those three-quarters, about half had had sexual intercourse, and less than a quarter of their hookups had become an official relationship.

"Ask them, in the days after a hookup, how they feel," said Stepp. "Happy? Confident? Strong? Independent? Or are they checking their cell phones to see if the other person called? If it's the latter, maybe what they are really after is a relationship, not a hookup, but if they are really and truly happy—go for it."

LANE TWO

Shannon T. Boodram, 20 at the time of writing, Ontario

IT WAS JULY OF 2001 AND I WAS SWEET SIXTEEN, DOING some big things. I was on the warm-up track, getting my body ready for my first race in the World Youth Track and Field Championship in Debrecen, Hungary.

I sat in the middle of the field, stretching my legs while a bunch of butterflies were doing lord knows what in my stomach. I looked up and saw one of the other girls on Team Canada coming toward me. The team was a collection of athletes from across the country, so I had only met some of these people a few days prior. If this had been any one of my regular teammates, she would have known better than to bother or talk to me close to race time.

"Nervous?" she asked, sitting beside me.

"Always."

"Aren't you going to watch the 100 meters? M is running now."

I looked up at the big screen that was set up so competitors could watch their teammates run from the warm-up area just outside the arena. A bunch of boys were setting their starting blocks in their skintight suits. Then the camera panned across the eight competitors and did a close-up on each athlete as the monitor displayed his name and the country he was representing. It's one of those details I will never forget: ALEX, GREAT BRITAIN, LANE TWO.

"He is freakin' gorgeous!"

"But you can't see his teeth. You know British people all have messed-up smiles." My teammate nudged me, then laughed at her own comment.

I ignored her remark; she was irritating me and distracting me from the Adonis on the screen. I had honestly never seen anybody that good-looking before in my life, not even on TV or in a magazine. He was mocha skinned, probably half black and half white, with a clean fade and slanted eyes. The race started, and as my friend cheered for our teammate, I just kept my eyes on Lane Two.

I went on with my day; I ran my races and looked around like a madwoman to catch another eyeful of Lane Two, but he seemed to have vanished. As soon as I finish competing, I am always in a magnificent mood, and some of the other Team Canada girls and I walked around, checking out guys and taking pictures of the cute ones for a calendar we had joked about creating.

The following day, after I completed my other races, I went on a stakeout (more like a stalk-out) to find Lane Two and get a picture of him. I found him in Great Britain's main tent, but coaches and trainers surrounded him, so I decided to wait on the field until they cleared out. After about half an hour of waiting, I came to two conclusions: The people were never leaving, and I looked like a frigging idiot.

So I finally decided to bite the bullet. I got up off the ground, strolled right into the tent, looked at Lane Two, and said, "Picture?" as I pointed at my little disposable camera.

"Sure."

He stepped outside the tent; I took my picture and said my thanks, then took off. You ever see one of those movies where the girl gets around the guy she likes and makes a total fool of herself? I speed-walked my way out of the warm-up area and onto the main road to catch a streetcar back to my hotel.

Just as I reached the sidewalk, someone yelled, "Canada! Canada!" (You have to say it with a British accent to get the full effect, so go ahead and read it again.) "Can I get a picture of you?"

I told him that it would have to wait until I came back, after I had showered and gotten out of my track clothes. He said when will you come back and I said I don't know. He asked if it would be easier if he just came back to my hotel with me and waited for me in the lobby. I said if you want. He did.

He told me his name was Alex. He may have been just less than six feet, and he was half and half, as I had suspected. When I tell you this guy was beautiful, I'm not exaggerating. As we walked toward the streetcar stop, people were literally turning their heads. Several girls from Bulgaria even tugged his shirt as they passed, but he smiled and freed his arm while he continued walking and talking with me. I felt really special.

We got off the streetcar and walked into my hotel, past the lobby, and toward my room. Conversation was just flowing, and the nerves that had consumed me an hour before were nowhere to be found. When we reached my room, he just stood awkwardly by the door.

"You can sit down. I'll only be a few minutes. I promise."

He sat down on the bed, then motioned for me to join him. "You have the most unbelievable eyes. Didn't know that Canada made beautiful girls."

I nodded, then escaped into the bathroom, where I could blush in private. I had my shower and got dressed. When I opened the bathroom door, he was on my bed, stretched out in just a pair of shorts.

"Sorry, it got hot in here since you had the shower running for so long."

"Yeah, I had to wash my hair. You can take that picture now."

"Not with that on. You have to put something Canadian on." He fingered through my bag and pulled out a T-shirt. I walked over to him, took off my shirt so I was wearing just a bra, and stretched out my hand for the shirt he had chosen. He gave me his hand instead and pulled himself up so he stood centimeters away from my face. He was so close I could feel his erection. *Oh my gosh!* We kissed, then went to the bed and kissed and touched and kissed.

Things were moving too fast, and I was not sure how to stop it or if I wanted to stop it. Part of me wanted to make a bond with him that would make our distance seem like nothing. Another part wondered what it was like to be a part of someone so beautiful. And the sensible side of me sat back like an invalid all the while, as the ignorant voice inside me encouraged, *He's wonderful—who better to give yourself to for the first time than someone you adore?*

"Come inside," I invited foolishly. *This is what is going to make us special,* I thought as I peeled off my panties and offered my vagina for the first time.

"You're sure?"

"Yes."

The next motion was so swift, it's hard to say exactly how it happened. He slid his boxers to the crease under his knees, smiled softly at me, and then attempted to push his hardened member in me unprotected. For some reason, I did not want to watch; I closed my eyes and bit down on my unsteady smile.

Ouch! My eyes shot open as he tried to push his way inside my vagina. He tried again but was still unsuccessful. *What are you doing?* my common sense screamed, making its first appearance during the whole ordeal.

He began to move in toward my throbbing crotch once more, but instinctively I moved my hands up to obstruct his momentum. He fixed his eyes on mine.

"Wait, do you have an STD?" I blurted out. I'm not sure why I bothered to ask, honestly—like he was actually going to say, "Yeah, Shannon, I'm HIV positive" or something. But I guess I felt like I had done my part to protect myself.

"No, of course not. You have to relax your muscles down there, okay?" he said, moving my hands away and kissing me on the forehead.

I exhaled, then focused on making my body limp. He pushed again, but when he still couldn't fit, he applied more pressure. The pain was ridiculous. My eyes started to tear up. He pushed a little harder and finally broke through. I felt something snap inside me; then the pain was gone and replaced by a feeling of nothingness. Maybe it was numbness—I'm not quite sure how to explain it.

So this is the first time, I thought, lying on my back with my hands clasped around his neck.

The next day was the final day of competition. I ran my relay races, and Alex met me in the warm-up area afterward and did my cooldown with me. It was really neat just jogging, laughing, and sharing tiny pieces of myself with someone I hardly knew, yet who knew a part of me that no one else in the world did. Even though sex had been a huge physical letdown, I was still pleased to have been so close to someone I believed I really cared for.

"You're pretty nifty, eh," I said in my best lumberjack accent.

"And you are one swinging babe," he said, doing possibly the worst Austin Powers impression I have ever heard.

I smiled and kissed him just below his lips. He looked at me unalarmed and smiled back.

The meet organizers had set up a street party outside my hotel for all of the athletes to attend, so we both went back to our separate hotels to get ready. By 10:00 PM, my roommates had already gone down, and I was hurriedly fidgeting in the mirror when I heard a knock at my door. It was Alex. I let him come inside. I knew we meant to go downstairs, but somewhere in between my naive nature and his ulterior agenda we found ourselves kissing and sexing once again. While he pushed his body into mine, I lay thinking of a million and one girlie things: what our kids would look like, fantasizing about us being the world's superstar track couple, wondering how we could move around our distance. I could feel his body stiffening inside mine, and I held tighter, not prepared to let him go just yet. I liked being so close to him this way. It made me feel important, like I was the only one who could make his body roll this way. All of a sudden, he yanked free of my grasp and rushed out of my body. I knew something had gone horribly wrong.

"I think I got out in time."

"No! I don't think you did!"

"Sorry."

I sat there silently wondering if it really was a big deal or not. I brought my head to his chest. "Now what?"

Alex glanced at his Timex. "It's almost one. The bus will be leaving soon, and the coaches are going to get angry if they knew I was up in some girl's room."

I was jarred. He slid out of my arms, got dressed, and yanked me up to hug goodbye.

"Wait, I'll walk you."

He glanced down at his watch again, then at me. "Hurry, then."

I got dressed and tried to match his speed as he exited my space and flew down the stairs. There were so many things I still wanted to talk to him about. He reached the lobby and stopped once we exited the front doors. I grabbed both of his hands and raised my green eyes, which he'd told me he loved so much, to meet his.

"Goodbye, love." He gave me a peck before loosening my grip and quickening his pace.

I stood there, numb. I let him get a few yards away before I found the words and called out his name, then ran to meet him. I pulled him in close and kissed him deeply, then waited for him to make the next move, waited for him to ask the question that was weighing down my tongue, wanting him to ask when he could see me again.

He opened his eyes and smiled at me. "I have to go before I get in trouble." He took off again with renewed speed, and I never did get his phone number or email address, nor did I ever see Alex of Lane Two again.

Confused about how I felt about my short-lived relations and Alex's reaction, the next day I told one of my teammates what had happened.

"Shannon, you dog!" was all he said before breaking into a fit of high-fives and laughs.

Had I done something right? I left my unsettled feelings alone and decided to leave the past in the past, but unfortunately, this memory was unable to forget about me.

Shortly after I got back home, the dreams started. I dreamed I saw Alex and asked him all of the questions I should have asked weeks ago: How many partners have you had? Why don't you carry protection? What will you do if I get pregnant? How do you feel about me? Where will having sex leave us? Alex had no answers.

I felt so disgusted with myself for wasting my virginity on someone who didn't give a damn about me. I had pawned myself off for nothing; it hadn't even been physically pleasurable. I was embarrassed, I felt low, but I was determined to right my wrongs by twisting the truth. I told my best friend what had happened and laughed about how I didn't care if I ever heard from Alex again.

"Yeah, I got his number, but who wants to call long-distance? It was just sex."

I described every erotic detail that I could think up and bragged about how amazing it was. It turns out I was a good liar, but the worst was yet to come.

Less than three weeks after having sex with Alex, I got an irritating itch in my vagina. I had no idea how to deal with these strange side effects or where to go to find out, and I sure as hell was not going to my family doctor. So, being the little girl that I was, I told myself to wait for it to erase itself.

Six months later, and no miracle—in fact, it had gotten progressively worse. I broke down one evening and told my older sister what I had done and how I was feeling. I cried. I had never been so embarrassed in my life.

The following week, she took me to a sexual-health clinic. I was terrified and I begged her to come inside the office with me, but she refused. After all, I was grown enough to have sex on my own. The nurse asked me questions, and I cried during the whole Q&A period. I had to get undressed from the waist down, and the doctor came in to see me. To my surprise, the doctor was a man, and I instinctively hid my nakedness and cried again. The nurse was called in, and she assured me that I would be fine. She stayed with me while the doctor did a Pap and drew blood for HIV testing. In two weeks, they would have my results and I would finally get some answers.

I cried every night. I was sure that I had something, but the thought of HIV scared me the most. For the past six months I'd gone on living, not knowing that I could be dying. What was worse was that I could have been putting the people who really loved me at risk.

After those two weeks, I went in for my results: I was healthy. I have no idea how, because the things I felt were so real. The doctor suggested that my condition may have been psychological, since I had been so worried about it, or perhaps it had been a recurring yeast infection that had cleared up on its own. I left the clinic feeling alive, and I vowed to never put myself in the line of fire again. My best friend bought my story, but the worst was yet to come; I got caught up in the lies, pressure, and fictitious stories of sex. I wanted to feel empowered, I wanted to be the girl every guy wanted, so I turned myself into someone that I am not proud of.

Looking back now, I realize that getting an STI and feeling the physical consequences might have been the best thing for me. Maybe then I would have felt the effects of my irresponsibility, truly learned from my mistakes, and made the necessary changes to stop myself from disrespecting and misusing my body again.

CREASE IN MY SHEETS

Shannon T. Boodram, 21 at the time of writing, Ontario (based on a relationship I went through when I was 18)

WELCOME TO MY THOUGHTS 3 AM . . .
Damn is sex meant to be this deep?
I claw at the mattress clenching the sheets with my teeth
I think I might just pass out from all this God damn heat
I do this for love but I know he does this to release
Tighter he moans so he can feel that extra piece
Water runs down his face but it's I that weeps
Hips move methodically as they press and retreat
Kiss his salted flesh but to me it tastes so damn sweet
Ten minutes of his love make a girl feel elite
And all these emotions just so he can release
Our rhythm breaks I feel his hands getting weak
I realize my time as his baby is coming to a cease
Then his body moves jagged as he frees his natural grease

Moments later . . . "You know I'd like to spend time but I gotta say peace"
And now I'm left to contemplate what just happened to me
And now I'm really questioning if his love will ever be
Have my soap opera teachings lied blatantly?
Could it be that sex is truly not love's currency?
I quiet my brain and listen to the door click behind his retreat
All the while staring at the vacant crease in my sheets

FRIENDS?

Stacy Rees, 22, Florida

JOSH AND I STARTED OUT AS LONGTIME FRIENDS. I HAD always had more guy friends than girls anyway.

I worked for his parents, we went to the same school, he was dating a girl in my circle of friends, and we even lived on the same street. We were inseparable, and I truly believed he could do no wrong. Josh was a senior, about eighteen, and I was young for a junior, only sixteen, but in a town this small, that really didn't matter—he was my best friend and I was his. I helped him through the breakup with my friend, and even though he ended up hating her, our friendship lasted.

I remember very vividly the day this all changed. When I think back on it now, I realize that I carried a huge crush for Josh the whole time we were friends but never openly admitted it to myself or anyone. In my mind, he was the embodiment of everything I thought was cool and special. Thinking about that day now is like watching one of those horror movies where you want to yell at the main character, "Don't do that!"

A whole group of us had decided to skip school and go to "the Creek," a small river area, to party. We were all down there swimming and drinking, no problem, but then one of my friends became very ill. Josh offered to leave early and take her to my house, because my grandparents were out of town and she could sleep it off there without getting in trouble. When we got to my house, I took care of my friend and tucked her in to the extra bed. Josh and I were supposed to be at school, so we had time to kill. I was tired and told him I was going to lie down. And that's what I did, and moments later he joined me to do the same. I wasn't alarmed—this wasn't the first time we had shared a bed—and besides, this was Josh. I fell asleep.

I woke up to his hand rubbing my stomach. He was spooning me and had lifted my shirt to rub my bare belly. I had no previous experience with any kind of sexual physical contact with a guy, so I was shocked. I turned over instinctively and he kissed me. I must have looked as shocked as I felt.

"Are you okay?" he asked me, like this was a normal, everyday thing.

What could I do? This was Josh, the best guy I knew, right? So I nodded yes and began kissing him back. Soon we were both naked and he was doing things to my body that, if I'd been thinking clearly, I would have realized were horribly embarrassing. I mean, I had never even so much as made out with a guy, let alone been naked in front of one. But I kept telling myself that this was Josh and I trusted him not to do anything that would hurt me. Looking back now, I see that I was the only one worried about someone other than myself. I hate to admit this, but in the back of my mind I was thinking, *This changes everything; from now on we will be much more than friends. This is a big step, and he must care a whole bunch about me to be doing this with me.* I was guilty of the same thoughts that I had ridiculed other girls for having. Sex to some changes nothing; it's simply a physical act. Who was I to think my circumstances were special?

"I'm going to try and put it inside you now, okay? I think you're ready," he said, looking at me like I had some kind of clue what was going on.

But everything so far hadn't been bad; some of it had been very nice. So again I reassured him I was right there with him: "Okay, if you want to." I whispered those stupid words with a wobbly smile and no idea what I was saying. If *you* want to?! What was I thinking! What about what *I* wanted? Somehow I had completely left one of the biggest decisions of my life up to someone else.

He pushed inside a little bit, and I'm sure my gasp of pain must have penetrated his lust-hazed brain, because he said, "It's better if we do it all at once. Just relax."

Relax? What was he saying?

Obviously, the position we were in was not going according to his plan, so he situated my legs differently and then, when he was satisfied with where I was, he tried again. Josh, the guy I had trusted with all my secrets, gave one impossibly hard thrust and it felt like my insides had ripped apart. The pain brought instant tears to my already foggy eyes. It was at that instant I knew that this wasn't just "something" to do. This had been something big, and I had just wasted it. He began to move, and the pain gradually faded into nothing. After that point, he made no more efforts to make it more pleasurable for me—he just kept going until I felt his body tense and I knew he was done. Josh rolled off me and went into the bathroom to clean up, I guess—hell, I had no idea what he was doing. I just lay there and thought, *Okay, he's going to come out here any minute and explain what happened. He's going to tell me things are going to be different between us now.*

He came out talking, all right: "It's way later than I thought it was, and I have to meet my parents for dinner. Umm . . . you might want to shower; I imagine you're pretty messy right now. I'll talk to you later."

With that last comment, he walked over and kissed me on the forehead before walking out of my house. I lay there with a vacant mind for a few moments before I sat up to go shower. I looked down at myself, only to learn that I was bleeding. I wasn't all panicky about it, because I had heard some girls do. What was appalling was that he'd just left me there, knowing that this had happened. *Messy,* he'd said. What an understatement.

Much later, things like pregnancy and disease came to mind once I realized we had not used protection. I then did what all girls do when in distress: I called my best friend, Anna. Since I wasn't the type to be upset over unimportant things, she rushed over to my house. She walked in and saw me bundled up in sweats on the couch.

"What in the world is wrong with you?"

"Anna, I messed things up real bad, I think." I couldn't even look at her as I said it. For something I had never really given much thought to, my virginity had suddenly become a big deal on the very same day I'd lost it. No, I won't say "lost," because it's not like I woke up and I had misplaced it—I had willingly and foolishly given it away.

"I had sex with Josh."

She just looked at me. Here we were, two opposite sides of the coin. I had never really been taught to give much thought to my virginity, and she was a good Christian girl who was waiting for marriage. Anna sat down beside me and held my hand. "Tell me what happened."

I told her everything, all the while thinking it sounded like a dream I had imagined. Questions like: Does this make me a slut? Is he going to tell everyone?

Anna, of course, said all the sensible things, like, "Josh should have taken the time to talk to you. He was the experienced one, so he should have had the sense to use protection."

She offered support without judgment. All I can say is, if a situation like this arises, tell someone—someone you trust—and tell them the *truth,* because keeping it in will undoubtedly cause the guilt to eat at you. I told Anna, and I know that her words and understanding salvaged some of my self-worth—not all, but some.

I then went on to convince myself that I was in love with Josh. I pined after him, still playing the role of best friend, letting myself be heartbroken every time he dated another girl. In between his girlfriends, I would let him use me as a sexual doormat, only further tricking myself into thinking we would end up together one day. Never once in all those years did we ever talk about what had happened. Honestly, the thing I regret the most about the whole situation isn't losing my virginity; it's the fact that I didn't hold him accountable for his actions. I certainly didn't do it by myself. I should have talked to him. After all this and all the intimacies we shared, we still have never talked about that day, or any of our sexual encounters.

I truly regret what I gave up in adolescent stupidity. I let myself be used and, in a sense, abused by a selfish person under the guise of friendship. But in hindsight, not all the things that came of this were bad: Now I realize how much stronger I am and how much more I am worth. I feel no shame for what I did, only a twinge of regret at the wasted opportunities to talk.

Josh and I have a tentative friendlike relationship currently, and I am working on being less of a pleaser. Now, whenever younger girls ask me about my first time and what should they do, I say, "It may not seem like a big deal to you now, and you might not realize how much it will change you, but it will. So hold on to it as long as you can, but if you do decide to have sex and it turns out not to be love, talk about it with him, whoever he may be. Let him know how you feel and what you've done. There is no reason why you should carry the burden alone."

Like they say, it takes two.

THAT KIND OF GIRL

Michelle D'Souza, 22, New York

"WE HAVEN'T HUNG OUT IN A LONG TIME, HUH?"

"Yeah, I know, haven't had any time for boys, really."

"Well, there's your problem: Boys can't keep you interested. What you really need is a man."

There was a long, silent pause; I was thinking and he was thinking. We had tried that whole more-than-friends bit but had settled for being acquaintances months back. I don't even know how we got into this conversation. It probably had a lot to do with the hour. Word of advice: Don't talk on the phone past 1:30 AM—you're asking for nothing but trouble.

"I want to come see you," he said, interrupting my thoughts.

"Where would we go? Neither of us drives."

"My cousin will drive me over, and then we can hang out in the front. We'll be really quiet. What do you think?"

I think that my parents are light sleepers and I have a dog that may have a barking fit. I think that we are two sixteen-year-old kids who probably can't afford to spend the rest of our lives grounded. But I also think that you're kind of cute. . . . "No, if we were outside my dog would bark nonstop."

"So I'll come inside. We can go in your basement or something and talk."

"Maybe. I'll call you back, and you tell me if your cousin will drive you."

I pressed disconnect on my cell and exhaled until my head felt light. Was I going to do this? Sneaking a boy into my basement—the idea excited me and made me insane with anxiety all at once. Kind of like a James Bond mission or something. And if my little mission impossible failed, then I would have to face immediate annihilation. I glanced at the clock, flipped open my cell, and dialed.

"Hello?"

"Yeah, it's Michelle. So what's going to happen?"

"I'll be there in five or ten; my battery is dying, so I'm going to leave it to charge. Where should I meet you?"

"Uh . . . at the side door, I guess. I'll bring my dog out, so hopefully he won't bark."

"What are you going to wear?"

What am I going to wear? I glanced down at my underdeveloped body, then envisioned my underwear drawer, littered with teakettle-embroidered panties and sports bras. "Uh, just my nightclothes."

"Okay, got some of those Victoria's Secret silks?"

This boy obviously spent many a night fixated on his mother's magazine collection. "Something like that. What does it matter?"

He ignored my remark. "All right, remember: Be outside in, like, ten minutes."

No goodbye followed—just the hurried *click* of the line. *Holy shit, I guess I'm going to do this.*

I waited outside, feeding my dog biscuit after biscuit. If my parents came outside, I'd just tell them I was letting him go pee. Truth is, it was me who had to go. I was so nervous that the pressure on my bladder had me tap-dancing. It had been only seven minutes or so, so I raced inside and relieved myself. As I tiptoed back to the side door, the inevitable happened: My dog was barking like crazy. I quickened my pace and grabbed the box of treats.

"Biscuit," I hissed.

My dog's head reared around and cocked to the side, then he ran toward my inviting gesture. My guest of the hour stood there looking nervously at me, wearing a loose-fitting wifebeater and blue jeans with his brown hair clumped together over his eyes. Had he just showered, or was he really nervous?

"Why didn't you wait outside the gate?"

"I did for a little, but I didn't see you or your dog, so I was going to knock on the window. Then once I got inside, it was too late."

"Well, you have to go now. It's too risky."

"But my cousin already drove off," he whined.

"Well, call him back."

"With what phone?" he asked flatly, patting down his pockets.

Shit, he was right. He had to use my house phone. I motioned for him to wait, then crept back into the house. Silence. It was as though the whole barking fiasco had never happened. I popped my head out the door and waved him and my dog back into the house. He grabbed my hand, and immediately a swarm of butterflies dove into my stomach. As I guided him through the house and down the stairs, I could hear his breath exploding in nervous spurts. At least I wasn't the only one.

When we got to the basement, I turned on the light in the bathroom and closed the door so there was a passive glow in the sitting area. He sat down and I chose the opposite love seat and stretched out.

"What do you think your parents would do if they saw me down here?" he asked.

"My dad would probably twist you into a pretzel, and my mom would call your mother."

"I could probably handle your dad."

I couldn't help but laugh. Who was this wiry-bodied, prepubescent, can't-even-fill-out-a-wifebeater-from-Wal-Mart's-kid-section young boy fooling?

"What's so funny?"

I had to hide my face in the pillow to keep from bursting into a loud cackle.

"Okay, so maybe I don't look tough, but you'd be surprised," he mocked himself.

Despite his efforts to roll with the punches, I still could not get the picture of him standing up to my father out of my head, so I kept laughing. Then, without warning, he pounced on me, sat on my stomach, and pinned my arms to the couch.

"See, I'm not so weak after all."

"Please," I said as I rolled him off me, sending us both crashing to the ground in a wrestling fit. After a minute, he regained control over my limbs and then triumphantly stated, "Now you're mine."

"I guess I am."

He kissed me full on the mouth, then nervously pulled away. With that, I grabbed his hair and tugged it until his mouth met mine again. He flattened his body and put his hands behind my neck, softly tugging my hair. We continued kissing, and as I savored every tantalizing tongue twirl, his hands and mind roamed in other areas. Ten minutes later he was tugging at my clothes and unbuckling his belt. This situation was spinning out of control. I tried to hold his hands, but he wiggled them away and gave me a mischievous grin as he lowered them.

Was this what I wanted? Yeah, I guess I kind of wanted him to come over and make out a little, but this was going too far. Did I like him like this? Did this mean we were going to be a couple? If I told him to stop, would he think I was an immature tease? As my mind raced in a million directions, I finally got the reprieve I was praying for. As if he sensed my fear, he got off of me. I sighed; at least he was having the same doubts.

"Something told me to bring some. I'm glad I did." He shuffled around in his jeans pockets and pulled out two condoms. Shit.

He smiled at me, then lowered himself back on top of me and began kissing me again. I wondered if this was a good time to tell him that I didn't want him like that, but next thing I knew he was awkwardly unfolding the colored condom over his penis, so I said nothing. And when it was happening, I felt nothing; I thought maybe he was doing it wrong. He swung his dick in and out of my body, just like they did in the movies, but I wasn't feeling those explosive effects that other girls on TV seemed to have during sex. I was bored and actually quite bothered by the feeling of his body inside mine.

When it was finished, he kissed me on my nose and smiled as if he was all too satisfied with himself. He walked over to the coffee table, picked up the phone, and dialed.

"Come back. Meet you out front."

He then turned back to me. "I didn't know you were this kind of girl." He grinned.

"Oh."

"Well, I'm going to get out of here before your parents come down. You were breathing kind of loud. How many times did you orgasm?"

Is this guy delusional? "Don't know."

He walked over as he tucked his undershirt into his jeans. "Maybe we can do this again, huh?"

I just smiled and got up to lead him out the way he had come in. Once outside, he sped toward the gate, then turned back and sang out, "Thanks!" And then he left.

That word made me feel sick as I played it over in my mind. *Thanks*—what a perfect way to sum up that evening.

To my surprise, he called me first thing the next morning on my house phone!

"The phone," my mother said testily, as she waved it in front of my sleepy face. "It's a boy."

I wasn't allowed to date when I was sixteen, so my mom was never enthused when boys called the house. I had gotten around the issue a lot by claiming that they were just friends or that we were in project groups together. I rubbed my eyes and took the phone from her; she sat on my bed. I instinctively opened my cell and noticed I had missed his call—*shoot*—and now my mom was staring at me like she was trying to see right into my thoughts. What was so important that he had to call my house? I collected myself and did the routine I had perfected before I'd convinced my mom I needed a cell phone.

"Hello?"

"Hi, Michelle, it's Kyle. I need to tell you something."

Oh my God, I had to shut him up before he said something my mom would overhear.

"Listen, I just woke up and I don't have the notes on me right now. I'll call you back in half an hour or so.

We ended the conversation, and my mother announced that she was leaving for work soon. I kissed her, then returned to my bed.

I wondered if he had called to ask me to be his girlfriend. I guess it was the only thing to do—I mean, we did have sex, and although I wasn't a virgin, I still wasn't a slut. The more I thought about it, the more I warmed up to the idea. Maybe getting sex out of the way was going to be good for our relationship; now we could focus on other things. As soon as I heard my mom's car drive off, I hit the recent-callers list.

"Hello?"

"Good morning, baby. I'm surprised you're up so early. What's on your mind?" I smiled on my end. I could get used to this.

"Well I wanted to call you as soon as possible to let you know: I . . . uh . . . was looking at the condom after I left your house, and there was a tear in it."

My heart sped up to an unhealthy rate. My life was over.

"So what are you going to do about it?" he asked.

"I don't know. What am I supposed to do?" I was panicking.

"I'll ask my cousin, then call you back."

A few hours later we were in front of the pharmacy, debating who would go in. After losing a game of Rock Paper Scissors, he still refused, so I went in. The receptionist eyed me and rudely informed me that I needed a prescription from a doctor. My eyes started to water; there was no way I could go to my doctor. She sighed and pushed a card across the table for a sexual-health clinic. "They can help you," she said, then waved me off.

I went to the nearest pay phone and called the number. They booked me for an appointment the next morning, which was a Monday, meaning I'd have to skip school. That was a risk he was unwilling to take, so I went alone and ashamed.

That night I phoned him, really wanting to talk, wanting to make sense of the whole situation so I didn't feel as dirty. But my hopes were shot down as he came to the phone annoyed after his mother called him and informed him who it was.

"What's up?" he said hurriedly.

"Nothing. I went this morning. I don't feel so good now, and I just need someone to talk to."

"Uh, you'll probably feel better tomorrow."

"It's not only that I feel sick; I also just feel . . . I don't know, like, weird about what happened."

"Oh. Well, I can't talk now anyway. Anna is over."

"Anna? I thought you guys broke up."

"I never said that."

I hung up the phone, hurt, angry, and confused. But one thing was clear: I had been used. It wasn't even like I'd had feelings for him before, so why did this have to hurt so badly? I spent the next few days phoning from a blocked number and hanging up, praying that he would contact me so I wouldn't feel so unwanted.

Be careful what you wish for.

Two weeks later, he called me and asked if he could come over later that night, or, as some may say, early in the morning. I was actually relieved that he had thought to call me, so I agreed and promised to look sexy. After he'd rejected me, it was as though I was on some desperate mission to prove that I was good enough.

He came over that night, complimented me, told me he missed me, then undressed me. As I held his body close to mine, I realized that I had somehow formed some serious feelings for him. I didn't want to stop seeing him, and I was unsure how to remove sex from the equation without disappointing him, so I disguised my feelings for him in a friends-with-benefits situation, in hopes he would realize that I was the complete package and not just a midnight fling. What I didn't factor in is that most guys are able to separate sexual desire from emotional interest.

Months after our sexual arrangement began, I finally realized he had no intentions of falling in love with me and I told him that we could no longer be friends, or whatever he wanted to call our relationship. I hoped he would ask me out in order to keep me near, but he just nodded and let me know that if I ever wanted to sleep with him again, I just needed to call. Thankfully, I didn't take his advice, and once he realized I had no intention of doing so, he started telling others that we'd had sex.

About a month after I stopped being his pleaser, I became aware that news of our arrangement had just begun to get around. Some of his friends even contacted me, hoping to "get to know me better." I told those creeps to get lost and hoped no one I knew would hear about me and Kyle, since he went to a different school—but once again, I underestimated reality.

I exited my last-period class and proceeded to the spot me and my friends always hung out at. I stopped in front of them as they buzzed and scurried around like a bunch of coked-up squirrels. Once they spotted me, everyone's energy immediately dropped. A friend rushed over to me and hauled me away from the group.

"I've been over there defending you; tell me it's not true. Did you sleep with Kyle?"

I glanced over, and everyone's eyes were on me. If I denied it, Kyle might come to my school to confront me in front of everyone.

"Yeah, once, a long time ago," I half confessed.

"Damn, I never thought you were that kind of girl."

STILL

Jay, 21, Maryland

I AM CURSED.
Enslaved to a feeling that is not returned,
Casually spoken words
And callous remarks
Continue to crush the pieces of my broken heart.
Even though I knew my place from the start,
My part
Was just a needed sexual release
And nothing more,
Yet every time I know I shouldn't surrender,
I fall to his tender touch,
So slow and exploratory,
Hands snaking around my waist,
A mouth on a place
Just below my face.
For a moment I feel loved,
I feel special,

I am tempted to believe the lies his hands tell,
But I know it will be to no avail,
Because whatever feelings his hands portray,
His heart does not harbor in any way.
And yet I continually let my heart betray
My mind and common sense,
Letting him touch me again,
Because in some twisted way
I think that in validating his belief
That I am a whore,
I can cling to his perception
Of me
So that his rejection
Of me
Won't hurt as much anymore,
Because now I am the very thing he abhors,
And yet some part of me still adores
Him.
I wish
That I didn't feel like this,
I Wish
That I Hadn't,
That I Didn't,
That I Don't,
But I Have Strengthened My Resolve,
So Now I Won't,
But I Wish
That Everything Wasn't The Way It Is.
I Miss
The Simple
Rich
Friendship.
Truth.

I'm not one of those outcast Lifetime girls or a smutty ho, but I'm not perfect either. I have a pretty normal life. I had great parents, I came from a good home, I didn't have low self-esteem, and I'm not ugly. I'm intelligent, funny, and silly. No words can ever truly express how much I wish I had waited for someone who loved me for these qualities.

If you choose to have sex, take a lesson from my experiences: *Sex will not make someone love you.* Whenever you have sex with someone, you are giving a part of yourself totally to them, so instead of giving my husband the true amount of what he deserves—all of me, untainted—he will be receiving all of my heart but a used body as well.

BACKSEAT BASEBALL

Charles Keeranan, 20, California

"CHARLES, DID I EVER TELL YOU HOW HOT YOU ARE?" asked Joanne, while she was blowing cigarette smoke out of her mouth.

We were sitting outside of a party, both of us trying to get some fresh air after being enclosed in a room of sweaty bodies, loads of alcohol, and ear-popping music for a couple of hours.

I starred into the night sky, trying to regain my senses after having had too many shots of vodka and rum. I turned toward Joanne to better face her. She was wearing a gray tank top that displayed her cleavage and low-cut jeans, causing the straps of her G-string to spill over her pants. I let my eyes run over her body—I love summer.

"Joanne, I know I told you that you're hot because you look hot every time I see you," I responded with a distinct slur of words, trying to make as much sense as possible.

She laughed after I made my remark, then kissed my cheek, holding her position, pressing her weight into me for a couple of seconds until she retracted. I noticed that she had been drinking as well. Her face was a little on the red side and there were tiny bags around her eyes.

"Aw, you're so sweet," she said.

Out of one part instinct and two parts gratitude for her drunken flattery, I leaned in and kissed her on her cheek as well. My lips felt good when they made contact with her warm, soft skin, and as soon as my lips left her cheek, she quickly gave me a long kiss right on the lips. All of a sudden, a simple exchange of thank-yous turned into a full-on make-out session. With our tongues screaming for more, my mind began to race, trying to figure out where we should make our moment of lust a little more discreet. You see, I'm the type of person who isn't into PDA, or watching other people's PDA. I racked my brain for an after-party spot for Joanne and me; we couldn't go back into the house party because every single room was occupied by at least ten people; the back yard was out of the question because rolling over a spot where someone threw up isn't one of my favorite things to do. All of a sudden, after mulling the thought over for half a minute, my drunken brain came up with the obvious destination: We could go to my car.

I pulled back from her lips. "Hey, let's go to my car."

"Why, how come we can't stay out here?" she asked me quietly, as if we were doing something wrong.

"I just don't want people to notice and start pointing fingers at us or anything. Plus, we're able to talk more in my car." Of course, the last part was a lie—I wanted to use my mouth, all right, but not for talking, per se.

"Okay, that sounds like a good idea."

And off we went to my car, which was parked a block away. Holding hands tightly, we quickly walked down the empty street as the rush of excitement grew between us. The thought of doing something sexual with her at that very moment filled my mind like air in a balloon, while the rest of the things—including my good old morals—were deflated.

The walk was shorter than I remembered, and just like in those old movies, Joanne slid neatly into the passenger seat while I got behind the wheel. Closing the doors, we instantly began to make out once again. I suppose both of us were feeling the same thing about each other at the time—the feeling of pure lust.

But shortly after the doors closed and the kissing began again, my mind started to plan what to do next. Kissing each other passionately was cool, but did she want to take this to the next level? That was when I decided to take my chances and find out. Foreplay was something I enjoyed because, to me, it was like getting the luxury of happily passing three of the four bases before hitting a home run. I was already on first, and now it was time for me to make my way to second. The position of my hand slowly and smoothly changed from holding the back of her head to exploring the area of her vagina. My fingers did all the work, by unbuckling her belt and unzipping her pants. I constantly checked to see if she didn't want to go through with it, but she didn't say a word or make a motion that she wanted me to stop.

Hearing her moan and say my name increased my excitement, and I knew I was ready to experience those feelings for myself. Lucky for me, Joanne quickly grabbed my leather belt and began to do the same thing I had done just a few minutes earlier to her. She did everything in such a hasty and somewhat violent fashion that it made me feel like I was in one of those movies where the two main characters are about to engage in an intense lovemaking session, violently tearing their clothes away from their bodies as fast as they can in order to get down to business. Once my privates were exposed, she began to do a little foreplay of her own while I made my way to third base.

With things moving in all the right directions, the only thing left was the predictable ending of sexual intercourse. I took it upon myself to lure Joanne to the back seat of my car. Sex was definitely the only thing that consumed my thoughts at that point.

Here's a quick sexual education lesson for you folks: Now, typically, when guys are presented with a chance to engage in a sexual act with a good-looking member of the opposite sex, they will take the offer faster than a race car with a full tank of gas. I was just doing my job as a male to do whatever was necessary to accomplish the ultimate goal of getting laid. And it seemed Joanne was on the same page.

I stripped her of the clothing I'd admired in the beginning of our encounter, and in turn she assisted in taking off my clothes. Putting on a condom was an obstacle in itself, being that the amount of alcohol in me was a little above my limit. But once I was able to put it on properly—after a few fumbled attempts, I admit—our sexual activities ensued. And yes, home run.

Well, more like hitting the ball out of the park but being stopped before you run around the diamond. We were only a couple minutes into it before she told me to stop. At first I thought she realized it was time for her to go home—she was still living with her parents, since she was only eighteen—but that wasn't the case at all.

"Charles," she panted, trying to catch her breath, "we can't do this, it's not right."

"Why not?" I asked in confusion. I thought it felt right to me.

"Because . . . I have a boyfriend," she said with an irked expression on her face.

Although she looked beautiful in the nude, she was absolutely right. She did have a boyfriend, a commitment that I knew she took very seriously, because before our little incident she'd been talking about how great a guy he was and how he treated her well, something that she wasn't used to. I let out a long, heavy breath and got ready to move, but then I noticed that she wasn't budging.

"What?" I asked in response to her stare.

She paused for a brief moment. "Don't you have a girlfriend, Charles?"

It was then I realized that I'd made a terrible mistake; I had honestly totally forgotten that I was committed to someone else. Even though my girlfriend and I had been going out for only a little less than a month, cheating was cheating, and I don't think it is right to cheat on the person you've agreed to have an intimate, loving relationship with. But there I was, caught with my pants down in a moment of my own hypocrisy.

"Let's just keep this between us, okay?" Joanne said meekly, a far cry from the sexual vixen I'd been humping moments before.

"Okay, will do."

I went home that night feeling smaller than a dust mite. Months after our rendezvous, both of us were single. I didn't know why Joanne broke up with her boyfriend, nor did I want to ask her. The reason why my relationship ended was because I lost interest. That, and I made out with another girl at a nightclub. I guess you could say my inability to keep my dick in my pants has been a problem in many of my past relationships. But I'm starting to see things for what they really are now, and in all honesty, even though I thought I got a home run on that night with Joanne, I have realized it was actually a strikeout. No one won and nothing was accomplished.

THINK

Justin, 20, Pennsylvania

I SEVERED THE LINES, TIES ARE BROKEN
It's like trying to get on the bus with no tokens
Took something away, so sacred with sympathy
Never really caring, or showing empathy
Premarital sex was something I expected
When I was done, feelings were always neglected
Whether her emotional stability was intact
Integral part that helps relationships from going in retract
I created an emptiness that always will be inside
Her virginity was lost, that she can't hide
Just took it away, and created a major void
We all get old, just like throwing out toys
Now she will always question people's motives and plans
That trust she had sunk like quicksand
Did he love his last partner or am I just another try?
A question that will be asked every time . . . why?

I wish I could take back that sexual experience
Then I wouldn't have this sense of interference
For meddling with her wholesome purity
I see in her eyes a new sense of insecurity
All the things we did and the things I said
Were they merely plugs just to get her in bed?
But the connection that two make when sex is performed
Is much greater than any consequence that can be endured
Your souls meet and you form as one
So when I took that away that's when our troubles begun
She thought that we were always going to be together
But the sun didn't last, got stormy weather
Now she's wishing that we never met
What we did was fake, and she highly regrets
Looking back, her virginity was much bigger than me
I changed a good girl and tarnished her prosperity
I severed the lines, ties are broken
It's like trying to get on the bus with no tokens.

SHE'S PIGEON-TOED AND WEARS A SCARF

Michael Villo, 19, California

"SHE'S CUTE, ISN'T SHE?" DAVID SAYS, SMOKE TRAILING from his lips. A grin cuts his face, exposing teeth that shouldn't be white—but they are.

"Sure," I reply. My head throbs from the bourbon we finished.

He begins again, glancing at me as he lowers the volume on his stereo: "Have you met her friends yet? Her friends are . . . " He cups his hands around imaginary breasts, a smile still across his face. "Oh . . . you'll like them." I nod and stare out the window at all the homes with pitch-black windows.

We leave David's car, our bubble of smoke rising in wisps, as we make our way back to the only house with kids on the porch. Inside, the pulsing dance music chisels at my skull. Minutes after my reentrance, after a few petty conversations, I am left with a red cup in my hand, alone. David is off and about with that girl in the white dress he can't shut up over.

I muse alone for a bit, failing to strike a conversation with a brunette in a green dress. Her eyes never meet mine, and I look for any excuse to leave. I rush off to the bathroom; toilet paper is scattered on the floor along with empty red cups. Dust and drops of water dot the mirror as I check my pupils, my acne, my teeth. *Is my collar straight? Is my shirt wrinkled? Why did I say anything to her at all? Relax. Ignore her and act as if you didn't say anything stupid.* I fix all my clothes and pop a zit before heading back out to the throbbing mass.

After a few more self-made drinks, I find myself talking to a girl named Rebecca. Her overbite distracts me. I have trouble looking at her face, but we talk—or she talks and I mutter in response about her school, books she's read, politics, and so on. I wouldn't be interested in this girl anywhere else; I make the effort, though, and she can't tell the difference. We talk some more, and I feel a little better after she gives me her number, but she doesn't budge from the sofa. I leave her after a minute; I don't have the patience—either I'm not handsome enough or she's too sober.

There's another girl, though. Our eyes meet from across the room. Her name starts with a *D*—Danielle or Denise or something like that. She's pigeon-toed and wears a scarf because she's insecure about the size of her breasts. I like her face, though. After a few more drinks, all I can see are her glossy lips joining and parting, but my thoughts are elsewhere. I finally decide to take her hand in mine and lead her to the back yard. There are tons of unknown people talking; I don't look them in the eyes when I walk by. It's just going to be me and her right now. Cock blocks have ruined enough of my nights.

Danielle asks, "Where are you taking me?"

"There's so many people. I just want to hear you."

"I know, right?" she says, squeezing my hand a little tighter.

We're under a tree now. People don't notice us amid its bare branches.

"I think you're . . . gorgeous. It's not the alcohol talking, I swear." I concentrate on speaking without a slur.

She smiles. "That's so sweet of you. You're hot yourself, mister."

Our noses are touching. I'm drunk enough not to care how lame I probably look. Then our lips meet. Her lip gloss is sweet. We're sloppy kissers at this point.

I feel as if we've been dating. She begins to tell me everything: how her ex was here, how he brought some girl named Sarah over. How she was nervous about moving to the dorms at her college. She starts to tear up. I hold her close, kissing her forehead. I don't want her tears ruining her makeup.

"Let's have another drink" is all I say.

Her eyes are glazed over enough. "All right."

HER HAIR IS SOFT; AUBURN CURLS FILL MY FINGERS, MAKES them curious. It smells like lavender shampoo also, but the stench of her vomit ruins it all. She's gripping the shaggy mat covering the linoleum floor, heaving into the toilet bowl.

"I'm so sorry. . . . " Her trembling voice fills the tiny bathroom. Saliva is clinging to her lips.

"It's okay. Are you done?" I ask, after a few more of her wet coughs convince me that there's nothing else. I put her pale arm around my shoulder and lift her. Her made-up face glistens under the yellow lights; I can see every pore of hers. Would it be wrong to call her beautiful at a time like this?

I maneuver us through the halls, past chatting couples and drunken idiots. We reach a tiny bedroom with ruffled sheets and clothes littering the floor. I lay her on the bed and she curls up under the sheets. Danielle's eyes are sunken and glossy. Her hand reaches under my shirt.

"Do you need water, babe?" I ask.

"Yeah, can you get me some?"

"Of course. Wait a second."

"Come back soon, okay, darling?"

I don't even respond. I stumble out of the room, passing people whose faces are nothing but fragments. I reach for a red plastic cup in the kitchen, an empty one next to a puddle of soda. Bottles of Jäger, cognac, vodka, and cheap beer are scattered about the counter. I wash out the cup and fill it with tap water to bring back to her.

She's waiting for me, the bedsheets completely covering all but her face, her brown curls warming her shoulders.

"You look cozy, babe. Here's your water." I show her the cup and she smiles.

Locking the door behind me, I step over all the scattered clothes and trash. She drinks the water greedily. My eyes never leave her glossy lips. Finally, she puts the cup down. My hands are on her shoulders and my lips reach hers. There is no *what are you doing?* no *stop, please.* Instead, her arms wrap around my neck and she pulls me closer. A faint acidic taste is still on her tongue, but I keep kissing her, getting in bed next to her. I can feel the crumbs beneath the sheets. I can feel her. And that's all that really matters. The dance music is still pulsing from the living room.

A thrust. A jerk. Her gasps for air. Moans.

She has a birthmark on her smooth, flat stomach. She has nice thighs. I can finally smell her hair, for once. Our clothes are in a pile on the floor somewhere. She doesn't respond when I call her "bitch."

I leave her pale naked body among the ruffled sheets. She's fallen asleep and I couldn't even shut my eyes. I just lay there, thinking, *I probably hurt her. She'll wake up with bruises all over her thighs. God, she'll fucking hate me. I can't be next to her when she wakes up. She'll ask questions and I won't have answers.* So I put all my clothes back on and place hers neatly on the bed. I can't be here when she wakes up, so I rush out quietly.

Rebecca is lying on the couch still, sleeping. She must have a gift for making men give up. I stare at her for a moment, watch her sleep, count her freckles. She is beautiful when her mouth is shut, when you can't hear her voice or see her teeth.

David wanders out of the hallway to the front door. His face is tired; I notice the circles around his eyes. When he notices me, his smile creeps back into place.

"Hey, let's head out."

I follow him back to the car. I can see my breath in the cold. It's still dark out, but now the streets aren't empty. People are pulling out of their driveways to go to work.

"So how was the girl in the white dress?" I ask David, my head throbbing.

"What?" David asks, unlocking his car doors.

"You know, the girl in the white dress? The one you were talking about all night."

"Dude, her name's Veronica." David twists his key in the ignition, and his sedan roars to life.

"Well, how was she?"

David grins again, showing his perfect teeth. "Fool . . . I gave her the business." He pauses. "But who was that girl I saw you with on the couch?"

A nudge on the shoulder makes me look him in the eyes for the first time. "Um . . . Rebecca? I got her number."

"That's it? Not even a blow job?" David looks at me, shocked and angry.

"Fuck you. There's this other girl, too—Dianna, I think. She wore the scarf and the yellow blouse. I made it with her; she's passed out."

A laugh escapes his chapped lips. "I love these nights!"

He pulls into the road and begins driving toward the main street, back to our homes. The drive is quiet but the stereo is not.

"What are you doing tomorrow?" David asks.

"You mean tonight?"

"Yeah, there's a party at Mike's house."

"I'll check it out."

"Kim is going to be there."

"Yeah, I'll be checking it out," I say as I stare out the window. The road is filled with morning commuters; my mind is just as clogged as the streets.

What was her name? Does she remember mine? She doesn't. I hope she doesn't. Should I have gotten her number? God, what is that smell? Did her perfume rub off on me? Or is that David who stinks? Danielle . . . Denise . . . Dianna? What was her name? My eyes stay fixed on the crowded streets while my hands lay on my lap, lonely.

The party the next day was the same. So were those that followed. No names remembered, no faces. Just images, just fragments of voices. But nothing to hold on to. Nights starting and ending in David's filthy sedan, him driving like any reckless teen and me in the passenger seat. We'd share stories, or at least the interesting parts, all starting with "I was so drunk. . . . " He'd actually look interested, and I, well, I let my mind wander. To be accepted, to be a man, well, that was what I had imagined it to be.

BROOKLYN NIGHTS

Alyssa Varin, 21, New Jersey

THE BASS PUMPED OUT OF THE SPEAKERS, TRAVELED through the gyrating bodies on the dance floor, and pulsed up over the clouds of evaporating sweat. It traveled up my legs, through my bones and veins, moving every cell in my body. I glanced to my left and spotted a cute girl with short brown hair taking pictures with a fancy digital camera. I sipped my beer, building some confidence with each mouthful. She was the photographer for the party, and she was snapping pictures of drunk, sweaty queers as they danced along to beats mixed on a MacBook.

I was trying to dive headfirst into the New York lesbian scene. I had skated on the outskirts for years, letting my older friends test the waters first. Now, at twenty-one years old, I finally had my turn. After a few beers, I left my insecurity on the barstool, walked right up to her, and said, "You are absolutely adorable."

She smiled, took me by the hand, and led me to the hot, crowded dance floor. Her fingers on my waist set my nerves on high, yet I still felt slightly comforted by the closeness of this mysterious stranger. We danced for a while, so close that I could feel her breath on my cheek. She was reading me through my movement, through my glances, trying to answer every question she had without using words. I could see her inquisitiveness in her eyes, and I wondered how much she could decipher about me between the sway of my hips and the nervous look in my eyes.

Before we knew it, we were among the last people left in the once crowded Brooklyn nightclub.

She looked deep into my eyes with more intensity than I felt comfortable with and said, "I don't normally do this, but do you want to come back to my apartment?"

Millions of answers flooded my head in a matter of seconds. *Of course. No, I should probably go home. Why the hell not? What exactly do you think is going to happen when we get there? This could be an interesting experience. I might need a few more drinks first.* At that moment in my life, I wanted to never miss an opportunity, to say yes as much as possible, and to always be open to new experiences. I decided I would let her take me home.

"Do you have cats?" It came out faster than I could filter it.

She laughed. "Yes, I do, actually. Why do you ask?"

"Oh good," I said. "I like cats. . . . "

We walked down into the subway, arm in arm. Her eyes looked much older in the harsh subway lighting. She had left her youthful, boyish appeal in the dark club, and on the G train she suddenly became a tired, weathered woman. She was, after all, nearly ten years my senior. I started to feel dizzy with regret, but I pushed the feeling back down, deep inside of me. *I need to be open,* I thought. As we exited the subway, even the familiar Brooklyn streets felt foreign and strange. Yet there was something about her that made me feel like I could pretend to be someone else. Or maybe the city did. It's hard to say.

We walked through her gate and up the stairs to her studio apartment on the third floor. Where I'd typically feel awkward and nervous, I was calm and confident. Despite her age, she reminded me of an overzealous teenage boy who had discovered his own sexuality for the first time. Her forward nature came across as borderline annoying, and nothing about her awkward attempts at sensuality were remotely attractive to me.

I sat on her small sofa and focused my attention on her cats, trying to avoid excessive eye contact. I was convinced that if she looked into my eyes for too long, she would be able to see that I was unsure about the whole situation and slightly disinterested in her. She sat across the room and stared at me while I petted her cats and talked to them like they were my new best friends.

"You're trying to figure out the world, aren't you?" she finally said, never averting her eyes.

"I guess so," I replied, slightly unsure where she was coming from. "I'm always trying to make sense of everything around me. How can you tell?"

"There's so much inside of you. You're searching for something—I can see it in your eyes."

I didn't want to be that transparent; I didn't want her to actually see me. I wanted to hide in a different version of myself so she wouldn't know that the chemistry was draining out of our exchange with every passing second, like sand in an hourglass.

After that, we just made small talk. "Do you smoke?" she asked. I knew she didn't mean cigarettes.

"I don't make a habit out of it. But I enjoy it once in a while."

"Awesome! I'll roll a joint."

I'd never felt so relieved to see pot. I inhaled the musky smoke and held it tightly in my chest, letting it out slowly like a deep, quiet sigh. We passed the joint back and forth as she talked endlessly about her life. At some point in the middle of the conversation, I realized I hadn't been listening for quite some time. I almost wished she had gotten me drunk first. Perhaps that would have numbed my increasing sense of discomfort and made the experience slightly more enjoyable—and if I was lucky, I'd forget the whole thing in the morning.

Two joints and a cup of coffee later, my anxiety was peaking and I was ready to crawl out of my skin. By the time we made it to the bed, it was after three in the morning. Our mouths were dry, and the rhythm was enough to put me to sleep. She didn't kiss with tongue, which baffled me. Her loose skin felt old and tired in my hands, something I was not used to. She grunted oddly, and her breathing was choppy. I found myself pretending she was someone else, anyone else: a recent ex-girlfriend, another girl I'd slept with a few weeks before. I longed to find a source of comfort in a situation that I'd let go too far, yet I could not find anything. She was nothing even remotely close to familiar, and I couldn't wait to close my eyes and find solace in my dreams.

In the morning I slept for hours, through my classes and obligations, to avoid confronting my mistakes. The sun crept through her window, tickling my face, daring me to rise, but I pressed snooze and reset my phone's alarm more times than I could count. I wasn't exactly sure why at the time, but now I understand: Not a single part of me wanted to open my eyes and accept the reality of the long, tiring night before. I wanted to pretend it never happened, that I wasn't in some strange apartment in Brooklyn, and that she wasn't sleeping, breathing loudly, next to me.

I finally arose and announced that it was time for me to leave. She rolled over, sat up, and smiled. She gently stroked my naked back as my eyes desperately searched the bed for my clothes.

"I'll make you some coffee," she said, as she climbed off the bed and walked toward the kitchen.

I quickly got dressed and packed up my things. In a few minutes she returned with a pink mug of hot coffee. I sat awkwardly on the edge of her bed as I drank it and stared deep into the cup. Maybe I thought I'd find meaning in the swirling soy milk—answers in the rising steam. Instead, I only found more questions: *Why do I feel so awkward? Why did I agree to stay over in the first place? Will she be upset if I don't call her? How many minutes before I'm far away from here? Why do I feel like I'm on the outside looking in?*

She insisted on walking me to the subway, which I agreed to because I had no idea where I was or where I was going. I forced a goodbye kiss but refused a complimentary sweatshirt, even though it was so cold that I couldn't stop shivering. I'd never felt so relieved to walk down into the subterranean depths of New York City. I escaped on a C train, bound for Manhattan, and never looked back.

GOT QUESTIONS ABOUT CHAPTER 1?

THE HOOKUP

You keep tossing this word around, but what does it mean?

Two people (or more, I suppose) without any official obligation to or affiliation with one another who decide to participate in a no-strings-attached sexual encounter. Hooking up can mean anything from kissing to full-blown sexual intercourse—as long as it's steamy and no one is expected to call the next day, anything really goes.

BEING USED

How do you know if you're being used for sex?

If the person wants to see you only late at night, when everything else is closed, or only when an unsupervised space is available. I realized that this was happening to me when I was out with my friends at a theme park and I saw the guy I was sleeping with. He walked by me and just nodded. I called him back, and he seemed anxious to get away; his eyes were darting everywhere but on my own. I spent the rest of the day on the lookout for him, and when I finally found him later in the day, he was among another group of girls. That same night, he phoned me at 3:00 AM and asked me to come outside.

If someone "hits it and quits it," what does that say about you?

It depends on the situation. In some circumstances it could mean that the other person has commitment problems and is too blind to see all the wonderful things you have to offer. Other times it could mean that you are not presenting yourself in a manner that commands respect. You have to look into your own situation to find cause for the action.

Why do people continue to have sex with people who they aren't in a relationship with?

I can't speak for everyone, but in my own experience it was the only way I got to spend time with the guy I really cared for. If I did not offer some form of incentive, I didn't believe that he would be interested in me. Although this game that I was playing made me feel inadequate, lonely, and unpretty, I continued to use my body as bait for some time.

FRIENDS WITH BENEFITS

Jay, 21, Maryland

What does "friends with benefits" mean?

Jay: Friends with benefits are friends that you have some sort of prearranged—or totally by chance, depending upon how the relationship comes about—agreement in which you and that person have some sort of sexual interaction without the ties or responsibilities of a committed romantic relationship.

How do you transform a friend into someone you have sex with, too?

Jay: Most of the time this happens by accident; the lines of friendship are blurred at one point or another, and neither person makes a move to stop it. "Friends with benefits" is also a term used for people who really weren't friends in the first place. In some cases, the couple talked as more than friends or even dated before deciding to continue having sex with no strings attached. This usually happens after one person decides they are not romantically interested and the other person wants a way to hold on to the relationship. A lot of girls use the friends-with-benefits thing to try to sway their lover's emotions through sex—it doesn't work.

Then you fall into a pattern of sexual conduct which you may not be totally comfortable with but have gotten used to. However, friends with benefits can be anyone, and "benefits" doesn't mean just sex.

Is there such a thing as no-strings-attached sex?

Jay: Not really. With sex being an extremely close-contact activity, the chances that the incident will be an isolated night that neither party ever thinks about again are pretty slim. You may not realize it at that moment, but there are always strings: emotional, physical, mental, spiritual. . . . The biggest string of all is the thread of being used. In many (if not all) of the friends-with-benefits relationships, someone is being used, whether they realize it or not. And of course there are the physical consequences, which can become extremely complicated since sex or sexual behavior is all you are agreeing to.

LOSING YOUR "V-CARD" (VIRGINITY FOR GIRLS)

Was intercourse extremely painful?

I would not say extremely painful, but yes, it did hurt. Others say there was no pain, and some cry for dear life and often bleed; it depends on your specific situation, as well as your feelings about it, and it varies a lot among women. Some people have to try several different times because it is too painful. That's normal. Go at a pace that is comfortable, and stop if there is excessive bleeding or an unbearable amount of pain.

Is it better to get it over with, with someone you don't know?

To each their own, but in my opinion—*hell no.* It really is an experience that I have kept with me always, and for me to have to think back and remember that I tossed mine away to someone random makes me sick to this day. On top of that, it takes a lot of understanding; you want to be with someone who cares about your comfort level and is willing to stop if it gets too painful for you. Since it is such a monumental experience, you also want someone who will hold you, kiss you gently, and assure you that you have made the right decision.

SELF-ESTEEM

What does self-esteem have to do with sexuality?

How you feel about yourself reflects on everything you will ever do in this world. Your self-esteem can either make or break your sexual life. If you understand how wonderful you are as a complete person, people won't see you as an easy target for no-strings-attached sexual activities. If others know that you value yourself, the only people who will step to you are the ones who think the world of you as well.

Do girls who are promiscuous just have low self-esteem?

Promiscuity comes as a result of many different circumstances. Sometimes it's a chosen lifestyle, sometimes it's a form of attention seeking, and, yes, sometimes it's because the person has low self-esteem. They might feel like other people won't like them or try to get to know them unless they provide sexual favors. Unfortunately, people who use sex as a Band-Aid for their lack of self-confidence usually end up making themselves feel even worse. It eventually becomes a cycle where the person is continuously trying to solve the issue with the problem.

HOMOSEXUALITY

Alyssa, 21, NJ

When did you realize you were homosexual?

Alyssa: There was never a definable moment when I realized I was a lesbian; it was more like a gradual thing. For as long as I can remember, I had crushes on girls, even if I didn't know what that meant. In middle school, I finally admitted to myself that I was in love with my best friend, which was the first step toward understanding and accepting my homosexuality. For a while I told myself I was bisexual, because it was easier to swallow. One day I wrote, "I'm bisexual" in my journal and quickly scribbled it out. But even the simple act of writing those words down made it real, and even though they were scribbled out, they still existed underneath the extra ink. I was fifteen when I came out to my friends and family, and it felt like a weight had been lifted off my shoulders.

At what age did you have your first queer experience, and what happened?

Alyssa: I was lucky to find an older lesbian to confide in at a summer camp I worked at for a few years. When I first came out, she helped me realize that I wasn't alone and I wasn't the only one with these feelings. When I was fifteen, she introduced me to her best friend, who I dated for almost a year. My first girlfriend was very butch (looked and acted very masculine), and most people thought she was my boyfriend, so in some ways I eased into the queer world.

Were you terrified?

Alyssa: Not at all. I spent many years thinking about these confusing feelings, and by the time the opportunity came around, I was more than ready. I knew exactly what I wanted. In fact, I think I was more excited than anything. It was a whole new experience, a whole new chapter of my life opening up right in front of my eyes.

Who is the last person you would ever tell?

Alyssa: My queerness is not a secret—it's who I am and I don't feel the need to hide it from anyone. I'd rather be a platform for positive social change and use my voice to educate others, comfort those who have yet to come out, and inspire them to do so. There is a lot of work to do in order for queer people to be equal members of society, and we need as many allies as possible.

What was it like as a queer in high school?

Alyssa: I was completely out by the time I was a sophomore in a small, rich, conservative town, and at that time, I was the only out gay person in my school. Naturally, I received stares and sneers in the hallway, and someone even carved "dyke" onto my locker junior year. There were times when it was very hard to want to get up in the morning for school, but I tried not to let it bother me. The teachers were very supportive and protective of me, and I had a lot of very good friends who accepted me regardless of my sexual preference. I was being true to myself, and that's all that mattered.

LESBIAN HOOKUPS

What does lesbian sex include, since it's not possible to have traditional vaginal/penile intercourse?

Alyssa: I honestly haven't been asked this question in a long time, but for some reason it always makes me smile. There are a number of ways lesbians have sex, and these ways can differ between individuals. However, deriving pleasure from fingers, tongues, toys, or pure old friction is certainly the main ingredient. There's always a level of creativity, and the experience two women bring to the table can have some influence over that. I've found that even straight women who are very in touch with their sexuality can find pleasure in lesbian sex. That's right, I said it!

Is hooking up prevalent in the queer community?

Alyssa: The queer community is no different from the heterosexual community in terms of sexual behavior. We hook up too! We have one-night stands, friends with benefits—all that hooking-up stuff. Of course, we also have committed relationships.

What did you learn from your experience with hooking up?

Alyssa: This was not the first time I've hooked up with someone like this, but something about the experience has stuck with me. Perhaps it was a combination of the vastness of the big city and my own eagerness to experience something new that left me feeling empty and regretful. Unfortunately, it took a long, tiring night of regretful sex in the city to figure out that the meaning I'm constantly searching for can't be found between the sheets of a stranger from a club. It's something that can only be found inside of me, and I now carry that lesson with me every day. I still see the girl once in a while, and I'm sure we'll remain some sort of friends/acquaintances.

How do lesbians practice safe sex?

Alyssa: In terms of oral sex, lesbians can use dental dams or Saran Wrap. It's my understanding that some people advocate wearing latex gloves as well. As with any sexual experience, there should always be certain precautions taken to make sure all parties involved are as safe as possible.

HOOKUPS THAT STAYED HOOKED

Amethyst, 19, Washington

How do you view hookups, since yours resulted in a positive experience?

Amethyst: First off, I'll come clean and say I haven't had too many hookups. I had one (which you will read about in the next chapter), and about six months after that I met a guy who I thought would be another hookup . . . but he ended up becoming my boyfriend of two years and running! Judging from what I've personally experienced and observed with my friend so far, I think hookups are a fun, chill way of enjoying sex with someone, minus the complexities of being or pretending like you're in a relationship.

How were you able to maintain control of such a casual relationship?

Amethyst: It was surprisingly easy, especially considering that it wasn't a onetime affair. I had to really know myself and understand what my partner and I desired from this relationship. For me, a hookup is a temporary physical relationship with another person. If you think you're hooking up but start to feel an intimate connection with your sexual partner, or that your self-esteem is based on this relationship, that's where the line starts to get blurry. If that happens, you should definitely step back and reevaluate your own desires and feelings to see the situation for what it really is.

When do you think hooking up can actually be a positive thing?

Amethyst: Hooking up can be a fun, enjoyable experience when you understand your desires and know that just plain hooking up is really what you want. It goes without saying that full consent—willingly engaging in sex of your own accord—is key to having a good hookup; actually enjoying the company of your sexual partner helps, too. Sex is a really intimate, intense experience; this can be an amazing thing, but oftentimes people use sex as a way to boost their self-esteem and to mask their insecurities. This isn't to say that you won't have a great time hooking up with other people if you're insecure about yourself; it just means you have to know that remedying insecurities requires internal self-reflection, and the act of hooking up isn't going to help you do that. Lastly, I think your own attitude and judgment toward hooking up will really affect how much you enjoy it, both in the moment and when you think about it afterward.

CHAPTER 1 CHECKPOINT

ARE YOU A PLAYER?

Would your hookups fall down or would you dominate the field? The general spirit of hooking up is being down for whatever, with few questions asked. It takes a certain kind of person to make it work in his/her favor. After all, just because you're a player doesn't mean you're not getting your ass kicked by the other team. Take the quiz below to see if you're a true player or if you're better off stepping back and reassessing your approach to sexual relations.

If you had sex with someone for the first time, the next day you would:

a) Check my phone to see if they called
b) Call the person to talk about where we should go from here
c) Forget about it and go on with my day
d) Get to work on securing the next hookup

Someone calls and asks if you want to come to their house at 3:00 am, so you:

a) Ask them politely why 3:00 AM and why not 3:00 PM
b) Tell them I already have plans with my pillow and sheets
c) Tell them I'll stop by if I'm still awake
d) Go to their house at 3:00 AM. Next question.

At a party you meet someone you're really attracted to, and you make out. At the end of the night they say bye without asking for your number, so you:

a) Call them back and ask for their number
b) Find my friends immediately to vent about what a jerk that person is
c) Shrug and look for someone else to talk to
d) I'm the one who probably walked away first

Someone from your town whose profile pic is pretty hot messages you, "What's up sexy what/who do you do for fun?" So you respond:

a) I really like ice cream and action movies, what about you?
b) Respond? I deleted that message.
c) Hey back, cute stranger. I do who and what suits me at the time. You?
d) Hey, sexy. Are you free, like, right now? (Then I search their profile to see if they have any hot friends.)

You met someone at a family function. You talk on the phone and hit it off, then decide to go on a date. The person suggests their house Friday at 9:00 pm. You reply:

a) Sure, we can go back to your house after we do something else first.
b) No thanks, I have an early morning Saturday; what about 5:00 PM on Friday?
c) Cool. Are your parents going to be home or at least asleep?
d) Let's make it 11:00 PM. I have another date first.

Out of choices a, b, c, and d, which did you circle the most? Check below to see what this might mean about what's on your player card.

You answered mostly:

a) It seems like you're more interested in a committed relationship than you are in just-for-fun random acts. You may also find that you have trouble expressing this to other people, for fear of coming across as too needy. Playing it cool is fine, but if the other person is pretty forward about their intentions and you're choosing to be quiet about your own, don't be surprised if in the end, you don't get what you really want. Your player card needs to be revoked before you hurt someone or yourself.

b) You're not interested in casual hookups at all, but you don't even need to see that in writing—you already know this about yourself. You're not a player, and you certainly don't play games with those that you suspect are.

c) You're not technically a player, but you don't mind hooking up with one or tinkering with the title yourself every so often. You seem content to go with the flow and have few long-term expectations for potential partners. Nobody is going to break your heart or sweep you off your feet anytime soon. For that reason, you don't get a player's card, but you can certainly have a season pass to all of the games.

d) Erase, replace, embrace a new face. You love them, leave them, and don't flinch. Love and lovemaking are your oyster. No arguments here—you are a player.

CHAPTER 2

AND THEN I SAW STARS . . .

INTRODUCTION

Her eyes danced with lust, his lips dripped with desire. They walked in unison to the exit without one word exchanged between them. Once outside the noisy club and away from the prying eyes of the world, he grabbed her ass and squeezed it as hard as his johnson had become. She let out a whimpering cry and pressed her lips tightly against his to keep from screaming out in ecstasy.

They ripped, clawed, grabbed, tore all of their clothes away until even their underwear lay in a limp, defiant pile behind the Dumpster. He raised her body onto his waist—his bulging biceps seemingly unaffected by the effort—and then, with one lustful blow, he entered her. The woman's eyes shot open and a single tear tumbled down her cheek and onto his O-parted mouth. She moaned with intensity and orgasmed. It was so wonderful, so perfect, and such a complete load of crap.

THIS SCENARIO PLAYS OUT A MILLION TIMES OVER IN movies, books, and even advertisements. Sometimes the setting is different, sometimes the relationship is a little more formal, but the formula is pretty much the same: Girl and boy with no official affiliation have an impromptu sexual encounter without any foreplay whatsoever, and the female goes wild with pleasure. So I made sure to include a chapter that would set the record straight. Not to say that this scene isn't realistic—I'm just saying that you may have a better chance of being struck by a bull than you do of relating to two-stroke pleasure tales like the one above.

This chapter was by far the most difficult to recruit writers for. It seems most people believe that sexual education and talking about positive sexual experiences don't mix. I mean, how can we teach people about sex if we admit that it can be wonderful?

I completely disagree with the notion that we shouldn't be teaching young people about how great sex can be. It is important for teens to know the parameters of a healthy sexual relationship so they are better able to judge whether they are in one. After all, would parents and educators prefer children went by TV's standards—or, even worse, music's standards—of when the time is right?

And for the record, no, you will not just *know* when the time is right. You have to educate yourself about what these "right things" are beforehand. Patience and high standards will help get you through this difficult stage. Finding the right things in a world that glamorizes the bad stuff takes plenty of work. Remember, the world is full of billions of people. Positive sexual experiences are created only through mutual adoration. Anyone who thinks you are less than wonderful is not worth your time. If you are adamant about finding someone who makes everything right, then you need to spend some time and get to know a lot of people before you settle for the first person who wants to have sex with you.

The first step toward finding a sexual partner who will help you understand the beauty of your sexuality is getting to a place where you yourself have an appreciation for the beauty of your own body. The gift and the curse of a woman's body is that it creates so much pleasure for her partner, but often that same pleasure is not reciprocated. Guys may be able to find sexual release with almost anyone, but the female body is an instrument that takes time to master and understand. When I was in high school, I believed that the clitoris (an erectile organ whose sole purpose is to provide pleasure) was inside of the vagina. Why else would women in porn cry out during vaginal sex? Later on I learned that the clitoris is located outside of the vagina, and for this reason many women do not experience orgasms from sex without direct stimulation to the clitoris. It can be a lot to take in, I know. But that is why it is so essential to find a partner who is caring and willing to learn beyond the media and their friends' advice. Sex with the wrong lover, no matter what, is not the right decision for you, your body, or your emotional and physical pleasure.

The second step to a positive sexual lifestyle is to begin thinking of yourself as a vivacious, whole adult. After all, partnered sex *is* for adults. Being an adult means becoming fully aware of your complex responsibility to yourself and your loved ones. And though I did not want to hear this when I was younger, I fully believe it now. I'm not saying wait until you're twenty—after all, adulthood has little to do with age and the world to do with wisdom, self-control, and acknowledgment of the consequences of your actions. Just wait until you're confident enough and know yourself enough to make a decision that's going to be good for you.

The authors of the pieces you're about to read have had wonderful sex. By being assertive, honest, and compassionate with others, they were able to find a worthy lover with those same qualities in order to create a truly beautiful moment—void of regrets.

WONDER WOMAN

Amethyst, 19, Washington

IT WAS ON A PARTICULARLY HOT SATURDAY IN SEPTEMBER that I met Erik. Though he was still a boy by societal standards, he was five years my senior and was—to me, anyway—a full-grown, sexually experienced manly man: the perfect specimen for my very first sexual conquest.

I was at one of the nation's largest art festivals. It was a gathering of the biggest names in music, film, and dance, and it seemed like the entire city of Seattle had swarmed to the Space Needle grounds to experience their share of the excitement. The speakers in the stadium were cranked up to full blast, and a sweating, heaving crowd of concertgoers moshed and danced their hearts out to the New York Dolls. Having been born a generation too late, my friends and I couldn't care less about the New York Dolls. We adamantly plopped our butts onto the floor, determined to protest this outdated excuse for rock music and to save our energy for the act that really mattered (Garbage was up next). As we yelled at each other about current crushes over the deafening racket, someone who had been trying to weave his way out of the crowd tripped right over the four of us—together, we had formed a sitting roadblock.

"Hey! Sorry about that! Didn't expect to see anyone sitting down."

He was more charming than I had imagined a stranger could be and far more handsome than any other guy I'd ever crushed on. His perfectly mussed-up blond hair glowed rhythmically as the spotlights swept across the crowd. His eyes sparkled with apology—for having tripped over us—and with the happy satisfaction that comes with a summer day. And best of all, his lips framed a smile that was to die for.

"It's totally cool; we aren't doing much anyway. At least, until Garbage comes on."

It seemed that my friends were as instantly smitten as I was, except that they were much more outgoing. Before long, the New York Dolls headed offstage and were replaced by Shirley Manson, with her alluringly husky voice, and her entourage. As Shirley began to work the stage, one of my girlfriends began to grind with Erik, pressing her ass up against what I was sure was a sizable package, while I shyly hung back and admired the movement of his cut body from afar. (I later found out that he was a ski instructor *and* a gymnast—no wonder he had the kind of physique that made me want to jump him then and there, never mind the fact that I was still a ninth grader, never been kissed.) Apparently, my hungry stares didn't go unnoticed, because as he halfheartedly gyrated his body to keep up with my friend's frenzied teenage dancing, he would occasionally swivel that beautiful head of his over to give me a wink. By the end of the night, when I was feebly dancing with my other friends, distracted by fantasies of getting with this veritable sex god, he started to reach over and fondle my ass, giving it a little pinch every now and then, accompanied by that signature grin of his.

We exchanged numbers at the end of the night, our ears ringing from the deafening concerts. I definitely wouldn't say I was smitten—that would have implied that thoughts of him occupied my mind at all times. No, I was in lust, and frequent thoughts of him made me wet constantly. The fact that he was a college senior and I a high school senior did not deter me one bit. I remembered that, coincidentally, my tutor was a student at the same university, meaning that I had ample opportunities to meet up with Erik. I began to devise a plan in my head to get in his pants.

Over the period of a month or two, we met up a few times after school to get a bite to eat or romp around his university district with our tongues flicking at our ice cream cones. We flirted the entire time, managing to incorporate sexual innuendoes into our conversation even when talking about the most mundane topics.

"So the other day, I was cooking at home . . . " (he had made it abundantly clear that he was practically a gourmet chef, always inventing new dishes with eclectic ingredients) " . . . and I mixed this new drink called 'Sex in the Kitchen,' and it was uh-*maze*-ing!"

"Huh." I smiled coyly. "Perhaps we should try having sex in the kitchen while drinking Sex in the Kitchen."

His eyebrows shot up and a sparkle gleamed in his eye: "You think so?"

We were nowhere near a kitchen, but I might as well have been leaning up against a granite countertop, holding the red plastic cup in my hands. This was a game of imaginary truth or dare, and it was about to get interesting. "Yeah, I do," I matter-of-factly replied, with a teenage smirk plastered on my face.

His only reply was a big smile, teeth slightly parted to reveal just the tip of his tongue sticking out at me.

By the time Halloween rolled around, our bodies still hadn't made contact for more than a few consecutive seconds. So I asked him to meet up a couple hours before I was planning to attend a party a couple blocks from the university campus, making sure that I was decked out in full Wonder Woman regalia. My costume was every guy's fantasy, and I was sure Erik would not be immune to its sexual appeal. Not only was it scandalously revealing, I had gone to great lengths to ensure that I looked exactly like the comic book character: I had thick silver armbands (though mine couldn't deflect bullets), the gold headband, the apple-red boots, and the golden lasso. Who could resist?

I felt a jolt of satisfaction when his jaw dropped at his first sight of me: I liked that I had this kind of power over him. We wandered around the campus aimlessly. Our conversations might as well have been in gibberish, because at this point we were just talking to defuse the sexual tension. As our heels clicked on the brick pavement near the graduate library, a misty rain began to fall. The raindrops grew fatter and we soon found ourselves running through a downpour, searching for any door that would open and lead us to shelter.

"Over here!" he yelled, as he flung open an unlocked door.

We rushed inside and found ourselves in the basement of the administration's building. Droplets of rain trickled down the smooth sheen of my hair to land on my shoulders. This time, I didn't damn the ubiquitous Seattle rain because I knew that my glistening, exposed chest and my soaked costume worked to my advantage. I was still breathing hard from our frantic run. I took in the sights of the dead-silent basement and the exposed pipes running overhead where a tiled ceiling should have been. It wasn't the most picturesque place to receive my first kiss, but that was the last thought on my mind. Erik smiled just before taking a step toward me, pinning me against the wall, and bringing those lips to mine. For the first time, my tongue swirled around another wet tongue and my wet skin was dried on clothing instead of a towel. My breath caught in my throat and I coyly bit my lip, looking at him. Though it wouldn't happen for another few months, I was sure then that I would do him.

Two weeks later, I was straddling him on a park bench in a beautiful grove on campus. Trees reached their branches out to form a natural ceiling for the amphitheater, which was prominently framed by four Roman columns, but I was oblivious to the scenery. I was intent on extracting my pleasure from Erik's lips as we made out aggressively, our hips pressed against each other's. I was *so close* to getting what I wanted from him—why were our jeans in the way?! Oh, right: This was a public place.

His tongue traced the outline of my lips and I returned the favor. Occasionally, he would break the kiss and suck on my lips instead. By the time we were done, two hours had passed, the sky was pitch dark, and I was more sexually frustrated than ever. My mouth was noticeably plump from our marathon make-out session. For the next few days—until the swelling died down—I would run my tongue over my lips, reminiscing about our little romp, eager for more sexual satisfaction the next time I saw him.

Personally, I think he hesitated to initiate full-on intercourse until I celebrated my sweet sixteen. Although I was a senior, I had skipped a few grades, so I was young. We enjoyed our time together immensely, for the most part just making out, and sometimes rubbing our naked bodies together as we did so, feeling the heat build up between us and between our legs. We rarely talked, doing so only to avoid awkward silences. The fact remained that he was a full five years older than me and the age of consent in our state is sixteen—the thought of having illegal sex might have creeped him out a bit. We never talked about it openly or anything, though, since it was clear that we were just frequently hooking up, no strings attached, plain and simple. And in the meantime, until my birthday rolled around, waiting for "the real thing" was far from boring and involved lots of oral-sex orgasms for me!

Another couple of months passed. Knowing that I was about to become sexually active, a close friend gave me a box of condoms and lube for my birthday, along with a book called

Exhibitionism for the Shy. I read that book cover to cover . . . twice (don't judge! I'm a fast reader!), and from then on, I always kept a condom in my wallet and a mini-bottle of lube in my bag. It certainly came in handy the next month, when Erik and I met up just before Valentine's Day. I don't think he knew we would have sex that day; it was supposed to be another lunch "date," which entailed lunch, making out, oral sex (if we could find an empty classroom), and a cordial hug goodbye. But I put on my favorite lacy, mesh panties and a silky balconette bra with little roses printed on it, ready to lose my virginity and begin the first of what I hoped would be many sexual experiences.

Somehow, we ended up in the bowels of the mazelike university medical center, without even having had lunch first. This part of campus was completely foreign to me: Each door looked like every other one, and though the wings were designated by different letters of the alphabet, I couldn't tell one apart from the other to save my life! I trusted him to find us a private spot, and we soon happened upon a teacher's lounge tucked away in a quiet corner of the building, away from the busy labs. We opened the door, glad to find nobody inside, and saw an old conference table surrounded by dingy upholstered chairs and a sad-looking mini-fridge. Judging from the looks of the place, nobody would be spending their lunch break here anytime soon, but we unpacked a couple notebooks and textbooks and scattered them around the table so that we could pretend to study just in case anyone walked in on us.

When we were finished with the technicalities, Erik moved closer to me, wrapping his arms around my waist to pull me closer. As we kissed, our tongues fighting for dominance, he wound my hair around his fingers and gently pulled. I unbuckled his belt, leaving him to undo the rest while I wrestled my way out of my own denim. In no time at all, I found myself lying back on the table with my butt on the edge while he knelt down and ate me out. I had no doubt that Erik had been with more than his fair share of girls and women: I climaxed, but it wasn't enough.

I motioned him up from between my legs. "Guess what? I have condoms and lube in my bag."

His eyes hit me dead on, then disappeared just as quickly as he rushed to my bag. Before I knew it, he had expertly rolled the condom on and I was about to have sex for the first time. I took a deep breath as he slowly pushed his way in. I was as sexually curious as I was inexperienced, so I'd read a lot of stories about this moment. I expected a bit of blood or a sharp pain as he stretched the hymen, but all I felt was that initial stretch, which melted into fluid pleasure. I experienced my first climax from actual sex.

He smiled. Erik was the kind of guy who was all about giving sexually. Though he would willingly go down on me for hours at a time for the duration of our "hookup relationship," he never asked for a blow job in return, which I was grateful for. My guy grapevine tells me that blow jobs are practically a holy event in terms of sexual experiences, so I'll never know why he never asked me to give him head. All I know is that it allowed me to lay back and take all the sexual pleasure I needed from Erik without ever having to actively give in return.

That day, I reached my peak of multiple, small orgasms, and, seeing that I was satiated, Erik peeled off the empty condom and threw it in the trash instead of pounding away until he reached his happy place. Good thing, because almost immediately after he did, we heard the doorknob turning. Like superheroes, we jumped into our pants and buttoned them within a matter of seconds.

"So, you said the midterm was next Friday, right?" I asked nonchalantly while packing up my books.

"Yeah, I'm pretty sure. I'm going to have to study lots this weekend, though."

The woman had walked in to fetch her lunch from the fridge. My cheeks were flushed bright pink. The room had that suggestive musky smell of sex, and a condom was sitting at the bottom of the trash bin. But she didn't notice anything . . . or if she did, she didn't even flinch or bat an eyelash, or whatever it is that one's supposed to do in such awkward situations.

Erik and I flashed each other playful smiles, elated to have gotten away with such high-risk sex. I was already thinking that this would be a great story to tell my friends, and I'm sure the same thought was running through his mind. We hugged each other goodbye and walked to our respective bus stops to head home for the day.

NOTHING BUT YOU

T.C., 20, Florida

THAT FEELING OF HIM THAT NIGHT CREATED A SENSE of ecstasy
That I thought could only be imagined in those sensual dreams
Way deep under my sexual frustrations in the midst of my mind.

That thing he does, that makes my toes curl
And the way his lips softly caress my earlobes
Sends this sensation up and down my spine, making me scream silently, internally . . .
For him to pleasure me even more.

It wasn't the penetration of his rotations between my walls
But the way his touches spark an internal fire even when my clothes were on.

The gentle way he removes my Victoria's Secret panties
Sends this warm front of anticipation of what may occur next.

After minutes of him teasing me with his tongue
He becomes acquainted with my Mac lip gloss
And makes love to me with his endless kisses.

As I whisper in between, "I love you," so that he knows.

Laying on top of me he carefully spreads my legs, then positions
Me comfortably in the middle of the bed.

While looking me straight in the eyes, he finally proceeds
To enter into my domain, in sync we release this moan of pleasure
Smiling back at one another as we let each other know
We felt the same damn thing.

Every moment possible we indulge in each other's kisses
And he always remembers to hold my hand
Assuring me that our hearts are truly connected.

He is the only one that pleasures me endlessly, making me climax
Way past cloud nine—and enjoys the sight of my orgasm, making sure
I get mine. . . .

Because my baby makes love to me
Making me feel the way that no other man can.

IN BETWEEN ROOTS AND WINGS

Gabrielle Unda, 18, Ontario

WHEN I WAS GROWING UP, MY FAMILY LIFE WAS ALWAYS different from my friends', though it took many years for me to understand that ours was the one considered "abnormal." How was I to know that a mother doesn't typically swing from episodes of intense mania to suicidal depression on a daily basis, or that a father usually spends more hours in a day at home than at work? My life was all that I had ever known, so I never bothered to question it.

With hindsight, I see now how little of my childhood was stable.

Because of my father's long-term commitment to his employer, we would move across the country once every few years. Beyond encouraging my love for travel, this nomad lifestyle taught me to never become emotionally dependent on anyone other than my family: There was no reason to get attached when I knew that at any given moment, my whole life could change.

The stressful, unstructured conditions of our household destroyed the traditional roles found in healthy family settings. They also allowed for important boundaries to be crossed. By the time I was twelve, I had been repeatedly sexually abused by at least two men. Although I was intellectually and emotionally mature for my age, I never understood the full impact of these incidents. All I knew was that I had been betrayed by two of the most important people in my life and felt that I really was all alone. After that, unsure if I should trust anyone ever again, I decided to keep pushing forward, as independently as I could.

A lot of things changed once I reached high school. I immediately began testing the limits of my newfound freedom. In no time at all, I was rolling up my uniform's kilt, paying more attention to my appearance than ever before, and loving all the attention that I was getting from guys. I had never been much of a follower, but this new world managed to drag me right in. My sense of self was vulnerable, and I didn't notice the speed at which things were happening.

Ignoring my parents' decision that I was still too young, I had a boyfriend within the first two weeks of school. It wasn't that there was anything special about him—come to think of it, I doubt that I ever really liked him. It's pretty scary to think that I would have gone out with anyone at that time—it was my way of feeling as though I was finally in control of my life. Up until then, I had always been both studious and rule abiding. Shocked by the sudden change, my friends were pretty pissed off the first time I skipped class to go make out with him.

There I was, sitting by the soccer field outside, with an alien tongue in my mouth that belonged to someone who I knew next to nothing about; so much for my long-awaited "romantic" first kiss! The whole time we were out there, only two things kept going through my mind. First off, I couldn't get over how strange it felt, and secondly, *How do I make this stop?* Just like that, I had found myself feeling powerless in yet another uncomfortable situation.

The following weekend, still pushing the limits of my independence, I went downtown with some friends for three days of live concerts. That weekend was my first introduction into a world of drugs, booze, and rock 'n' roll. I'd already been forced into growing up too quickly, and the rest of my life was progressing at a similar pace. Fortunately, fate stepped in.

On our second night there, my friends and I were having the time of our lives, dancing in our bras and singing along during Gob's set. Apparently, this happened to catch the eye of a good-looking guy who was walking around looking for his friend. He came over and started talking with my friend Gen, right behind me. He told her that he and his friend had been split up while crowd surfing, and then decided to wait with us. The next half hour went in slow motion; I was definitely on cloud nine. I couldn't stop myself from glancing back every few minutes to check him out. Each time I did, he would look me in the eyes and we would both smile.

When Gob was done playing, he had to get going. He hugged each of my friends goodbye, and I deliberately waited to be the last in line.

As soon as we had our arms around each other and his mouth by my ear, he whispered in the sweetest voice that I had ever heard, "You're really pretty."

Somehow, those three small words instantly erased all thoughts of the guy I had been seeing. My tummy was filled with butterflies and I couldn't have had a bigger grin on my face. As we pulled away and stared each other in the eyes, some sort of metaphysical field drew us together . . . then there it was, my romantic first kiss. Unlike my previous experience a few days before, the next few moments felt magical.

Realizing suddenly that my friends were cracking up at how random it was to see us kissing, we unwillingly pulled away. From there, I went to see my friends, who were all giggling and teasing me, and he left to find his ride home.

"So . . . what was his name?" asked one of the girls.

When I finally came back to earth, I suddenly realized that we had kissed before we had even talked.

I shrugged and said, "I don't know, but I guess it doesn't really matter anymore."

By that time it was getting late, so we started the long walk toward the park's gates. Halfway there, we had to turn back for a sweater we'd left behind where we were dancing.

As we were leaving for the second time, the mystery boy unexpectedly showed up. This time we made a point of introducing ourselves: His name was Andrew and he lived about forty minutes away from me.

Andrew then explained to me, "When I met up with my friend and told him what happened, he sent me back to track you down so we could exchange phone numbers."

It's astonishing, really, that he was able to find me at all; there were way too many people there for it to have seemed even remotely possible. To this day, I still can't bring myself to admit that our meeting was likely coincidental. In any case, I'm just thrilled that it happened.

When I got to school Monday morning, I had planned out exactly what I would tell my boyfriend. But as soon as I saw the look on his face when I found him, I understood that the news of what had happened must have already reached him. Considering that we had only been together for about a week, he definitely overreacted. Although I admit that I felt bad at the time, I am glad to say that I broke up with him that same day.

In the few weeks that followed, I spent endless hours online and on the phone with Andrew, getting to know him. My father may not have been pleased with the expensive long-distance phone bills, but I was so stoked about it all. What amazed me the most was that every time we would talk, the conversations would flow really well. There was never a single awkward moment . . . well, none excluding the time that my mom and my brother overheard me asking him about his previous sexual experience: "So tell me the story about the girl you fingered. . . . "

Thankfully, neither of them would have dared repeat it to my dad.

ANDREW WAS IN ELEVENTH GRADE AT THE TIME, EVEN though he was only about fourteen months older than me. I figured that it wasn't a big deal since most of the girls in my grade also dated older guys. As with all of those other girls, the age difference definitely affected the relationship's pace and dynamics. The biggest difference between the two of us was that he had been in more previous relationships than I had. Luckily, that experience turned out to be what made him realize how special what we had really was, and in the long run convinced him to stick around when it would have been easier not to.

Since we were both too young to drive, we spent months convincing our parents to give us rides on the weekends. Considering how my dad felt about my having a boyfriend at that age, I'm pretty sure he only agreed to it so that my parents could still be involved in my life and question me about it during each long drive. They would even go as far as to call his house before I'd go over, to make sure that we were never home alone together (which might have been extremely embarrassing if his parents wouldn't have been the same way). We knew that they had good intentions, but when things started to get more physical between us, it was annoying as hell.

During those first few weeks of getting to know each other, Andrew asked me about my previous relationships. I felt comfortable with him and knew that I needed to be honest for things to work out between us. He ended up being one of the first people I told about the sexual abuse that I had endured. He was shocked by the news, but still managed to be patient and support me when I would talk about it. Knowing how my past had affected me, Andrew never once pressured me into doing anything that I wasn't completely comfortable with.

The way we saw things, we spent all week talking and getting to know each other, so it made sense to spend the few hours we had together on the weekends exploring the physical side of the relationship. With our parents always on the lookout, we were forced to resort to the most absurd public places to hook up. Most days, we would "go for a walk" and come back hours later with terrible excuses for why we were gone for so long. That worked out fine until winter came along: Trust me, there is nothing sexy about sitting outside in the snow, decked out in gloves, toques, winter jackets—with frozen, well, frozen everything. That didn't stand in the way of our hormones, though; it simply meant we needed to be more creative.

In the first year that Andrew and I were together, we became extremely close. He stayed up on the phone all night with me when things were rough at home, and I was there for him throughout his parents' messy divorce. Even though we spent more time with our other friends than together, Andrew and I had become an essential part of each other's lives. I can still remember exactly how I felt looking at us through his hallway mirror, when I first knew for sure that we were in love.

He was behind me with his arms wrapped around my waist and whispered gently in my ear, "I love you."

I nearly melted before telling him that I felt the same. The more comfortable we became with each other, the better we were at knowing our bodies. For the first time in many years, I was fine with being naked in front of someone else. His compliments and ways of appreciating my body helped me gain self-confidence in the way I looked. I was discovering what it was like to explore my own sexuality in a safe and healthy way.

At the end of our first summer together, my parents left for a weekend to drive my brother to his university. As soon as I found out that I would have the house to myself for the weekend, I wasted no time in inviting Andrew over. I spent the whole day cleaning my room and decorating it with rose petals and candles. We hadn't ever discussed being ready to sleep together, and I wasn't expecting it to happen—all I wanted was a romantic night alone together.

He lied to his mom about where he would be overnight and took buses to my place. When he arrived, I ran a warm bath for us to relax in. The relaxing didn't last very long; we were all over each other and decided to move to the bed. It was the only time we had been alone together overnight without having to worry about getting caught. It must have been a combination of atmosphere, opportunity, and curiosity that led to what happened next.

With nothing on our minds except how badly we wanted each other, things were moving really fast. I wasn't sure where the night was taking us, but decided that it was better to be safe than sorry.

I gathered up some courage and managed to say, "Babe, maybe you should wear a condom . . . just in case."

Since we weren't sexually active with anyone other than each other, we had never used a condom together. After a few clumsy and awkward attempts, we were finally able to get one on right. I guess by that point, it felt as though the only thing left to do was to give it a try.

"Are you sure?" Andrew asked, and I responded with a nod.

I lay down on my back, anxious to feel him inside of me, and soon felt the weight of his chest press down against mine. As we looked deep into each other's eyes, he gently pushed himself inside.

He must have been able to tell that it was painful by the look on my face, because right away he asked me, "Are you okay? Do you want me to stop?"

I answered quietly, "No, it's fine. Just go slowly."

He buried his face into my shoulder and began moving himself in and out. With my hands holding tightly on to his strong back, and taking in the smell of cologne on his skin, I remember thinking to myself, *Thank God it's Andrew and not someone else!*

Even though it felt good, I couldn't concentrate. My mind was racing and I was overcome by a tidal wave of different emotions: *Does it feel good for him? Are we doing this right?* Although I was very unsure about everything that was happening, I wasn't at all scared. As always, I knew that I was safe in his arms. That night, as I lay in bed next to him, I felt that we were closer than ever. It wasn't as though something had changed between us; I just felt that we were both content.

For the next couple of weeks, I started to feel different; I could barely recognize any of my emotions. There was some kind of emptiness inside of me that I knew could only be filled by Andrew. He was the only thing on my mind, and I wanted desperately to be with him each minute of every day. Thankfully, he was just as much of a sweetheart as always and I was easily comforted by the stability of our loving relationship.

We later discussed what had happened that night and agreed that maybe we were both still too young for sex. Neither of us regretted having lost our virginity to each other, but we decided to wait until we felt more ready to try it again. It wasn't until much later that sex became a regular part of our time together, and only then were we able to enjoy it fully.

It has now been almost four and a half years since Andrew and I first met, and I am proud to say that we are still going strong. It hasn't always been easy, but we've both managed to hang on tight through the ups and downs of our roller coaster–like lives. Even though I've always been surrounded by wonderful and supportive people, I'm not sure how I would have handled my teenage years without Andrew by my side. Whose hand would I have held during my father's funeral? On whose shoulder would I have cried when I felt as though my world was sure to implode? With Andrew I have been able to rediscover trust through a loving, yet not interdependent, relationship: something that few people in my position are able to find. Thanks to the love that we've shared, I've learned how to feel comfortable with my sexuality. I now see that it is a beautiful and positive part of who I am.

STATE OF CONFUSION

Jamie Reid, 24, North Carolina

I LOGGED ON TO THE OPEN CHAT AND CHOSE A SCREEN name that pinpointed my intentions. With a thousand doubts running through my mind but one relentless urge, I typed in . . .

Curious: female from NC, looking for first experience

I stared at the screen, barely breathing, watching others' comments appear and fade, but saw none that responded to mine. I shook my head nervously and then I typed it again.

Curious: female from NC, looking for first experience

This time I got a response.

MDee6000: Hey Curious. How are you?
Curious: I am fine and you?
MDee6000: I am good. What part of NC are you from?
Curious: Greensboro. And you?

MDee6000: Durham.

Curious: Oh ok, that is not too far from . . . that may be about an hour away.

MDee6000: Cool Deal. So what are you here looking for?

Curious: To be honest I really don't know what I am looking for. I just know lately I have been fantasizing about the touch of a woman. So here I am.

MDee6000: Sounds like you are sure to me.

Curious: Well I guess you can say that. So what are you looking for?

MDee6000: A new friend. The last one I had became a little clingy. So what is your status?

Curious: Status?

MDee6000: Married, single, boyfriend?

Curious: I have a boyfriend. And you?

MDee6000: Married.

Curious: How old are you?

MDee6000: 25. And you?

Curious: I just turned 21.

So it began. . . .

That night, after having my first encounter, so to speak, I sat with my hands behind my head, thinking of the moments, sightings, and conversations that brought me to this place. To be really honest, some of those times I was left in a state of confusion. I would ask myself daily who I was becoming. It was getting harder by the day to look at myself in the mirror. Even looking at the man I was supposed to be in love with was becoming harder on me by the moment. I wondered how I could explain to him that I was changing and I wasn't sure if it was for the better or the worse. Now, don't get me wrong, my heart and soul were deeply in love with my boyfriend, but my body seemed to yearn for more, so how was I to come up with an explanation for him? I could feel myself withdrawing from him. I was no longer fiending for just his touch. I simply wanted the touch of someone else.

As time moved on, I continued to battle with myself. I thought about the saying "curiosity kills the cat," but I could feel my curiosity about being with a girl growing all the time, so I suppose I was about to be dead. I would find myself fantasizing while lying in bed with my boyfriend. I would fantasize about him, her, and me, and then my mind would just flash to just her and me. My body responded in ways that his image could not inspire. I was beginning to drive myself crazy. I knew it was time for me to act on my feelings, but I didn't want to hide it from my boyfriend. So I decided to ask him how he felt about bisexual women.

"I have a question for you," I said.

"Sure, but can it wait until this show goes off?"

"Naw, I really want to talk to you about this."

"Okay, you have my attention."

Here goes nothing, I said to myself. "How do you feel about bisexual women?"

"Why do you ask that?"

"Just to have a conversation with you."

"Whatever. Those chickens that you call friends are always putting something funny on your mind. I keep telling you that they're bad news. They don't care anything about you. Why do you continue to have conversations with them?"

"I didn't ask you that question for you to bad-mouth my friends. And for your information, the girls and I were talking about it only because we were watching a movie and it had a little to do with that. So can you please give me your opinion?"

I had to quickly defuse that argument before it even happened. See, my boyfriend couldn't stand my girls. He felt they filled my head with nonsense. But my thoughts were not influenced by anything they had to say—my mind was already made up. I wanted the experience and I wanted his opinion.

"All right, since you really want to have this conversation. I personally don't think it is right. I see those types of women as greedy and selfish. They want to have their cake and eat it too. They need to choose between the two lifestyles. Either it's gay or straight . . . there is no in-between." I sat there and let his comments sink in. "What are your thoughts on it?"

"Personally, I don't care. I feel that it is their choice, and if that is what they like to do then there should be no problem. It is about the freedom of choosing."

"So would you get down with a woman?" I sat there for a moment and debated if I wanted to give my real thoughts or what he wanted to hear. In his eyes I was the perfect girlfriend. I took care of our family, my house, his house, managed to go to school full-time and work a full-time job. I never questioned him about where he had been or who he had been with. I wasn't the type of girlfriend who didn't trust her man.

So I answered him the way he wanted me to: "No, but if you wanted to, I would do it for you."

"You would do it for me. I figured you would say something like that. You are always putting me first. Baby, you are so giving, I could never replace you. We are going to be together forever."

"Forever."

But fate has a way of nudging us toward our desires. A month after that same conversation I was sitting on that same couch, crying on my roommate's shoulder, not because I had strayed, but because my boyfriend had. I found out that he was spending time with another young lady. I realized that I was the only one worrying about someone else, so I decided to do something just for me. I would suppress my feelings and thoughts until then.

After my roommate left, I sat down at my computer and began searching singles' sites. The only reason I chose to go the online route was because I didn't want to get anyone around me involved in my search. Plus, I had already seen what this type of thing could do to my friendship with some of my friends: They turned against my roommate when she came out to them. So turning to them was out of the question.

I know what you are thinking—the Internet is not the safest way—but I felt I could disappear without a trace.

After I typed those first words—"female from NC, looking for first experience"—and MDee6000 responded, it became much simpler. We got the basic stuff out of the way. I had a kid and she didn't, I was going to school full-time and working a full-time job, and so was she. I was five-foot-two and so was she. We found that we had a lot of things in common. Personally, I wanted to know more about her. After our first conversation, we talked every day online. Once I felt comfortable enough, we traded pictures with each other. She was beautiful. She was one of those natural beauties—you know the ones—who need no makeup. I was definitely attracted to her and nicknamed her Pretty Lady.

After months of talking online, she offered me her phone number. We would talk on Saturday nights when I got off work. I would talk to her until I got home to my cheating boyfriend. Oh yeah, he was still seeing that girl. My roommate and Pretty Lady were the only ones who knew why I took extra hours at work and stayed away from him so much.

One Saturday, the routine changed: He called to say that he was taking our daughter out of town to visit his family and they wouldn't be back until Sunday night. A night of peace and no worries was all that I could see. I called my job and asked my manager if they really needed me to come in. She told me I could have the day off, so instinctively I jumped in the shower—as if I had somewhere to actually go. So I decided to call Pretty Lady.

"Hey, Pretty Lady! How are you doing?"

"I am good. How are you doing, girl?"

"Good and bored."

"What, you're not working today?"

"No, I took the day off, and I have nothing to do."

"I'm shocked you're off. Boyfriend must be gone." She felt I was a certified workaholic, but she knew the real reason.

"Yes, he took the baby to visit his mom."

"What are you going to do with yourself?"

"I want to go shopping, but I hate doing that alone."

"Well, I'm game if you want to come down this way."

"That sounds like a plan to me. I haven't been to the mall there in a while."

"Well, you come on down here. I will be here all day, and I'm not doing anything today." She gave me directions to her house; it was exactly forty-five minutes away. I drove the speed limit while my mind raced to the possibilities. Was today the day?

When I arrived at Pretty Lady's house, she was waiting for me outside on the porch. As she walked toward my car, I began to get butterflies in my tummy. She opened my car door and sat down. I inhaled deep and heavy—yes, today was the day.

"Hey, girl!" she greeted me.

"Hey, Pretty Lady," I said shyly.

"It is so good to finally meet you. Your pictures don't do you any justice. You are even more beautiful in person."

"Thank you, I try . . . the same to you."

"Thank you. Are you ready to shop?"

"Shoot, girl! I was born ready." She gave me directions on how to get to the mall from her house, and we hit the beltline.

We spent three hours at the mall. I found out that she was just as silly as me. I hadn't laughed so hard in years. When we got back to her house, the day was still young and I really didn't want to go home. I could tell that she didn't want the day to end either, so I decided to stay. We watched movies and ate popcorn and talked more about life. I even checked out her wedding albums. I was lost in my own world when she asked, "Have you talked to your boyfriend?"

"About what?"

"About your curiosity?"

"Well, we talked about it. His answer was that he couldn't get down like that."

"How did that make you feel?"

"A little uneasy, because I felt my thoughts of wanting to try something different were a form of cheating."

"So, did it change your mind?"

"No, because it is something I really want for myself. I have been going through so much with him. I can only worry about myself, since he is not."

"Is that chick still calling you?"

"Yes, and I am tired of it all. So I am just going to do me."

"Let me do you."

I stopped breathing and looked up at Pretty Lady's soft yet sincere expression.

"I'm sorry," she continued. "I've been holding that in all day. I have wanted you for a while now. Please don't think that is all I want from you; I really like the friendship that you and I are building. You don't have to do anything—I will just do you, and you won't have to do anything to me."

"Okay."

"You know that this will only be between you and me."

"Yes," I replied, speaking from pure instinct, not allowing myself to second-guess my feelings for the first time in what felt like forever.

"I will still be your friend after the fact. And if you don't like it, it will never happen again."

"All right, I'm game."

"Good." I knew at that very moment I had reached a point of no return. And I was about to get exactly what I wanted. . . .

She began touching me in places that had been unveiled only by the hands of a man, but her touch was softer—gentler. I wasn't sure if I was supposed to be feeling this good. So I took my mind off it and imagined that she was a man pleasuring me. But once I opened my eyes, I was thrust back into reality. She was not a man and there was nothing to imagine. I was getting my first experience and I liked it; I enjoyed her touching my body. I felt like my body was lifted up and floating above me. I was making sounds that I had never heard escape my body as she caressed my inner thigh. Her tongue was very skillful, and she was working my body over and over again. I kept thinking how new and wonderful this feeling was, something that I had not been able to experience even with my boyfriend. I felt a warmth rush over my body, and I knew the ultimate was coming. A fire had been lit in me that no longer could be extinguished. I never thought my body would succumb to the touch of a woman. I knew at that very moment that this was now a part of me. I wasn't in love with a woman, but I was enjoying the touch of one and for some reason I wanted to reciprocate the gesture. But I knew I wasn't ready for that.

I don't know how many times I came for Pretty Lady; I just know it was too many to really count. I was at a loss for words for what she was doing to me. When my breathing became regular again, all I could do was look at her and smile. As our eyes met, hers reassured me that this was our little secret.

That whole situation was four years ago. For once I had found the strength to do things that I wanted to do. I was happy with my choice. But being the thinker that I am, I worried about what others would think of me. Was I gay now, since I liked it so much? No, I wasn't—I still had a passion for men. Call me greedy, even judge me if you like. I had grown tired of what everyone else wanted me to be. The girl who never opened her mouth and said what she really wanted out of life. The one who attended the college her parents wanted her to. I even befriended the right girls so that I could get into the right sorority. I had to find my identity inside of myself, so today, I stand as a sexually free woman who has no doubts about her sexuality. I am Bisexual.

POPPING

Crystal Coburn, 25, Ontario

BEFORE I CAN GIVE MYSELF FIVE MINUTES TO THINK IT over, Aaron is already maneuvering his four-door over the curb, through the playground gravel, and onto the middle of a pitch-black soccer field. As he's about to position us at center stage—void of any audience—all I can think about is, *Thank God I don't have to pee.* Sex on a full tank is no fun.

After he parks the car, he leans over and kisses me, his girlfriend of seven years, then quickly exits and motions for me to grab his jacket. As soon as I get out and round the right front headlight, he's all over me all over again. We're moving so fast, yet my brain is working so slow. I hop up onto the hood before he can spread his jacket. In that instant, I realize the *way-too-hot* heat on my back from the hood of a recently driven car is more than I was ready for. Instinctively I arch, and if it wasn't for his quick hands, I would have fallen off.

All I can manage is a breathless "Oh shit."

"Don't worry, you won't fall."

In the next instant his zipper is pulled, my black Vicky's are dropped, and I'm gripping the wipers in a desperate attempt not to fall off. Just like that, I forget about the heat and discomfort and focus on his face, contorted but so honest. His movements cause my back to wax the old paint new again. Every jump in my body creates a ripple-effect popping sound sure to leave a dent.

I'm thinking, *If this were kids dropping bricks onto his car, he would be livid.* But it's not. The damage is unimportant; he's increasing his pace as the night air causes his nose to run. I can't help but stare at the clear sky and wonder if constellations are big pictures taken of moments just like this. I swear I see the stars realign in the shape of what we're doing in the dark.

This is what freedom feels like. I know what we're making is more than love. It's more raw, more human than that. It's about feeding the appetite that's discouraged in charm-school etiquette by misguided mothers, fathers, teachers, and media outlets. It's about proudly breaking out of the "good girls don't do that" mold and simply satisfying yourself and feeling good about it. Because even though what I was up to was hideously unladylike and the hot, sloping car hood made finding the easiest position absurdly difficult, it was wonderful—wonderful in the healthiest, most un-Hollywood way. Wonderful because that genuine awkwardness is what turned me on the most.

I NEVER HAD WHAT YOU WOULD CONSIDER A HIGH SEX drive. I was interested in sex once I experienced it, but to say that I was craving it all the time would be a lie. Actually, to say that I wanted it most days of the week would be a stretch. I don't know if it's because I had less sexual partners than fingers on one hand, or that the ones I had never produced any kind of orgasm. Maybe it was because I didn't even know what an orgasm felt like and basically completely accepted I would never have one. That's not to say that my past sexual partners didn't contribute to my "good enough" experiences; it was probably that I hadn't been emotionally stimulated enough to climax once sex was taking place.

Whatever the reason, my libido had been on cruise control for many years. I never tried new positions (doggy-style and missionary are not new), I never used other parts of my body to please my partner, and I *for sure* never considered having sex on anything other than a box spring. Not even the desk chair in my bedroom seemed appealing. To be honest, I always thought of those experiences as belonging to *other girls*—you know . . . freaks. Those were things porn stars did. Things far from anything I was willing to do.

It didn't help either that I didn't have girlfriends who would talk about these things even if I was curious about them. Me and my two friends Chantal and Natasha were all living under the "good girl" image, so to reveal anything that might suggest otherwise would change our thoughts of each other. My best friend Chantal didn't lose her virginity till she was twenty-one. So unfortunately, I never had an outlet to poke and prod with questions or confessions. I guess you could say that added to my active yet unexciting sex life.

It's wonderful how things can change, though, when you meet someone who not only has a sex drive that's through the roof but also wants you to get that high. Something changed in me when I met Aaron. It was basically instant: From one month after we met, when we started having sex, I became more . . . into it. Not just into sex but into the biological act: the touching and feeling, kissing and caressing. My unintentionally frigid walls were falling at a rate that I hadn't anticipated, and the best part is—I loved it.

Not only was Aaron a fun, loving, honest guy with swagger-right attitude, but the way he treated me was phenomenal. Like all men, he wasn't perfect, but he tended to my emotional and physical needs like no other man I knew. Inside of our relationship, I was able to improve my connection to my sexual self. This new comfort allowed me to feel okay to openly explore new adventures with him.

Before Aaron, I had never had sex in a car, in the shower, on a bathroom counter, or on a couch with the possibility of parents arriving home any minute! Those experiences were locked in Eric Jerome Dickey books. I never imagined they would become mine. We had done a lot over the first year of our relationship, which to me was exciting, but the momentum didn't slow down during the six years that followed. Being in a committed relationship made it easier to open up sexually, so as time went on I was learning to let go and embrace new passion. We had done a lot with each other, some things that were a first for me.

Who knew I would be breaking beds, scratching paint, and sinking my teeth into human flesh over a roaring clitoral orgasm that I didn't want his mom to hear? With Aaron, sex didn't only have three letters and one syllable. Sex involved intense panting, sweat dripping off the middle of my back, increased flexibility, overworked quadriceps, and more calls to the heavens that my churchgoing grandmother ever knew I made.

Funny enough, my belief in women finding their own happiness before pleasing a man has seemed to strengthen with each *yes!* I say to him. What I mean is that I now understand how a woman can be so in control by surrendering inhibitions and hang-ups. What I learned with Aaron was that screaming out, "You're the best I've ever had!" with my back in the shape of a boomerang was as empowering for him as it was for me.

THE ONLY LOVE THAT NEVER HURTS ME

Andrea, 20, Quebec

SHOWERING IS A DIVINE TREAT
Step into the icy tub and run my love
Turn the heat until it burns my feet
Release the center piece
I love the first time our bodies meet
The body of water
And the body of me
We play like two love-stricken birds
It rinses while I wash
Foreplay intensifies
Stepping coolly to the side
We both know just what's in mind
Lift the head and caress its tip
Change the setting to a jetlike stick
My vagina responds with a lustful reaction
For this love she has a strong attraction

In anticipation she releases contraction
Oozing out her exotic juices
There is no better, her throbbing profuses
I lower the head to meet her core
The body shudders, vagina begs for more
Lifting the labia and spreading my thighs
Give clit all the love water can comprise
Legs soft, body longing, eyes turn black
Soul moving in between this world and the other
The water massages me
The only unselfish lover
The friction so intense the pleasure too immense
Why women feel shame makes no damn sense
The body is exploding
I know for release she is loading
The time of completion I am secretly loathing
Contraction
Contraction
An incomparable orgasmic reaction
Body given in lends itself to the floor
The water still runs but I can take no more
My perfect lover taps my nipple
I lay limp, pleasure has me a cripple
I return the showerhead to the fixture
Breath heavy, body light
A sheepish grin crosses my face
See you tomorrow. Same time same place.

THE LIDO DECK

Laurence Anthony, 24, Ontario

MOIST, BUT NOT TOO WET; AGGRESSIVE, YET PATIENT; innocent, but experienced; and confident, but still shy—that's what kissing her felt like. We had kissed and explored each other before, but this was different. My lips, followed by my tongue, slid down her neck, passed her collar, traveled farther down toward her breasts. I slowly and enjoyably teased and glided over her nipples. It was extremely hot, and this was different than when we were on top of the Lido deck days before. This time, she didn't restrain my hands. Instead, she used her own and reached for my belt as I slid her pants off. . . .

Two years, six months, and eleven days ago—that was the last time I found love. In my early teens, I grew up witnessing many variations of it. I saw women cheated on and abandoned by their men. I saw men taken for granted and underappreciated by their women. My observations were combined with my mother's adoration for R&B and jazz music, which I woke up to every morning. I would listen to the lyrics about love:

finding it, losing it, wanting it, betraying it, and needing it. I was captivated by the idea of a feeling that I had never experienced outside of my family.

IT WAS FRIDAY AFTERNOON IN MIAMI. MY GRANDPARENTS chose to celebrate their fiftieth anniversary among the people who had helped get them through all those decades. Fifty years is a long time! My entire family and I boarded the cruise ship to celebrate my grandfolks' love, but the symbolism of the event would only occur to me long after I returned home. As far as I was concerned I was single, ambitious, employed, and boarding a ship to sail the Caribbean. Finding love was the farthest thing from my mind.

Darren, my younger brother, asked, "So, you plan on going off this week?" We were about to enter one of the lounges posing as a club on the ship. "Can I borrow ID?"

I smiled, having forgotten just how young Darren still was. "No problem," I said, "but don't come in for another twenty-five minutes. That should be enough time for security to forget a name and face."

He agreed and I hit the bar. Not long after, Darren came in. We had a few drinks and watched the other vacationers dance, flirt, and drink. Music was blasting in all corners of the lounge and hip-hop was the genre of choice. This was just fine by me and my brother, especially since not everyone can dance or move to hip-hop. We began a game of picking out the worst dancers. You know the type: the old man who routinely uses his "roll the dice" dance move or the young college guy who's certain he's starring in his own rap video, complete with hand gestures and signals, pouring beer on the floor and lip-synching T.I. lyrics to bewildered girls.

I left to get us more drinks at the bar. It was when I was returning with a mojito in one hand and a rum and Coke in the other that a young lady approached me.

"Hi!"

Judging from her uppity intro, I assumed she was either a cheerleader or a Miss Congeniality. I sized her up: Attractive? Yes. Energetic? Hell yeah. Conversation holder? We were soon to find out. So I stood with my drinks in hand and listened to her as we exchanged pleasantries.

"I'm Molly! I go to school in Columbus, Ohio! Where are you from?"

"I'm Laurence. I'm from Toronto."

This excited her even more. "Wow! I've never met anyone from Canada. Isn't it cold up there?"

Molly wasn't doing much for my opinion on how little many Americans seem to know about Canada. "The winters can be cold, Molly, for sure. Our summers can be pretty hot, though. So it's not always cold, and we do not live in igloos."

She let out a loud laugh—really loud. "I didn't think you lived in an igloo, silly!" She slapped my shoulder. "You're funny."

Molly was drunk. Not crazy drunk, but she was headed there soon. I entertained small talk with her for a couple minutes, but I was getting restless and was eager to return to hanging with my brother.

"I'm sorry, Molly," I smiled and apologized, "but I need to bring this drink to my brother."

As I began to walk away, Molly stated quite provocatively, "You can only go if I see you later."

"Of course," which was a half lie because although I was less than interested and one-night stands were not a top priority, it was a possibility.

I made my way to join Darren, who at this point was laughing it up with two college guys wearing jerseys and fitted hats. As I stood there listening to the Jurassic-age dialogue, I noticed a beautiful girl salsa dancing in a small group. It wasn't her light olive skin or her long black hair swinging (I'm more of a short-haired guy), or even the flock of men surrounding her, that led me to pause. Actually, it wasn't that girl at all. It was the young lady to her left that damn near caused me to go into cardiac arrest. I mean, my heart 100 percent stopped. I marveled. This girl was stunning. I don't mean stunning in the sense of overly dressed, or great makeup, or jewels, or even unattainable and hyperbolic physical features. No, she was the epitome of a word that had always stuck with me since an old teacher of mine had defined it for me years ago. Elegance is the combination of beauty and simplicity at the same time. That's exactly what she was: elegant.

I turned to Darren. "Bro, do you see that girl?"

Darren looked over. "Yeah," he said, then looked back at me. "I thought you weren't here for girls."

"I'm not, I wasn't, but wow, she's . . . " My feet started moving before I even realized that my mind was completely blank. I panicked, but it was too late to turn back. I went through every greeting, from "hello" to "bonjour" to "hey" to "what's up?" but nothing stuck. I took another step, and then the music stopped. The ship's captain was on the PA. All the younger vacationers on this cruise had a running joke about our captain, Stewart, or Stewie for short. Stewie had a thick Aussie accent and quite a propensity for saying words that just didn't sound exactly right together.

"Ladies and gents, this is mi final announcement for the eve. All adults are welcome to the Theater Room for a comedy show of such epic proportions. Please call a loved one to take care of your children, because you're all going to die laughing! See you there."

Stewie had just given me an in. I approached Miss Elegant with as much confidence and charm as I could muster and said, "Wow! That Stewie is pretty corny, huh?"

That was my line. That was my line! I mean, of all the things I could say, I actually thought it was decent and we could have bonded over our shared perception of Stewie's lame jokes.

Miss Elegant looked at me and said, "I actually like Stewie. Don't make fun of him."

Crash. Wow, it was a crash and burn. I had nothing to say—no rebuttal, no witty line, no comeback—and so I walked back to sit down, feeling defeated.

A few songs went by before Darren pulled up beside me. "You okay, bro?"

"I'm good. Just made a move and it didn't really go down," I said to him. He laughed. "Molly's starting to look good now, huh?"

I was discouraged. My ego wasn't crushed as much as I was inexplicably truly attracted to this girl I had just kinda-sorta met. It shouldn't have bothered me, but it did. As Darren left to head to the dance floor, I looked at the crowd and sipped another mojito. I was about to leave when a figure sat down beside me.

"Do you always sip drinks by yourself in a lounge?"

It was her, Miss Elegant, and she was sitting beside me, talking to me. She smelled great, really great.

"Not often, but it's not often I get rejected."

A smile, then, "You should try harder next time. I'm Felicia."

She wasn't the first Felicia I've ever met, but she was definitely the most beautiful.

"Laurence. It's nice to meet you."

"So, what are you doing here?"

"I'm here for my grandparents' fiftieth anniversary."

"Wow. That's amazing. Here I am thinking it's cool that I'm here on my spring break, and you're here for something like that. That's really awesome."

The words came out with such sincerity. I was genuinely surprised because you don't expect to find good listeners in a club. "What school do you go to?"

"I go to Cornell."

"Ivy League school, right?"

She nodded. "Yeah."

I had met an elegant, drop-dead-gorgeous lady with a sharp sense of humor who was not only comfortable in her own beautifully dark chocolate skin, but also confident and really casual. We got to know one another some more as the songs pumping in the background created the soundtrack for our first meeting.

As the night progressed we found ourselves on the top deck of the ship, known as the Lido deck. We chatted for hours about school, life, and whose country was better. She boasted about her Trinidadian and American roots, while I big-upped my Jamaican and Canadian background. It was perhaps the most honest and candid I had been with anyone—stranger or not.

"Well, Mr. Laurence from Canada," she said with a smile, "I'm kinda tired. I think it's bedtime for me."

"Cool. It was really good to meet you, even though you're Trinidadian."

"Hey!" She punched my shoulder. Unlike Molly, this was a welcomed, light punch. "I'm the coolest Trini you've ever met."

"You just might be; there aren't many cool ones to pick from."

She laughed. "Not many? Or not many who reject Jamaican Canadians!"

I had nothing.

"I'm playing with you," she said. "I'll see you around, I hope."

I was hoping the same.

When fate wants to intervene, there isn't anything you can do. Fight it, ignore it, embrace it, it doesn't matter. Before our meeting in the pseudoclub, I had never seen Felicia once on the ship, but now she was everywhere. We would meet randomly on various floors of the ship, and our conversations were as captivating as the first time. I was headed to the big dinner with my family on my grandparents' anniversary day, and as I was entering the dining room, Felicia was doing the same. Fate. She walked off to her table. I headed for mine, where Darren, my mom and grandparents, and the rest of my family were sitting. Before I took another step, I turned around and approached the hostess of the large dining lounge. "Do you have a pen I could borrow, please?"

She handed me a pen and I wrote:

I can't think of anything better to do on my grandparents' anniversary than to enjoy a midnight stroll on the ship, with the only woman on this ship more elegant than my grandmother. Ring me in my room if you think you know someone like that.

P.S. hoping it's you.
—L

After dinner, I returned to my room and checked my messages. "It's Felicia, I'll see you at eleven o'clock," her voice traveled over the machine.

It was the evening before we were to dock in Jamaica and we both found ourselves touring the ship. We ended up, once again, on the Lido deck. We had flirted and chatted for days, but it was when the two of us were alone, on that top deck, when the stars and moon provided a subtle light, that our lips finally met. It was beautiful. No corny words exchanged, just the two of us knowing that a kiss was wanted, and it was as well scripted as one could be. I would've been content with the way our lips felt together, but with the waves crashing below and the beautiful sounds of the night we found ourselves on a beach chair, caressing and kissing. I mean, inhibitions were erased, walls were down, and passion replaced every notion of common sense. I didn't know her and she knew less about me, but we were attracted to one another. I spent time kissing the right side of her neck, moving over to the left, making sure every movement I made was both gentle and a statement of my attraction. I caressed her thighs, exposed by her tan-colored dress, and began to slowly raise my hands up toward her . . .

"We should stop. Let's use some good judgment here. We don't know each other."

I was disappointed. I could think of no greater setting or stage for us to have had sex with one another, but instead of telling her that, I said, "Okay, let's just chill."

So we lay down and had another amazing conversation—I mean amazing. We just connected verbally so well that I was no longer thinking about sex. We traded stories, talked about the most random of topics, then finally fell asleep on the deck. When we woke up the Jamaican flag was hoisted high above the ship as dawn was breaking. It was undoubtedly the most romantic evening I had spent with anyone.

We spent the rest of the week getting to know each other. Then, on our final evening on the ship, out of sheer curiosity/duty/frustration/adoration, we had sex. It wasn't like the Lido deck. There was no moon, no stars, just waves crashing below. It was awkward. We put two beds together to form a queen size and I fell in between the cracks during our passionate session. She laughed out loud and I laughed with her. Our lips met over and over again. Moist, but not too wet; aggressive, yet patient; innocent, but experienced; and confident, but still shy—that's what kissing her felt like. We had kissed and explored each other before, but this was different. My lips, followed by my tongue, slid down her neck, passed her collar, traveled farther down toward her breasts. I slowly and enjoyably teased and glided over her nipples. It was extremely hot, and this was different than when we were on top of the Lido deck days before. This time, she didn't restrain my hands. Instead, she used her own and reached for my belt as I slid her pants off. We looked at each other and once I pushed inside, we didn't stop until every position was explored.

It wasn't what happened during our sexual experience that was touching. It was the cuddling, the spooning, and the honesty that came with it. It all felt natural and oddly comfortable. I told her I was a horrible snorer and she accepted it. We woke up hours later and prepared to say goodbye. I had my laptop with me and played Erykah Badu's "Next Lifetime," a song about two lovers who want to be with each other but can't. I wanted to spare Felicia and myself the phoniness of pretending to, or promising to, chat/call/write when it all seemed kind of pointless given the distance. She offered me her number, which I mentally recorded rather than physically wrote down, and I gave her my business card. It was the most awkward and unemotional goodbye you could imagine.

I was hungry and wanted to grab food before my family and I left the ship. I headed to the Lido deck, and as I stepped off the elevator and entered the main area of the deck, Felicia, who I had just given the worst goodbye of all time to, was sitting down, smoking a cigarette and having breakfast. I approached, undeterred and more confident than the first time we'd spoken. We had a breakfast that lasted over an hour, and our laughter on the Lido deck replaced the awkwardness in her bedroom hours before.

She caught her breath after a heartfelt giggle. "You're pretty cool with your clothes on."

My family and I boarded our plane back to Toronto. I knew from that moment on Felicia would be heavily on my mind, but I sincerely didn't anticipate that as soon I dropped my bags beside my own bed and opened my laptop, she would be on my screen.

Hello Mr. Laurence Anthony,

It's Felicia. I just got settled in at home. My trip back was great. It's nice to be home a.k.a. "the place that's better than your wack country!" I just thought I'd write you to say hi and hope you got in safe. It was a pleasure meeting you. You may not be the most exciting person I've ever met . . . but you're alright. Call me sometime and hopefully I'll talk to you soon. I'm off to unpack!

—Felicia

I responded, then she responded back. We conversed via email for weeks. Then one day I phoned, and once again we were on the Lido deck, wrapped in our own worlds until the sun rose and reminded us we had to start our days separately.

After a few weeks of constant contact, I stopped. Mentally, I was back in that bedroom on the ship, worried that I was getting myself involved in something to which there was no good ending.

Then one Sunday evening I caved and called. After that I decided I was going to see Felicia even though she lived in Ithaca, New York, which was a good five-hour drive from my home. But you know what, it could have been forty hours—I didn't care anymore. I didn't care that I told myself I was avoiding love. I didn't care that I was opening myself up to an emotion I'm not sure even existed between us.

When I boarded that ship, it was two years, six months, and eleven days since I had lost love. When I arrived in Ithaca, knocked on Felicia's door, and waited, I didn't know if there was love waiting in return for me, but I was ready to find out.

GOT QUESTIONS ABOUT CHAPTER 2?

GREAT SEX

What makes a sexual experience positive?

A lot of different things, but the only universally correct answer is you. You make an experience positive. If it's okay with you and you are happy with all aspects of your decision, then it's all good. Your life, your body, your call.

How do girls climax?

The wonderful thing about being a female is having a diverse sex life. The majority of girls climax through clitoral stimulation, but some have reported climaxing through vaginal intercourse. I have even heard stories of women experiencing climax just by being touched sensually on their backs or by being caressed by their lover.

What is this G-spot and where can I find it?

The G-spot/female prostate/urethral sponge is a small area located about an inch or two into the vaginal opening, toward the pelvis. What I gather from conversations I've had is that some like the sensation of it being touched, some do not feel much when it is touched, and some don't like it at all. Each woman reacts differently, depending on her partner/toy, mentality, arousal level, and unique body makeup.

What is an orgasm?

Scientifically, it is a series of rapid nerve and muscle contractions that results in a wave of sensation. Many people experience different effects and responses, so orgasm is generally a personal state. There are innumerable books, classes, and even religious practices that are designed to help women attain this state; don't worry if you're not an expert at age eighteen.

Is it uncommon for girls not to reach orgasm during intercourse?

Not at all. Despite pornos, movies, and soap operas that show women going absolutely wild from just intercourse, most women do not reach orgasm from it. Researchers predict that anywhere from 60 to 70 percent of women cannot achieve orgasm from vaginal intercourse alone. A lot of women need clitoral stimulation to reach their climax; the clitoris is the only known body part whose only function is to create sexual pleasure. It is made of the same tissue as the head of the male penis and has twice as many nerve endings. Sex also has much to do with the mental, and if there is no trust or adoration between lovers it's difficult to reach orgasm, so if you don't feel much pleasure during intercourse, that does not make you weird or frigid.

What makes someone "good in bed"?

Being receptive to their particular partner's needs, both emotionally and physically, while maintaining a standard of respect.

GREAT SEX—MEN

Laurence Anthony, 24, Ontario

Why all the fuss about penis size? Does it make sex better?

Laurence: Penis size definitely has an effect, but not always a great one. I've been with women who have felt really small to me, and a large penis can be too much. Some women don't even like a guy behind them if his penis is too big. But I feel that no woman, despite what she might say, wants a small-penis guy. The size, in my experience, means something, but not everything. A guy needs to know how to engage his partner, and that, more than size, will determine how good sex is.

Why do you think men tend to want to have sex more than women?

Laurence: Men and women both want sex. Some women want it more than men, but I agree that men mostly want it more. I honestly believe it's a natural, biological thing. Also, from an early age men are told to pursue women, and I think there's some sociological aspect to the sexual desire men have. Women are better at controlling that, or at least not being led by that desire as much as men.

What is the recipe for a positive sexual experience?

Laurence: Wow. That's a tough question. The recipe for a positive sexual experience is a strong desire to be pleased and to want to enjoy and stimulate yourself and the person you're with. I think you can have great sex with someone you love and someone you really dislike. I've done both and I can honestly state that sex with someone you love and are very attracted to is infinitely better. One-night stands are great, but a connection and an emotional investment in the person you're having sex with ensure a more positive sexual experience.

How do you know that you're a good lover if so many girls fake orgasms?

Laurence: Confidence and trust are just as important in the bedroom as they are in life. If there's no trust in the person you're having sex with, then there's no point having sex, because you're second-guessing him/her and yourself. You'll be worried that he/she isn't being truthful, and that will mess with your head and performance. Confidence is huge. You need to believe that you know what you're doing and if you make love with confidence, not cockiness, things usually work out.

What makes someone "good in bed"?

Laurence: Listening and being intuitive are important. Communication (verbal and physical) in the bedroom is crucial.

MASTURBATION

Andrea, 19, Quebec

How do girls masturbate?

Andrea: Most girls find sexual pleasure by themselves by stimulating their clitoris. The clitoris is about half an inch above the vagina and is covered by vaginal lips. Some people use their finger to massage it; others prefer to use their showerhead or a vibrator that they can place on top of their clitoris.

Do you feel dirty after you have done it?

Andrea: No, when I was younger I felt a bit strange, but now I just see it as a way to treat myself, like eating a bowl of ice cream. Like anything else, if it becomes addictive, that is when you have the real problem. Other than that it is completely normal.

Why do some pornos show girls masturbating with stuff like cucumbers?

Andrea: Really, I'm not sure, but I think it is arousing for males because they imagine themselves as the banana or what have you. Not only is this practice generally uncommon outside of pornos, but it is also unsafe to put foreign objects inside your vagina.

BISEXUALITY

Jamie Reid, 24, North Carolina

What makes someone bisexual?

Jamie: I feel what makes someone bisexual is being potentially sexually/romantically attracted to both men and women. If you get off on something that diverges from the heterosexual norm (e.g., watching girl-on-girl porn), that doesn't make you bisexual. In all honesty, I personally think that kissing another girl and liking it doesn't make you bisexual either. Just doing it one time doesn't make you bisexual; I think it only shows that you wanted to experiment.

Is bisexuality a state of limbo until you're fully homosexual?

Jamie: Not for most people. Most people who identify themselves as bisexual really are attracted to any gender, but there's a spectrum. Some people who are very attracted to the same sex but only a little attracted to the opposite sex might eventually identify as homosexual instead of bi, but most bi people I know seem to be truly bisexual.

Do you have a preference?

Jamie: Being a bisexual woman myself, I prefer men over women. I think men and women satisfy different needs. There are times I may not want to be manhandled; I may just want to be caressed. I feel that women tend to know what another woman wants, while on the other hand a man has no idea what we mean by "Baby, please be gentle."

If I was to find the right man to share my life with, I would bring it to his attention that I am a fully active bisexual woman. He at that time has an option either to accept it or to disagree with it.

Do most people just think you are confused?

Jamie: Being bisexual is often difficult because I don't feel accepted by the gay or straight communities. I have run into this misconception mostly with people in the gay community. My old roommate was a lesbian, and her friends that she would have come over to the house would try to find out if I was a lesbian as well. She would just let them know that I was bi but preferred men. They would then give me nasty looks, as if I was wrong and I needed to choose one or the other. As for my straight friends, I know who I can tell and the ones I will never tell.

Do you think that bisexuality is just a trend for most girls?

Jamie: I am a really observant person, and I have found that bisexuality has become a trend for women of all ages. I think that many young girls are doing the bisexual thing to please their male mate because it is such a turn-on for the guy. Another reason why some females turn to bisexuality is the lack of attention from the opposite sex. If there are certain things that people may like and their partner is unwilling to do (e.g., oral sex), they tend to turn to the same sex to give them sexual satisfaction.

MAKING LOVE

T.C., 20, Florida

In your experience, what is the difference between making love and having sex?

T.C.: In my experience, when you are making love you are emotionally—not just physically—connected to your partner. Everything is just so much more intense: the way you look into each other's eyes, the way you touch each other, the way it feels when the person you're in love with says, "I love you" every chance they get. All of your feelings are heightened to another level. To me, sex is just about "getting yours." It's all about temporary pleasure. When I make love, I can feel the butterflies in my stomach days later just thinking about the way my partner touched me. After sex, the pleasure I felt during is usually long gone.

How do you know if the person you're making love to is not just having sex with you?

T.C.: Because he is primarily worried about me feeling every inch of pleasure possible. He spends a lot of time kissing me and does things like stroke my hair, hold my hand, kiss my forehead, and rub my back after we're finished. He massages me all over because he knows it makes me feel special and he knows I love it. To top it off, he goes and gets us a big cup of cold juice and will feed me some snacks as we lie there together in bed and he tells me "I love you" some more. . . .

CHAPTER 2 CHECKPOINT

ARE YOU SPEAKING UP OR LAYING BACK?

If your partner playfully pounces on you, then presses their fingers to your lips and whispers in your ear, "Don't speak. Let our bodies do the talking," smile coyly, remove their hand, and retort, "You're going to want to hear what I have to say."

Research has shown that the most important component of a relationship is effective communication. Getting to know the way you and your partner communicate with each other can do wonders for your sex life.

Communication and honesty are often not the same thing. For example, if someone you're not the least bit interested in asks you on a date, your gut response may be *ew, never!* But your communication goal is not to offend the person who just complimented you, while letting them know that it's never going to happen. So instead you might say, "That's very sweet, but I don't look at you in that way; maybe sometime we can hang out in a group."

Better, right? You've gotten your point across while achieving both of your communication goals. The art of communication is a gift few have mastered. This multiple-choice quiz will determine if you're among the few or if you belong to the majority who could take a lesson on expression.

Circle the response that you think is the most effective communication approach.

1. Your partner has a new ear-licking routine that turns you off and makes you uncomfortable. You want them to stop doing it, so you tell them:

a) "Know the sound of a dog drinking water? That's what your ear routine reminds me of."
b) Nothing. It's not a big deal, and you don't want them to feel bad.
c) "I don't really like when people touch my ears. Do you know what I really like? When you kiss my neck. You're really good at that."

2. You're using the Internet on your partner's computer and you come across porn sites in their recent history. You're feeling weird about it . . . what do you do?

a) Don't say anything but try to be more like the porn stars in case that's what they want.
b) Freak out . . . they shouldn't be looking at that stuff in the first place.
c) Ask them why they frequent those sites, then tell them why it made you feel uncomfortable.

3. You overhear someone you are in a relationship with bragging about how many partners they've had. You are pissed, so you:

a) Walk up to them like everything is fine, greet their friends, then say, "Can I talk to you in private for a second?"
b) Act like you didn't hear it. People talk smack to their friends—no big deal. If they say it to your face, then get mad.
c) Walk right into the center of the group and publicly yell at them for being a scumbag.

4. You're fooling around with your partner, but are getting annoyed that what they're doing doesn't really feel pleasurable for you. What do you do?

a) Keep going with the flow. They must like it, so it doesn't matter if it feels good for you.
b) Give up on it altogether. If they can't please you, they shouldn't feel good either.
c) Use your words and body to show your partner what feels good, and encourage them to do the same.

5. While you're hot and heavy with your partner, they tend to use dirty talk that you find offensive. You let it go the first time, but they do it again, so you:

a) Respond with something equally offensive.
b) Stop them in their tracks and say, "Let's be free but let's not be disrespectful."
c) Curse them out and let them know the next time it happens, you've got a can of whoop-ass with their name on it.

6. Someone that you have thought about becoming intimate with says they don't like condoms. You reply:

a) "Do you hate them so much that you'd rather catch something or end up with a baby? If so, what other forms of protection are you cool with?"
b) Say nothing and decide to address your concerns down the road.
c) Lecture that person on the dangers of unprotected sex.

ANSWERS

1. Your partner has a new ear-licking routine that turns you off and makes you uncomfortable. You want them to stop doing it, so you tell them:

c) "I don't really like when people touch my ears. Do you know what I really like? When you kiss my neck. You're really good at that."

Sexuality is a very delicate place where people tend to feel most vulnerable. It's also a place where creativity should be encouraged. We all know everything we try isn't always awesome. If your partner is experimenting in the wrong area, gently guide them back on course.

2. You're using the Internet on your partner's computer and you come across porn sites in their recent history. You're feeling weird about it . . . what do you do?

c) Ask them why they frequent those sites, then tell them why it made you feel uncomfortable.

So much can be accomplished by using the word "why" effectively. Ask them why they like those kinds of sites. Tell them why you're uncomfortable with the thought of it. The best conversations start with that simple question, but make sure you hear their side before you begin to speak. The person will be more inclined to be honest if they don't think they're being put on trial.

3. You overhear someone you are in a relationship with bragging about how many partners they've had. You are pissed, so you:

a) Walk up to them like everything is fine, greet their friends, then say, "Can I talk to you in private for a second?"

Address the issue head-on, but be tasteful. Your partner should be made aware that how they speak in public reflects on you, and that disrespect, whether it's behind your back or to your face, is not okay. Their response will also show a lot about their character. When you request a private conversation, do they brush you off and try to save face? Or do they comply and hear you out?

4. You're fooling around with your partner, but are getting annoyed that what they're doing doesn't really feel pleasurable for you. What do you do?

c) Use your words and body to show your partner what feels good, and encourage them to do the same.

Speak now or forever hold your peace. Most people aren't mind readers, so if you do nothing, nothing will be done to fix the problem. You can help them with a simple nudge, a squirm, or a "hey, why don't you try this instead." Also, letting them know it is okay for them to guide you will assure them you realize you're not perfect either.

5. While you're hot and heavy with your partner, they tend to use dirty talk that you find offensive. You let it go the first time, but they do it again, so you:

b) Stop them in their tracks and say, "Let's be free but let's not be disrespectful."

Retaliating might reassure your partner that it's okay, and if you go along with it, your partner will continue to cross boundaries. You've got to nip it in the bud with direct eye contact and deliberation—if it's offensive, it needs to stop.

6. Someone that you have thought about becoming intimate with says they don't like condoms. You reply:

a) "Do you hate them so much that you'd rather catch something or end up with a baby? If so, what other forms of protection are you cool with?"

Reiterate the dangers, but don't hit them over the head with a holier-than-thou/you-should-know-better lecture. Again, ask why first. Their reasons may be legitimate, but know that it is always your perogative to set your own limits for sex, and to stick it to them. If you want to use condoms and your partner refuses, you can decline to have sex with them.

CHAPTER 3

CHAPTER 3

HAVEN'T BEEN QUITE RIGHT SINCE THAT NIGHT . . .

INTRODUCTION

I remember the first time I heard those words. I was sixteen, sitting on the edge of my friend's bathtub while she stared blankly at the smooth ivory-colored stick she was holding. Moments before, we had been laughing as she crouched in the silliest position, trying to urinate on the damn thing. Now that the test was positive, smiling was the farthest thing from our minds.

Pregnant.

In the movies, pregnancy is often associated with bliss; it's a cause for celebration—the celebration of life and the irreversible bond that a man and woman have created. But this was no movie, and there would be no celebration.

Two years later, the same friend shared news that was even more earth-shaking than her pregnancy had been:

"You know I've had HIV for some time, right?" she murmured.

I did not know, and at eighteen I stood frozen in shock at her casual delivery of such morbid news. I had read that

Baltimore, where I was attending college, had one of the highest STI rates in the United States, but no statistic could have prepared me for this experience. I wanted to hold her and wipe her tears away, but there were none in sight. She stood firm and collected.

"How?" I blurted out.

The story that she shared with me would forever change my perspective on sexuality.

THE FIRST TIME I WAS SEXUALLY ACTIVE—ACTUALLY, FOR the first couple of years of my sexual activity—I never stressed protection. Why should I? Perhaps people in places like Africa had to worry about diseases, but not me. I came from an affluent neighborhood and none of my friends or anyone I'd ever even heard about had contracted anything. Eventually I realized the raw ignorance of my rationalization. The truth came out years later. I *did* in fact know people who had contracted sexually transmitted diseases, but people don't go around advertising their disease status. It was only after I began my website that others felt comfortable enough to share that piece of their history with me. For those of you who don't think you know anyone with an STI, there's truth in the numbers: Nearly one in four sexually active teens will contract a sexually transmitted infection or disease.

This chapter tells the stories of young women who experienced physical consequences as a result of sexual activity. Their stories take you inside the authors' worlds and give you a unique opportunity to hear the voices behind the faceless images of your sexual education curriculum.

Before you turn the page and begin the emotional journey, I'd like to take a little time-out to recap some of the terms and definitions that everyone who is considering getting physically intimate should be familiar with.

Human papillomavirus (HPV): This virus is the most common and underreported STI in North America. It is the only known cause of cervical cancer, and some strains can cause genital warts. HPV is transmitted through contact of sexual organs, so condoms are not always able to do the trick. HPV infection has been linked to males or females with multiple sex partners.

Chlamydia: This is the most common bacterial infection associated with sex. Symptoms are yellowish discharge, inflamed genitals, burning while urinating, and a very harassing itch. However, most men and some women do not experience any symptoms. If it (or any other STI, for that matter) is left untreated, women can contract pelvic inflammatory disease (PID); women with chlamydia are also up to five times more likely to get infected with HIV if they come into contact with it. Chlamydia is spread through genital fluids, so a condom does help if it is worn at all times when genitals are exposed.

Gonorrhea: This disease affects the mucous membrane and causes symptoms similar to chlamydia's. It can also cause vomiting, fever, and bleeding between periods. Again, it often comes without any signs of infection and, if left untreated, can cause PID. Same prevention as chlamydia.

AIDS/HIV: HIV, the virus that can cause AIDS, is transmitted through semen, vaginal fluids, blood and breast milk. HIV is commonly spread through unprotected vaginal, anal, or oral sex, needle-sharing, or breast-feeding from an infected mother.

Herpes: Herpes can be contracted through spit, genital fluids, and skin-to-skin contact during an upcoming or existing herpes breakout. Herpes is treatable but not curable, and your best protection is to use condoms or dental dams during vaginal sex, oral sex, or anal sex.

Crabs: Crabs are lice in your pubic hair. Crabs can also spread to your eyebrows or scalp if your face happens to be near an infected person's pubic area. Once you have crabs you'll most likely know it, and the only way to prevent them is to be observant of your partners.

Scabies: Kind of like crabs, but scabies make a home in your skin, rather than your hair. Their poo can infect you under your skin and cause inflamed pimplelike bumps. This disease is associated with poor hygiene.

Urinary tract infection (UTI): This is not a traditional STI, but it can be linked with being sexually active. Symptoms include bleeding during urination, the urge to pee all the time, and general discomfort while peeing. Doctors recommend ensuring your partner's sexual organs are properly cleaned before allowing them to come in contact with your own to help prevention. It also helps to urinate after sex, and to use condoms.

Syphilis: These bacteria are contracted through mucous membranes and go through several phases. If left untreated, it can result in death. Just after an infection, a sore will develop at the site where the bacteria entered the body. Condoms can greatly help reduce the risk of transmission.

Yeast infection: Not a traditional STI, but studies show it is most common in sexually active women. Symptoms are itching, burning, genital inflammation, and a thick cottage cheese–like discharge.

Vaginitis/bacterial vaginosis: This is one of the most underreported STIs because most women assume it's a yeast infection. Symptoms are similar to those of a yeast infection, the difference being that women who suffer from vaginitis often notice an unusual strong "fishy" odor.

LGV: This attacks the lymph nodes close to your genitals, and if left untreated, swelling can cause bum blockage. This is a pretty uncommon STI.

Pregnancy: The big "p-word." When I was in sixth grade, we had a sex ed teacher who told us that women get pregnant when a man and a woman who love each other very much take off all of their clothes and hug one another very tightly. At the time I believed it, but now I know everyone has a pretty good handle on this concept, thanks to the high educational value of music and TV.

NEVER SAY NEVER

Olympia, 24, California

IT'S FUNNY HOW OFTEN WE SAY "NEVER." *THAT'S NEVER going to happen to me* or *I would never do that.*

I was fifteen years old, taking a break from being a good girl and ready to have some fun. I was living with my mother again because my father's wife and I couldn't get along anymore. I'd rather be mistreated by my own damn mama than by some stranger, so I said to hell with the wicked stepmother and went back home with my mother.

The first week that I was back, I started calling up all my old friends from around the way to catch up on what had been happening in the old neighborhood. My dad lived way out on the other side of town and I went to a preppy school in the burbs, so I was really missing my people. It was too late to switch schools, so I was forced to take the long trip and make the best of an awkward situation. I really didn't like my new school because all the girls were stuck up and all the boys were goofy, but I knew I had to find some reason to make attending worthwhile. And I did, in the form of a magnificent junior named Ron.

I already had a boyfriend, who was nineteen and out of school, but he was starting to get on my nerves with his possessive behavior, so I was looking for someone new to kick it with and Ron fit the bill. He was fine and chocolate with the prettiest smile, complete with dimples. After a couple of weeks of me wearing my skirts extra mini and my shirts really tight, he finally noticed me. We talked a little bit and exchanged numbers on the spot. He promised to call, and like a good boy he did.

We made plans to hook up one day, but the catch was, I had to cut school to do it. Now, these were my pre–bad girl days, so I really wasn't a pro at cutting school. The other thing was, he wanted me to bring somebody for his older cousin to kick it with. I asked my best friend, Belinda, to go with me and she agreed with a shrug; she cut school every day anyway, so this was no big deal for her. Ron called me the night before and instructed me to be ready and waiting for him outside of the drugstore by the school.

The next day Belinda and I were standing outside, smoking cigarettes and trying to look bored while we waited. These guys were older than us, so we were trying to play it cool like we did this every day, but I was as nervous as an illegal immigrant at the INS! When they finally pulled up, I was relieved to get inside a car before someone who knew my mama drove by.

Once inside the car, I introduced Belinda to Ron's cousin and they hit it off. Everybody was smoking weed, so I just played along and hit it like this was the norm for me. After driving for about twenty minutes, we finally arrived at Ron's cousin's house. He had a nice two-bedroom apartment decorated in all white—I mean white carpet, white everything! He worked for a local grocery store in the liquor department, so we had everything we wanted to drink right there: Hennessy, vodka, Goldschläger, whatever. Naturally, with all the alcohol around we started playing this drinking/domino game where every time you let the person opposite you score, you had to drink. Of course by the second hand, me and my girl were fucked up, to say the least. A few rounds later, my friend and Ron's cousin were passed out on the floor like old-time drinking buddies, and Ron inched closer to me.

"Let's go in the room," he whispered into my ear.

I agreed and we went off to the room to get "better acquainted." Now, I was no virgin at the time; I was sleeping with my boyfriend on a regular basis and I was just looking to try something new. Granted, I was a little drunk and my decision-making skills were off, but I wanted Ron just like he wanted me, so we did it. And did a good job at it too—that boy had skills!

It was about time for me to be getting out of school, and I knew that time was no longer our luxury. Ron wasn't ready to let me go.

He gave me that beautiful smile and asked, "Can we do it one more time?"

I looked at that beautiful face and thought over his proposition. We had used all of the condoms but I was still kind of on, so I said fuck it and told him he had to pull out before he ejaculated, and he did.

On the way home, we sat next to each other in the back seat and held hands. Everything was all good. I was even thinking about breaking up with my boyfriend so I could pursue Ron on a full-time basis. So the next couple of days were even better. I felt like I was walking on a cloud at school because Ron paid so much attention to me. All the girls wanted to be my friend because I had a junior on my jock, so to speak.

I hadn't heard from my boyfriend since before me and Ron, and to tell the truth I didn't really care why. I knew that Ron was where I wanted to be; I just chalked it up to good timing and pushed it out of my mind until my boyfriend was slammed in my face.

On a day like any other, I came home from school and swung open my front door, eager to unload my schoolbag. Before I could drop my things, my mom appeared at the front door. Bad sign.

"I received a phone call from Damon's roommate." (Damon was my boyfriend who had been AWOL for a few days.) "He informed me that Damon had raped his roommate's sister's friend and given her gonorrhea. Did you have sex with him?"

Words can't express the feeling that crept into my belly, not just because the answer was yes but because I knew that I would have to say that word to my mother. I nodded with my eyes locked on my backpack.

"Unprotected?" she pressed.

"Yes."

We scheduled an appointment for the following day to see my doctor. I started crying because I knew if I was infected, I had given it to Ron. My fucking life was going to be over at school. I would be known as the girl who was "burning men." So the doctor tested me for everything. When I got my results, I hardly felt surprised when he announced that the tests came back positive for chlamydia and gonorrhea. . . . I had never felt so dirty in my life.

On top of my doctor making me feel like an idiot, my mom cursed me out after we left. I cried all the way home. I didn't feel right in my own skin and I had no clue how I was going to tell Ron. An STI is a humiliation you want to carry alone, but my mother, my doctor, and the boy I cared for all had to know about my shame. I contemplated everything from running away to suicide on that ride home. In the end I decided to just tell him what had happened and hope for the best.

I called Ron as soon as I got home and explained what I had done and asked him to forgive me. Surprisingly he did, and thanked me for being woman enough to call him and tell the truth. I asked him to please not tell anybody about it and to get himself checked out as soon as possible.

"Thanks for being honest with me. You know, a lot of girls would have just not said shit and stopped calling."

After that phone call, I knew the next step was to find Damon. I think I was more upset by the fact that he had raped a woman than I was by the fact that he had given me something. I had been treated for it, so I was fine. I knew he had to know that I had found out about the rape by now. I didn't even think he knew about the STIs, and that's what scared me the most, the idea that he could be out there giving them to some unsuspecting girl. I kept trying to contact him if for no other reason than to tell him that he had an STI and needed to get treated. I eventually gave up trying.

I never thought I would contract a sexually transmitted disease. I never thought my boyfriend would turn out to be a rapist. I never thought I would be that girl in the clinic looking worried and sick. I always thought that this was the type of thing that happened to other girls—nasty girls. I was just trying to have a little fun; it seemed like no big deal to sleep with two guys at the same time. A lot of my friends did it and later laughed about it. It still scares me that I was so careless with not only my body but my life and other people's. I don't tell too many people about what happened to me because there is a stigma associated with having had a disease, especially one that is sexually transmitted, but I have put my feelings aside to tell this to you in hopes that you will understand the dangers of thinking it will never happen to you.

IT STINKS

Emma Johnson, 23, Ontario

DAMN. I FORGOT TO PUT ON DEODORANT.

My last thought before your call came through.

"Where are you?"

"In my car, on my way," I say, too quick to even remotely sound true.

Not that I was lying, I just had the words mixed up. See, what I had meant to say was "On my way to my car."

You hung up the phone without saying goodbye. Why the hell did I lie down for an extra ten minutes after I said I would get up and get dressed? When you called to say you were already at the gas station, I was butt naked on my way into the shower, lying like a rug, saying, "Cool, I'll meet you in five. . . . "

Now I stood at the front door with one shoe in one hand and my cell in the other, contemplating this serious dilemma: to run up and put on deodorant or not to? With the guilt of my lateness fresh on my mind and the freshness of my body in serious question, I made an executive decision and chose your time over my peace of mind. It's not as if we would be doing anything that would cause me to get hot and (Lord Jesus forbid) sweat.

I locked my front door and flew into my car, tossing my purse into the back seat. Like it was Indy I put the pedal to the floor, dropped my window, and gunned it. The wind stung my bare arms; I glanced down in shock like it was somebody else's doing . . . what the hell? Who wears a tube top—at night—in September?! I put my window back up, then mapped out our evening together with four words we wish all hygienically challenged people would subscribe to: discussion at a distance. I mean, I was kinda aiming to inspire you into a nice nickname like baby/butternut/beautiful . . . BO broad isn't quite making the wish list.

About one left turn from meeting up with you, I realized I had not factored in the motherfreakin' X factor: butterflies. As corny as this is, the thought of you warms me. Tart as the taste of lemon before it touches your tongue, my body responds to you just because I know you are near. Heat rose from my palms and I instinctively pressed my arms tighter into my body as if I could suffocate the inevitable.

I pulled into the gas station parking lot where we often met and saw your adorable face through your driver's-side window. I wanted to touch you.

Okay, plan B, I thought. I waved at you, then rushed past your car and into the small station's store, where I began frantically searching for some deodorant/baby powder/damn I'll take a box of Arm & Hammer! No such luck, and back to my discussion-at-a-distance plan I went.

I'm not sure when I forgot about the no-deodorant debacle. I'm lying. It's not a matter of forgetting, it's a matter of priority—like when your stomach stops growling because a massive headache moves in.

I used to think that the only reason we kept ending up in these hot, shirtless, gripping, groping, pressed-up, sliding, and ultimately "unsatisfying" scenarios was because of the venue. Today I was corrected.

We drove to the lake, got out of our cars, and walked with our fingers teasing each other's as our hands swung independently. But even with the smell of the lake (which is only so damn smelly because people like *you* litter in it), the herds of flies, the Big Brother glow of the nuclear power plant, and the sketchy midnight dog walkers, I could not keep from biting your lips as we stopped along the boardwalk to kiss. The sexual frustration of having the man you want yet having too much sense to allow your senses to take over is so hard on me that I feel it's only fair to share some of my pain with you.

Besides, damn you taste good . . . and oh boy you smell sweet . . . and Lord be fair don't touch me like that . . . and woo! who taught your ass to kiss like that . . . ?

We leave the boardwalk and fall in one pile into my car, where the kissing resumes. This moment is just between you and me—no one else. We're not slowing down but we're going so slow. You [illegible] so sweet—unravel me one kiss, one less piece of clothing, at a time. Oh my goodness, I'm losing control.

This scenario isn't new to me—you have tried to sleep with me many times before—but usually I'm able to stop things way before it gets this far. I close my eyes and I look for the closest fire escape to turn me off and get my conscience back on. I think of Robin Williams sitting on the toilet eating a bucket of KFC, I think of microwaved orange cheese and ham, I think of being in a small closed-off space with you, hot and heaving without any damn deodorant on.

"Emma. Relax."

I open my eyes and realize I'm breathing like a camel midroute between Egypt and Cape Town. Damn, that's pretty embarrassing.

Inhale. I draw in all the air my lungs can accommodate and let it go. I open my eyes. Yours are closed. I take this time and evaluate.

Here is a true confession: I'm so attracted to you, but at the same time our brief history has caused me to become so emotionally turned off by you. I have never had any intention of having sex with you. Whenever we've been close, there was always some recent nonsense that I could recall to make the moment too superficial to take on. There are wonderful things and not-so-wonderful things about you.

You're against a relationship, often hard to reach, and far too busy to keep a handle on.

. . . And then there's the wonderful. The face-value things that I've handed to you like a grocery list: your smile, your ambition, your humor, your insight, your arms, your lil' red patch of beard. Things that people who have known you for five minutes can cosign on. But there are a few things that time has added: your dedication, your admiration for beautiful things, your creativity, your ability to learn on a dime, your big dreams, even your little (sometimes a little annoying) questions. Finally, I adore how, when it really matters, you think about others miles before you consider yourself.

The last person in my life to be as close to me as you are right now told me something as I was pushing him away: *Just live, Emma—sometimes the moment is good enough.*

I wander back to our moment in the car. You open your eyes and stare right at me.

Inhale. I trace my lengthy index finger over your broad back. My fingers dip and dive in between the grooves of your muscles. *Holy!* There is this beautiful space on your body that extends from one tricep to the next that curls my toes and waters my mouth every time I think about it. *Exhale.*

Inhale. You take away my underwear, then put your face in between my legs to kiss the place you've never been inside. I squirm with appreciation and you squirm out of your boxers. I begin to feel nervous then terrified once you raise your chin from in between my thighs and lay down directly on top of me. I'm not a virgin but I'm not sure I'm ready for this either; I feel your hard buddy putting pressure on my va-jay-jay. *Exhale.*

"Promise me you won't go in?"

"I promise."

You say that, yet your hard, bone-dry boner puts even more pressure on the soft wetness between my legs. I contemplate fighting it—but instead I think, *I guess it's bound to happen sometime.* I know life is about good choices, but somewhere between the lines there has to be something written about stupid chances. I move my hips toward you, you ease inside of me. I bite my lip and mutter something I don't think I even hear.

Man, I can't believe I'm having sex with you for the very first time. Neither of us is wearing protection—that bothers me for a second, but then I shift my concern to how I should move.

I don't remember sex feeling like this, but it actually tickles a little bit. You go a little harder and I try to move my waist to keep up with you, but then you go a little faster and I lose all rhythm.

"Relax, I'll do the work."

I stop moving but you don't. I wait for the fireworks, anticipate the peak, but once again it doesn't come for me. I've come to accept that maybe my body doesn't work that way. So instead of being a downer I focus on the positive. I focus on your face, soft and deliberate. I focus on how careful you are, how much attention you pay to the little details. You bite your lip and put one hand behind your head, I think, *This guy is so adorable.*

Your movement becomes rough and jagged. Your eyes close, your chin raises, then you pull out of my body and come into the palm of your hand.

"I'm going to go clean up."

I'm kissed, then you step out of the car. I exhale my gratitude for the space between us right now; then I wipe, adjust, slide on, fasten, tuck in, and do a self-check. My chest feels light, my legs incredibly heavy, my armpits are a little unfresh but not horrible, my mind feels slightly stunned, and my conscience feels . . . okay, I think.

The next day you called and I felt a little more secure. I walked through Wal-Mart with my cell phone pressed to my ear, searching for a new iPod charger while I listened to you.

"Last night was special. I'm glad we waited."

"I'm glad too," I say, dragging out my "o." I feel my face blush and I hope others around me notice how happy I am.

The feeling of being with you is so lovely that it makes me tingle between my legs.

After a few days the tingling does not subside, and I wonder if it's such a good thing after all . . . then comes the discharge—milky and thick.

You are the first person I have slept with in the longest time, and there is nowhere else to look but in your direction. Shortly after the discharge, I notice a strange odor. Not just strange: gross and fishy.

The word "chlamydia" hardens in my mind before "strange coincidence" has a chance to. With great disdain, I make the phone call to the sexual-health clinic and book my Pap.

I hang up my cell and hang my head. *What happens after I find out the truth? Do I tell you? Do we stop talking? Do you turn around and accuse me? Do we act like it's no big deal?*

The appointment was just as uncomfortable as I would have imagined. The nurse made me feel like I'm the first idiot ever to not use a condom. And I kind of agree with her—at least on the idiot part.

"Your results will be in in two weeks. If nothing is wrong, we will not call. If something is wrong, we will call with the code name, and after you confirm it's you, we can share what we've found."

This is going to be a rough two weeks, I thought, nodding and wringing my hands. How wrong I was. Six days later, I received a blocked call. . . .

"Hello, this is Faith. Is Emma there?"

I squinted to see the time: 8:00 AM. My stomach tore in two and my morning breath felt flaky and coarse slithering down my throat. I hadn't had time to prepare mentally. The phone call in itself already told me all that mattered—something was wrong. I just had to find out what.

"Yes, this is Emma."

"Your Pap results came back okay. We found bacterial vaginosis."

"Excuse me?" I say, half relieved it's not herpes and half terrified I have no clue what the hell she just said.

"Bacterial vaginosis, it's an overgrowth of bad bacteria. It could be caused by a number of things: if you're not wearing cotton underwear, if you're eating a lot of sugars, if you do not clean yourself adequately after going to the bathroom, but there is no set cause. Sometimes you can get it from a new sexual partner who has recently been sexually active with another woman. BV can pass from one female to the next, but it's still unclear what role men play in transmitting the bacteria, since they technically cannot house it without a vagina. Still, it's not a possibility to rule out."

Bingo. I'll give you research. I've never had any vaginal issues before, and days after having sex with Bacteria Boy, I've got an infection.

She continued, "Sometimes the infection clears on its own. You can come in for treatment, but only if you notice the symptoms are still there."

I hung up the phone and logged on to the computer. BV can increase your risk of contracting other STIs, including HIV; BV can cause numerous other complications if left untreated. I called back the clinic and set up an appointment to come in the next day.

I wish I could say it was as simple as I got treated, then forgot the whole thing ever happened, but it wasn't. After leaving the clinic, I decided to tell you what I had been going through on my own.

"Look, after we slept together the first time I started to get very strange symptoms, so I went to the clinic because I thought I had chlamydia. It turns out I had an infection called bacterial vaginosis, and I think that I got this infection from you. If we are going to be sexually active, we should always use protection, and if you are going to be sexually active with others, you should tell me."

"Wow, I don't know what to say. I'm glad you told me and everything, but I don't know what I'm supposed to do with that information. Do you still want to see each other later?"

So we continued to see each other, but I have to be honest: I never looked at you the same.

"Why are you stopping?"

I rolled off of you onto my stomach, too embarrassed to look you in the eye. The smell of my vagina was horrible; it just kept coming back. I had already been treated twice and taken loads of vitamins, but my natural scent had been kidnapped by this unrecognizable odor. It was too embarrassing to bear.

A few weeks later we agreed we wouldn't see each other anymore. I've fallen away from you like a bruised apple on a battered tree. It's sad to say, but I can't help but see you as dirty. I can't help but see myself as dirty. I have become extremely self-conscious about my vagina—a place I used to adore—and I resent you for causing this disconnect between myself and my body. I think I stayed with you for so long because I didn't know who else would take me now, but everything runs its course, and unfortunately this incident has cut our trip together short.

"You're so disconnected, Emma, I don't know what you expect me to do."

"There's nothing to do," I explain, standing at your front door with my shoe in one hand and your heart in the other. To this day, I don't feel the BV has completely gone away. I still feel there is an odor that is not completely my own, and there are days when the discharge is more suspicious than others. I have read that BV reoccurs and some women have a terrible time ridding their body of it. Instead of explaining all of this to you, I just shrug. The look in your eyes is hurtful. I'm almost thankful when you turn your back to me. Without a word of protest, I slip my shoe on and turn away from you, closing your front door behind my heels.

IT RARELY IS NOTHING

Jaclyn Sanchez, 18, New York

MY CHEMICAL ROMANCE PLAYED IN THE DISTANT BACKground while we played our third straight game of Crazy Freaky Eights. Same traditional card game, but the loser has to roll what you would call a teasing die and perform the displayed sexual favor on the other person. This die is like any other six-sided, cubed gamepiece, but instead of numbers it has six different presex pleasures. You're probably more familiar with the novelty die that shows different sexual positions; I have that one too, but I didn't bring it tonight. See, this was only the third date I'd had with Frank. From what I could tell, he was a very sexual kind of dude.

On our first date we went to the movies, and midway through the credits he undid my zipper and started fingering me. He used my jacket to cover his hand, but anybody could have looked at the bobbing coat and figured out what was going on. Hence why I brought the tamer die to keep things from getting too wild. . . .

"I change it to hearts," he declared. I played along and put down a single heart, even though I could have played doubles and really messed his game up.

"Last card," he said.

I knew that he had a spade left, so I pulled out the eight that I had in my hand and changed it to spades.

He slammed his card down and laughed, "Yes!"

I never told him that I handed him the win, because it would have taken away from the pleasure of what I was about to do to him. I rolled the die and landed on an image of a guy sucking on a girl's breasts.

He pulled his shirt up. "Get started, Jacks."

I smiled seductively and flipped the die with my fingers, landed a girl giving a guy head, and then moved in on him. While I was kissing and licking, he was pinching and massaging my breasts through my shirt. Then he lifted my shirt and put his cold hands on my hard nipples. I sucked harder and he moaned louder.

"Come here, Jaclyn."

He was looking at me with a low intense gaze that I knew meant business, the kind of business I was trying to avoid. But things don't always go as planned, so I decided to just go with the flow.

I stopped, then sat on his lap. He kissed me, used his tongue, and worked his hands on my breasts. His hands dropped onto my lap, where he nearly tore off my zipper trying to get to my crotch. He fingered me a few times before gently lifting me off of his lap and laying my back down on the couch. His sexy expressions and gentle persuasions made me think twice about mentioning protection. He seemed like a pretty decent guy and I didn't want to risk making a beautiful moment jagged or awkward, so I let it happen. He easily passed through my vaginal opening and then began a slow, rhythmic grind inside of me.

"How does it feel?" (Nine out of ten guys will ask you this question, so girls, if you're going to have sex, you should consider preparing some interesting answers.)

"Like fat-free chocolate cheesecake, honey!"

He pumped faster, then slower. He invited me on top so he could massage my clit—my hot button. Obviously this guy was an experienced and wise lover. I never orgasmed, but it was fun. When he was ready to ejaculate he pulled out and released into the palm of his hand. I kissed him deeply once more before I let him get up and fix himself up.

As he walked away I glanced at his dazed expression, and for some reason a sickening wave of guilt passed over me. He wasn't my first. Actually, he was number four to get the goods and the second to do so unprotected, but something about his sexual aggression didn't seem so sexy anymore. It seemed like a warning signal that I really should have picked up on.

One piece of advice I'd like to share at this point: Never assume that you're the only one. If someone doesn't stress protection with you, chances are they don't with other people. Never assume that you are that girl who just happened to bring out that part of somebody else. If they did it for you, they probably did it for someone else.

"Using the bathroom," he called as he hobbled away with his pants around his ankles.

I lay back on the couch and closed my eyes, still feeling uneasy. *Should I continue laying here to see if he returns to lie with me or should I get dressed and act all casual?*

Frank returned moments later with my answer. He strolled back into the room midconversation on his cell phone. I sat up abruptly and twisted my body, hoping he didn't catch the disappointment on my face.

After that night, things between Frank and me were pretty cool. We talked on the phone, went on a few more dates, but nothing really took flight. In person we had a great time, but mostly because we barely talked. Over the phone we really didn't hit things off like I'd hoped we would have. He was a man of few words, I guess you could say, so how he expected to connect with anyone was beyond my reasoning. It kind of bummed me out because I had high hopes for the guy, but I remember thinking to myself, *At least I didn't invest much in him.*

Little did I know.

Three weeks after our evening of unbridled lust, I was in the shower just letting the water run over me as a million thoughts ran through my mind: schoolwork, boys, clothes, parent drama, etc. . . . I lathered my fingertips with soap and started washing my vagina, and that's when I felt it. That's when I realized how a casual experience that I had dismissed as nothing could absorb my everything within a matter of moments.

It was a raised bump on the skin folds around my vagina. I moved my hand around and found a larger fleshy bump just slightly inside the vaginal opening. I freaked and jumped out of the shower. I grabbed my vanity mirror and positioned it between my thighs. The bumps were pinkish, slightly paler than the rest of my vagina. The sight of them was absolutely nasty, and now that I had spotted them they had begun to itch.

"Probably just shaving bumps," I mumbled as I swallowed tears.

The following day I called the clinic and made an appointment to get these bumps checked out—just in case. I cleaned the bumps and put tomato juice and aloe vera gel on them, but they still wouldn't go down. Three days later when I had my doctor's appointment, I felt as though they'd tripled in size and I had even found a new, tiny one between my clitoris and my vaginal opening.

I sat in the sex clinic feeling incredibly sorry for and disgusted with myself. Everyone in the waiting room looked at least two years older than me and had their boyfriend or girlfriend sitting beside them. I'd sooner have spit on Frank than invited him along as a support system. How the hell didn't I see these warts on his penis? Why would he have sex with me knowing that he had this disgusting STD?

Eons later, the nurse called me into the room and had me sit down at a small desk while she sat across from me with a pen and paper in hand. "Hi, Jaclyn, I'm Liz. Do you mind if I ask you a few questions before you see the doctor?"

"Sure."

"So, you're sixteen?"

"No, seventeen." I felt relieved that I could offer a higher number.

"How many sexual partners have you had within the last six months?"

"Two."

"How long have you been sexually active and how many partners have you had?"

"Two years and four partners."

"When was your last Pap smear?"

"I've never had one before."

She asked me a series of other questions concerning my protection methods, HIV testing, and specifics on my vaginal growths. Then she led me into the doctor's office and handed me a paper gown.

"Get undressed from the waist down and fix your feet in these holders. The doctor will be in shortly." She smiled. I thought she seemed really sweet.

Several minutes later a small, mousy Asian woman came in. I was so relieved it was a woman.

"Jaclyn?" she said while she studied her chart.

"Yes."

"What are we looking at today?"

I knew she had the information right in front of her face. "I'm here to get a Pap test."

"Is there any particular reason?"

"I've got some, uh, weird cold sores down there."

She looked at me for the first time. "Let's have a look."

The Pap test was relatively painless. She gave me a topical treatment for the sores, and then I was sent into another room to have blood drawn for an HIV test because the nurse suggested I should.

The sores went away a few days later, but the sick feeling in my stomach did not. I didn't know how to act around my family. My parents had their twenty-first-anniversary celebration, but I faked period cramps so I didn't have to go. I felt alone; there was really no one that I was comfortable telling this to. In high school news of genital warts would probably spread quicker than I contracted it. I imagined the teacher displaying one of those nasty images in sex ed class: *Now, this student is a severe case of genital warts. Notice the gooey abrasions and bumps.* And now I was a living sex ed lesson.

Two weeks later I was back in the clinic, wiping away pointless tears and waiting for the doctor to come in and diagnose me. There were no ifs about my having an STD—what and how many was the real question.

"Jaclyn, the doctor will see you now."

I walked through the doors and into the tiny office on the left. When I went inside, a tall, roundish man was already in there, standing with a small grin on his face.

"You're here for your results?" he asked.

I nodded.

"Okay," he ruffled through the papers in the file he held. "Your Pap came back abnormal. You'll need to be treated for HPV."

I couldn't control my tears. "HPV?" I had never heard of such a thing in my life. I thought it must be some form of HIV.

"Human papilloma virus. It's what's been causing your vaginal warts."

"What? I don't understand. What does this mean? Is it fatal? Can I cure it? How do I get rid of it?"

The doctor nodded sympathetically at me. "You've never heard of HPV?"

He spent the next half hour discussing and answering my questions about my STD. HPV is caused by genital-to-genital contact and is the most common, as well as the most underreported, STD there is. There are over forty types of HPV; some cause genital warts, while others are cleared naturally by the body. The reason Frank never told me about his genital warts is probably because he never knew he was carrying

HPV; it is very rare that male carriers show any signs of the virus. But the most shocking piece of information is that HPV is the only known cause of cervical cancer.

It's been a year since that low point. Although I did get treated, doctors can't guarantee that the infection has been cleared, so I have to go in for Pap tests twice as frequently as the average girl.

Oddly enough, I was kind of lucky to get the warts. Without them I might have carried the virus for years and perhaps only realized its presence once it was too late to do anything about it. The best thing a woman can do to help prevent the spread of HPV is get Pap tested annually and reduce her number of sexual partners.

Unfortunately, I had to be reduced to a degradingly new low before I learned the value of these lessons, but I guess that all goes back to that cliché old saying: You live and you learn. But hopefully for you, you can read and learn.

CHECKMATE

Adam Smith, 21, Florida

THE FIRST TIME I BEGAN BANGING THIS GIRL WAS AFTER A drunken, pilled-out night at my house.

My parents had gone to sleep long ago and did their best to pretend like they didn't know what was going on. My friend had passed out on the couch in the living room, leaving me and this girl cuddling across from him. We hadn't as much as kissed when she got up to relieve herself in the restroom. After a couple of lonely minutes passed, I realized I needed to go and do the same. We met halfway from the couch to the bathroom door. She made her move. Check and mate.

We made out passionately as we maneuvered each other's clothes off and each of our bodies to my bed, a few feet away. I fell on top of her with heavy breath and one question.

"Do you have a condom?"

"No," she replied. "Why? Do you have anything?"

I told her the truth with a shake of my head, then shifted her thong from her hips to the floor as she removed her undershirt. There wasn't much foreplay before she insisted I insert myself inside her.

Although I was cracked out, I felt every endorphin flow from the top of my head to the tips of my toes. My body shook randomly on top of hers. She screamed out my name—I could hardly believe my mom or dad didn't come in to crash the party. I still had to piss and the room reeked of day-old fish, but we had done it. We had succeeded at killing off an hour of our miserable existences.

She put her clothes back on, as did I. There were no feelings of awkwardness between us, for neither she nor I was an amateur in the game of casual sex. I walked her to her car and kissed her goodbye, but it would not be the last time. We continued seeing each other for months afterward. I told her I only wanted a monogamous relationship, fearing more than one "depositor" could lead to a bad transaction. She agreed. Past relationships had forced me to succumb to a numbness that wouldn't allow serious feelings to arise for anyone. I wanted our relations to stay strictly sexual because I knew it was messed up from the start and I would be the one that got screwed over in the end. I was right.

A couple of months into this sextravaganza, I discovered what appeared to be a pimple on the lower region of my penis—on the shaft on the left side—while I was taking a piss. What I had thought was a pimple grew into a wart. I didn't know what to think of it at the time. Actually, I did have one thought: *Hey, warts grow all over my body—why not on my penis?*

I WOULDN'T FIND OUT IT WAS HPV UNTIL OVER A YEAR later. One doctor assured me it was nothing and sent me on my way. A doctor at a walk-in clinic in my town enlightened me. She told me it was HPV, told me it can cause cancer in men and women, and attempted to freeze what were now two warts off. The method extricated the cauliflower peak; however, the pimplish sign of the virus is ever present. So much for free love.

I still find myself having sex on very rare occasions after the human papilloma virus scare. I wear a condom so as to not infect the other person, despite their pleas for me to remove it. I became aware of how important using protection is when I was dating my most recent girlfriend. She was cool with not using a condom, a little too cool if you ask me, and got the HPV vaccine, which is only for girls. As far as I know, she doesn't have it, but just because you can't see warts, that doesn't mean you don't have HPV. In other words, if you aren't showing any physical signs of the virus, that doesn't mean you are not a carrier. Women can solve the mystery simply through tests; however, there are no HPV tests for men, even though it can cause anal or penile cancer if left untreated.

Now, two years later, I am still treating the virus with Condylox gel. It is applied topically to the infected area two times a day for three days, and then a four-day rest period is required before beginning the cycle again. It seems to be helping, although nothing is certain. It has been professionally brought to my attention that HPV can either stay with its host forever or go away on its own with some assistance. On top of the topical gel, I take vitamin E—when I remember—to strengthen my immune system. I do whatever I can to help completely rid myself of the wart-producing, cancer-causing guest that I let someone else bring into my body. What else can I do? There is no cure for HPV currently on the market . . . maybe the black market, but that's a whole other story.

SEX WITH YOU

Nikol Notiq, 18, Missouri

I GET EXCITED THINKING ABOUT THE THINGS THAT I could do to you, things to make you feel pleased and make you beg for more.

I love the way you savor every taste of me. You make my body explode into a thousand pieces, maybe even more. The look in your eyes is so erotic; the look of my body, you said, "is so exotic." You look at me and tell me my love is more than hypnotic: it's illmatic. I fiend for the moment of your love to come over me—it's like a clock on the wall, it's ticking away, every second I go by wishing to taste you again.

Role-playing with me while telling me I'm your Juicy Nubian Queen, the woman of your dreams, ready to reenact every part of those glass-house dreams. The touch of you makes me quiver; kiss my lips and they begin to shiver.

Wetness overflows my body like a tsunami. An earthquake awakes. Our bodies clash like ocean waves. Is that what my body craves or is it the thought of you? Imagining us making love while it rains, after drinking champagne.

You look into my eyes and say, "I want you more. I want to explore you. Baby, I adore you; I'll never hurt you, I promise to take it slow. Shush . . . baby, I'm here to fight those fears. It's going to hurt a little bit, but pain is pleasure."

And you were right because now I crave you. Like an addiction. I want to feel you against me. Sex games we play are crazy, but baby, every day is worth it. Because you know I'm driving you crazy.

SEX WITH YOU—THE AFTERMATH

The feeling was beautiful—wasn't that what you said to me?—but lately I've been feeling funny.

My body is not the same way it was when you last left it. I feel like I'm not myself, like I've become something else.

I look into the mirror and I don't see that seventeen-year-old girl with a banging figure. I see a girl (woman?) carrying your seed, and those Baby Phat pants won't fit.

This can't be me having a baby. What about my dreams? I had them too. You want to be a basketball player and your family sees sure to it.

Two months later I'm showing, little Danté is growing, but I'm homeless living here and there. You said I was your Queen, or was I just a girl to fulfill those nasty dreams?

Damn, I got to do what's right. Man, you should be here by my side. I called you and you didn't answer. I see you hanging with those girls while you are giving me those side glances like you want to help me. I say fuck you for hurting me. Who do you think you are? But I touch my stomach and realize that the deed has been done.

Now your seed is two years old and he looks just like you. I'm going to school, working on the figure you fucked up. But I'm happy I got mine and you're trying to get yours. You saw me today and realized who I was to you. Your son doesn't know you and it's going to be hard to explain who you are. You're looking in my eyes while I cry. These aren't tears of happiness but tears of sorrow, because now I don't know what lies you'll tell my son tomorrow.

WHAT IF

Lakia Williams, 22, Louisiana

I WOULD HAVE NEVER KNOWN THAT DREAMING SOMEthing that seemed so wonderful and sweet could turn out to be a nightmare. Looking back, I wish my dream would have never come true.

It was just an ordinary school day. I was in the hallway with my friend Iesha as the boys' track team passed through the hall. The rest of them were faded blurs as my eyes narrowed in on the star of the track team, Amaru. His eyes met my stare but only for a short while as he continued in the opposite direction. I shuddered with wonderment. What would it be like if this brother was mine?

Amaru was about six-foot-two, very muscular, with a bald head and a dimpled smile that would brighten up a grouch's day. I shook my head free of my daydream as I recollected my own makeup. I was about five-foot-eight, thick long brown hair, glasses, and on the heavy side—not fat, but, as some people would say, thick.

After they passed us, my friend turned around and said, "I saw you making eye contact with Amaru. Girl, he likes you—why don't y'all hook up?"

"Yeah, right. Come on, look at me and look at him—he sees nothing in me," I said.

We went to class, and during the middle of class I had to go use the restroom. As I was coming out of the restroom, I bumped into none other than Amaru.

"I'm sorry, I should be watching where I'm going," I said, feeling horribly embarrassed.

"Not a problem," he said casually. "I've been meaning to talk to you anyway."

"About what?" I blurted out.

"Us. Let's cut to the chase: I've been watching you for quite some time and I would like to get to know you, and after we get to know each other, maybe you can become my girlfriend."

I exhaled deeply and forced my words out as casually as my excitement would allow. "That's fine with me; I've been watching you watching me, so go ahead and call me sometime." I walked away smiling as I envisioned his eyes glued to my backside. I got back into my class and slid into my chair as though I was weightless.

"What's up with all that grinning?" Iesha asked.

"Amaru wants to hook up," I cooed.

"I told you so!"

I got home that day, did my homework, ate, took a nap, and waited for the phone to ring all the while. It finally did, and as I hoped, it was Amaru. From that day on, we talked to each other every night and at school and we went on dates. I soon became his girlfriend and we spent plenty of time with each other. Days turned into months and I couldn't feel happier.

Now, at this point me and Amaru had done nothing sexually. I wasn't ready, but I was still curious about what it would be like to take our relationship to the next level. One night we talked about it on the phone and made plans to spend a weekend together at a hotel nearby.

The weekend finally came and I was nervous as hell. On our way to the hotel we stopped for pizza and a movie to make our stay more comforting. When we got to the hotel, my nerves relaxed. Amaru had a way of making me feel so comfortable, and since he could see I was a little tense we did not rush things; we just ate, then watched the movie. We were talking and I was feeling so relaxed, but once the movie was finished Amaru turned on the stereo and the sounds of R. Kelly's "It Seems Like You're Ready" filled the air. I was immediately nervous again, so much so that I began to shake, and my heart was pounding so hard I swear he could feel it across the room.

"Are you all right?" Amaru asked me, eying me suspiciously.

I nodded, then he smiled and came over to caress me. Feeling his body against mine put me at ease, so we began to kiss. He laid me down and took off my clothes slowly. I pushed my mouth into an awkward smile, so Amaru slowed down, as he could see that I was not yet ready. We didn't end up having real sex, we just had oral sex. He took off my shirt, then my bra, and placed his hands on my breasts and started sucking like he was a baby drinking a bottle; then he kissed my chest down to my belly button. He slid off my pants, then my panties, opened my legs and stuck his head between them, and started to lick and suck my clit. At first it tickled; then it started to feel really good. I found myself making noises so that he knew what he was doing was feeling good. I placed my hands on his bald head and started rubbing it in a circular motion. He continued, faster. He was doing this for about an hour, then my legs started to tremble. A wonderful feeling swept over my body. It was something indescribable, something I had never felt before.

After he was finished, I kissed him thankfully and began to descend my kisses so I could give him the same pleasure that he had just given me. When we were done, we lay back breathlessly and fell asleep in each other's arms.

Two months passed after that special day in the hotel, and we had become closer than ever. It was time for us to be getting ready for the prom, and no question Amaru and I would attend together. As I perfected my look, I stared at myself in the mirror and was convinced I saw a woman. I was ready and this was the night that I would share the rest of my body with Amaru. I was finally ready to do what my friends were talking about.

We had a fun time at the prom, dancing and taking pictures, but I couldn't wait for the end of the night to see what Amaru had in store for me.

We finally left the prom and headed back to our room. As we entered the hotel room, there were candles and rose petals all over the place. The scent of strawberries filled the air. He picked me up and placed me on the bed as he hungrily took off my champagne-colored dress. He kissed every part of my body with soft wet kisses as he undressed me until there was nothing left to take off. He began pleasing me with his tongue between my legs. Those wonderful sensations crept their way up my body once more as I climaxed and then motioned for him to get undressed.

"Do you have a condom?" I asked breathlessly.

"We don't need it, it's our first time. Nothing's going to happen."

That's all he needed to say. I believed him, I trusted him blindly—some woman I was.

He entered me slowly, but the pain I felt was tremendous. I couldn't take it, so I tried to stop, but he stroked my hair and told me the pain would go away soon. I lay back down and he started moving up and down, round and round. After an hour the pain had finally gone and it started to feel really good. I closed my eyes and thanked Amaru for the special feeling.

"I love you, Kia," he stumbled through weak breath and then pulled my body closer to his.

The next day I was so sore I could barely walk, but all I could think of was this wonderful time me and Amaru had last night of sharing the experience of making love for the very first time. After that night we spent even more time together at school and going on dates; wherever he was, I was there. Life seemed amazing, but I've learned that things typically go very well before they get very complicated.

Weeks later, that wonderful feeling of being in love was clouded by the nauseating feeling in my stomach. I began to feel sick and I would throw up in the morning. My period was also unusually late, and even though I knew little about sex I knew enough to know that I may have gotten more than I bargained for. A few days later, the sickness still wouldn't leave and my period still hadn't shown up. I broke down and went to the drugstore to get a pregnancy test. Even though I suspected the truth, my suspicions still didn't prepare me for the results: I was in fact pregnant with Amaru's baby.

I sat down in disbelief as my mind began spinning in a million different directions. *Here I am, a senior in high school with my whole life ahead of me—how am I going to take care of a baby? How are we going to take care of a baby?* Amaru was a senior too, with a full scholarship in track and field at a top university. I knew that I had the challenge of a lifetime ahead of me, but I hoped that we could have them both: a baby and our dreams. But my hopes soon became very hopeless once I told Amaru the news.

"How the fuck could this happen?!"

His response deafened me; I was stunned momentarily as tears steadily ran down my face. "You said that it wouldn't happen, but it did, so what are we going to do about this?"

Hours later, I had his response. He didn't want the baby because it would mess up his plans for college and having what he wanted out of life. He said an abortion would be best, even though it didn't feel like the right choice in my heart. I must admit that I too was scared, since telling my parents, who did not even know I was having sex, would be extremely difficult, especially since the father had let me know what he wanted and it certainly did not include raising a child. My heart was broken—all I could do was cry—so I got in my bed, felt my stomach, and broke down. I felt so alone; how could someone who said they love you do something like this to you and back away at a time when you really needed that person to just hold on to?

I cried all night thinking back on prom night, asking myself, *Why? This is something that should have never happened. If only I would have made him put that condom on, I wouldn't be lying here in this bed crying my eyes out, pregnant. Why didn't we use protection?* But I knew it was too late for "what ifs"—I should have looked at the consequences the night I chose to have unprotected sex.

My decision to have an abortion was not an easy one, but it was one we both agreed on. My boyfriend didn't want the baby, and since I knew I couldn't take care of a baby by myself, it seemed I had no other choice.

The day I got the abortion, I woke to swollen eyes. I felt like a stranger in my own body as I went through my normal morning routine, all the while knowing what I had scheduled that same day. Amaru picked me up and took me to the clinic. I was very nervous, even more nervous than the day when we had our first sexual encounter. I really did not want to go through with this; I was just waiting for Amaru to say, "You don't have to do this," but he never did. Once we arrived at the clinic, Amaru paid the fee, then went back into the car. I couldn't believe he didn't even care for me enough to at least wait or even hold my hand. Right there, I knew what I meant to him and it had nothing to do with love.

I sat down for about thirty minutes. Then my name was called and tears ran down my face. I glanced at the front door once more, wondering if I should leave, but my feet continued on into the next room.

I went into the room, put on the nightgown, and lay down on the table. Part of me could not help but hope Amaru would burst through the doors, but I realized silly fantasies were what brought me to this place, so I shook that dream out of my head. The doctor told me to relax, but I was so nervous and too angry to relax. It hurt like hell! It hurt even worse because I knew he was removing my child, who I would never get to know or even hold.

After it was finished I put my clothes back on and rubbed my stomach. "There's no more baby," I said with tears rolling from my eyes.

The clinic doors shut behind me as I made my way back to the car, still feeling groggy from the procedure.

"Are you all right?" Amaru asked as I slouched over in the passenger seat.

I didn't answer him.

When we arrived at my house, I got out of the car with no words exchanged between us. As I made my way to my bedroom, the tears began. I lay down feeling like the saddest girl in the world as I used my sadness to put myself to sleep.

Me and Amaru didn't stay together very long after the abortion. I remembered the way he left me there, and his beautiful eyes I had once adored now served as a constant reminder of what we had done.

ABORTION

Derek, 25, British Columbia

"YOU'RE NEVER GOING TO FIND SOMEONE WHO LOVES *Seinfeld* and the Wu-Tang Clan," Chris Rock tells his audience. He goes on to explain that there's no such thing as a soul mate.

Sorry, Chris, but I found a girl who loves both. Add to that her love for steak dinners, her impeccable fashion sense, and her ability to roll the fattest joints of the sweet sticky-icky. She's like a lyric that my mind would keep in constant rotation.

I love her. That is to say, I used to love her, for everything on the outside that made us the envy of our friends, but the essential parts of what makes a relationship long lasting were missing. I felt the need to protect her from my own insecurities by keeping my personal truths past arm's length. I was worried she would reject me. I kept her from my parents because they wouldn't accept her for reasons that seem too numerous to count. With those realities underlining every step we took forward, we marched apart from each other, creating a distance. The one moment that should have pulled us tighter drove us apart.

A little over three years ago I went to her apartment, as I had every other day. We didn't hug or kiss when we saw each other. I followed her into her neatly decorated living room, where we sat across from one another. Before I could say a word, she told me that she was pregnant. In hindsight, my response to her confession was despicable.

I managed to fumble a monotone "What are you going to do?" past my lips.

I isolated her with six little words.

I made our situation hers. I exterminated any feeling of hope. I left her to fend for herself. Obviously, any other sentence would have been better than the one I offered. In my mind I knew we weren't ready to have a child. We were both students trying to survive by working jobs at night and going to school during the day. I just had no idea how to support her.

Weeks later she traveled alone out of town to have an abortion. Void of emotions, I went to see her the next day. When I saw her she was crying in her sleep because the doctors had sedated her. That was the only time I offered any type of comfort to her. I still hadn't realized that the grief she felt was to be shared. Days would turn into weeks, weeks would turn into months, and over those months we could never recapture what we had. It would take me all of that time to understand that I had lost a piece of myself.

I had always believed that men aren't supposed to be affected by abortions. We remain solid and upright through any of life's tests. We take on more responsibility to be sure that our partners have everything they need. We push forward because that's what we're supposed to do.

With twenty-two years of life behind me, I found out that I wasn't ready to be a man. By taking for granted my responsibility to her, my mind allowed me to release every single other responsibility I had. My way of mourning became my own self-destruction because I didn't know any other means to release the sadness I felt. My marks dropped, my friends slowly disappeared, and I turned back to a drug habit that I had defeated. I lived in my misery because underneath my shallow arrogance I believed it was what I deserved.

As I was bottoming out, she finally left me for her own benefit. I blamed her for being selfish then; now I understand how selfish I was. As parts of me kept decaying, I realized that I needed to fix those problems before I was taken over by them. A group of strangers showed me that mourning was the only way to release the guilt I kept wrapped around me. I pushed myself to honor and respect the memory of my child. The result of my grief was forgiveness for her and me. Men may hold their emotions close to them, yet they understand that those emotions need to be felt. By acknowledging a pain I so desperately tried to hide, I gave myself an opportunity to heal.

Now, with twenty-five years of life behind me, I've learned to celebrate my child who could have been. Quietly, I share each of my victories with the son or daughter that I never came to know. When I see doting parents tending to their children on the street, I smile because I know that one day that will be me. This minute I find myself blessed with good fortune, pursuing my passions with a new love who understands where my past has taken me while we take our first steps together.

A SECOND CHANCE

Lorie Singh, 25, Florida

PLAY (OCTOBER 2008)

"I'm pregnant," I said, looking over to him with tears rolling down my face and a positive pregnancy stick in hand.

PAUSE

Now, I know what you may be thinking, reader: Those three words (or is it two and a half?) instantly shattered my once hopeful future into "Oh God, my life is over! What have I done?" But you couldn't be more wrong.

PLAY

"I'm pregnant," I said, looking over to him with tears rolling down my face and a positive pregnancy stick in hand. He covered his mouth, trying to hide the oversize grin on his face and contain the tears (manly tears, I swear to you!) forming in his eyes.

"No way!" he said with this crazy happiness in his voice, followed by "Oh my God, I love you, this is amazing, seriously?"

And there it was. The way I had always pictured it.

I play that scene over and over again in my mind and think, *Damn, I am so lucky. This is the way it was supposed to happen. I love him more than words, and he loves me just the same, and we made a child together.*

Okay, so we aren't married and have only been dating for less than a year and maybe it isn't the "perfect" timing, but who cares! We're bringing a child into the world the "right way" . . . the right way according to us, of course, because let's face it: My "right" can be so wrong in the eyes of others. But to me, a child made from love and brought into the world with two full-time, capable, loving, and dedicated parents is all the makings of the right way, and screw all the watches that show "bad time."

This time was the *right* time, and this way was the *right* way. We would both experience something new and exciting for the first time, together. And knowing that, alongside the love of my life and father of my child, I finally found peace with my past mistakes.

REWIND (APRIL 2004)

"You're pregnant," the doctor said, looking up at me from the test results, gauging my reaction.

"Can you please check again? It can't be!"

I sat on the doctor's bench in hysterics over what I had just learned. The doctor looked at me with a sympathetic, yet at the same time *this is awkward,* look on his face and said, "I'll give you some time alone."

But that's just it. I am *alone.*

The situation was all too unreal. I asked him to wear a condom, and yeah, that broke, but that's what the morning-after pill was for, and those work, right? I mean, they're supposed to work, aren't they? A positive test result printout pressed between my fingers said otherwise.

Who cares now about how it happened—this is happening and . . . who is the father? I mean, I knew who he was but I didn't know *who* he was. Was he responsible enough to raise a child with me? Would he even stick by me? Did he have a good enough job to support the child? What kind of person was he really, and what kind of influence would he have on this child? I didn't really even like this guy to begin with, and now I'd be sharing a connection with him for the rest of my life? Is that what I wanted?

Now, had I had the wisdom to ask myself these questions before I decided to sleep with him, I could have wrapped this story at paragraph two, which, let's face it, would have bored you to tears. As much as everybody loves a happy ending, there is this need to complete the experience by watching the character go through a traumatic and life-altering experience. And you know I'm not lying.

But as vain as you may be, reader (just joking), I didn't go through all this just so I could someday write something that would entertain you. This was a rude awakening that forced me to reevaluate my choices and attitude toward the relationships I was keeping.

REWIND (JANUARY 2004)

"I will never be that stupid girl."

I've said it on many occasions as I listened to my male best friend repeatedly mock every girl he ever slept with and who begged for his continued attention.

That's the game, right? You hear it time and time again: Guys will say whatever they want to get into your pants, and then it's wham, bam, thank you ma'am. I watched this game in live action, week after week, as he blazed his promiscuous path, leaving a trail of emotionally attached and "stupid" girls behind. Knowing the reality of the game made me believe that I was better than it. I believed that sex was not something any girl should get emotionally involved in. I saw it as a game. A game every girl should learn to play and win.

So I beat them all to the punch and became completely emotionally detached.

"Thanks. It's been fun, but I have things to do today. . . ." "Don't bother calling me the next day, I'll be too busy. . . ." "I'm really only interested in one thing right now. . . ." Or (my personal trademark) "I *don't* cuddle!"

Not to mention bragging to all my girlfriends, and of course my male best friend, about my own power in promiscuity while mocking each man's performance from the "night before." *Now* who's the "stupid" one?

I was a player, I was powerful, I was winning . . . I was stupid!

FAST-FORWARD (APRIL 2004)

As I sat in the clinic parking lot, crying over the decision before me, I understood just how stupid I was. I didn't feel like a winner at all. I lost. I got pregnant, not him, and now I was bringing something precious into the world with someone who I didn't trust, or even like. Consequently, I was faced with one of the most difficult decisions a woman could make: Do I keep this child?

This was never the way I pictured it. This wasn't "right." The situation wasn't right. He wasn't right. The time wasn't right. What kind of life would I be able to provide this child without the benefit of a loving family unit, without a father figure? What kind of example would I be?

And once it was over, was I a horrible person? Did I even deserve a second chance at this? Could anyone ever love me knowing what I had done?

FAST-FORWARD (FEBRUARY 2008)

"Before we go any further, I have something to tell you."

I sat across from him with a large weight on my chest, fighting to find the right words. I'd had a crush on this guy for a year. He was smart, funny, sweet, crazy handsome, and just . . . all over astonishing, remarkable, beautiful, amazing, outstanding, and all the other words the thesaurus can come up with to describe "awesome."

Finally, we were on the verge of starting something amazing . . . but there was something that he needed to know, even if that meant bringing down my hopes of any future together.

"A few years ago, I found myself in a situation where I became pregnant by someone who I felt was the wrong person, so I had an abortion. Since making my decision, there wasn't a light-skinned child that walked by that I didn't come to tears over, thinking that he or she could have been mine. Not a day went by when I didn't question if I made the right choice. From that day, I vowed to myself that I would never put myself in that position again. I'm saying this to you now because I need you to know that there is no need for us to go any further in pursuing any kind of relationship if I know that you aren't going to be there in the event of any kind of 'oops.'"

Head hung low, I exhaled and raised my eyes to his to catch his reaction to what I had just said.

"From the moment I looked into your eyes, I saw my children," he said with deepest sincerity. "There is nothing that would make me happier than to find out that the girl I had an 'oops' with was you."

OCTOBER 2008

OOPS!!

The (wonderfully happy) end and the (wonderfully amazing) beginning.

DO YOU KNOW THIS MAN?

Sheila, 22, Maryland

"CAN YOU COME WITH ME? PLEASE." I TURN TO MY BEST friend and she nods. We both get up and head out of the waiting room and into the doctor's office. My breath is short and my feet are heavy, but I manage to keep my composure. *Don't make things harder,* I tell myself as I choke back a lump of tears. I promised myself I would not diagnose myself until the doctor did. If the tests came back positive, then and only then would I allow myself to cry.

Tracy had called me in a panic and told me to check my email. I begged her to give me details, but she refused—stubborn bitch. I opened the message; the subject read: "Do you know this man?" As soon as the image loaded, I immediately knew the answer to the question.

"Well, is that him?" my best friend, Tracy, asked for the third time.

"Yes," I responded.

"Yes?"

"Yes."

"So, what are you gonna do?"

"I don't know. I'm gonna hang up this phone and cry for a little bit, then I'll call you back. Cool?"

"Cool."

I replaced the receiver and did just that. I cried until my swollen eyes coaxed me to sleep.

THE IMAGE WAS OF A MAN NAMED DAVID MORRIS. I ONLY met him a couple of times, but there was no mistaking that grin. Deep-sunken dimples and a slight gap—if you didn't know any better, you'd think he was the kind that volunteered at an old folks' home.

The first time I saw that smile, me and a few girls were at the Powerhouse and my girl was talking to one of his boys at this table. The rest of us walked over and that cool, shy-guy smile spread across his swarthy skin. I say swarthy because I mean he was Cuban or something Spanish, a Taco Bell brother. As good looking as those men are, they are not for girls like me. It's not that I'm racist or anything, but my mom sure is and I know I couldn't bring a boy like that home to meet her. But it didn't mean that I couldn't bring him home. He was so hot—cute black curls, nice little smile—and even though he had on a button-up Hawaiian shirt, which was out of style, two out of four's not bad for a potential fling. I returned his smile, then put a little twist in my walk.

Turns out he was smiling at the pretty lights in the club or something, because he didn't seem to have any interest in me. There were four of them at the table and I was with, like, six girls. One of the dudes was really funny, so we stuck around the table for a few minutes. I kept shooting Mr. Taco Bell sideline glances, but he was on another planet, totally disenchanted with the conversation at the table and the people involved in it. Eventually we got up and ventured toward the dance floor and a couple of the guys from the table trailed behind, but not Taco Bell. He just stayed put. There was a remarkable innocence about his shy smile and solemn eyes that I found really attractive. But attraction coming from one direction is simply just obsession. I don't do obsession or crushes, so I moseyed my cute behind onto the dance floor solo.

I never achieved my objective that night, but one of my friends took down his friend's number, and the next weekend he had one of those "bring your friends and I'll bring my friends so we all can be friends" gatherings. Yeah, I put on a cute ruffled skirt and a gem-studded G-string and did my hair just in case Taco Bell happened to be there.

We arrived just before eleven. There were now eight boys, including you know who, and they had all already started drinking. The night got older, playing out on the same tip as the previous week. The clown of the group did most of the talking, and me and my friends just flowed with his conversation. Once all of my friends began drinking, the vibe switched and the raunchy talks began. Some had found their way to a basement wall while slow rock blared from the stereo system, inspiring them into a slow grind. Taco Bell just sat on the phone for the night. I glanced back in his direction and he caught me with a slow smile as he sipped his vodka cooler.

I turned to his friend. "What's up with your mute friend?"

"He's not a mute, just more of a serious guy. Go talk to him; you're the only reason he took the night off work and came tonight."

I took the goofy character's advice and sat down on the same couch as Taco Bell and folded my arms. Twenty seconds later he was off the phone. He followed my lead and folded his arms, then sat in silence. I inched closer, folded my arms, and shot him another glance, which he returned with another shy smile. He moved in again until our legs touched and we felt each other's skin for the first time. He held his head low and fixed his grin while his eyes were glued to the floor. I swung my legs over his thighs, played his game, and turned my head in the opposite direction. His hand slid up and down my freshly creamed legs. The touch of his hand made my temperature rise, but I could play shy just as well as he could. I moved my legs higher so they could rub against his manhood, and then, without notice, he ran his hand under my skirt and snapped my G-string. I gasped, then swung my head around. Wrong move. Our eyes met and he pulled my face to meet his moist pink lips. No one seemed to notice; if they did I really didn't care. We made out on the couch a little, but after a few minutes he seemed to get bored of that. He looked me in the eyes and flicked his tongue around so I knew he meant business. Taco Bell motioned to a closed door on the left with his eyes.

Moments later, we were rolling around on the battered futon. He broke from our intense romp and shot me a smile, got down on his knees, and slid my panties to the floor. He moved his face in as I flung my head back and braced myself for the immense pleasure of his wanting mouth. No such luck. He was pushing around down there like he was digging for gold. I tried to coax him away from my jewels before he did some permanent damage, but he was determined to "please me." So I did what most girls do and faked an orgasm. He raised his head with a victorious grin, then moved in again.

"No, no," I said breathlessly, "I'm too sensitive. I'm still feeling the effects of that . . . that performance."

"You're not getting off that easy!"

In a clumsy "I'm trying to be aggressively passionate" motion, he pounced on me until we both lay on the futon. He fumbled with his pants, then tried to dive on in.

"Condom," I said.

"Yeah, yeah, sure, I got 'em."

After another few awkward moments of fumbling, he slipped on a green rubber and boarded the mother ship with all the enthusiasm in the world and then some. It was bumpy and he had too many demands.

"Say you like it . . . oh yeah, girl, do that again . . . show me what you're working with . . . call me baby . . . " et cetera, et cetera. . . .

Shortly after, the "magic" was over. I got up and began scanning the floor for my underwear.

"Where'd you put my panties?"

"You won't be getting those back. It turns me on to know that you'll be dripping for me all the way home. I always keep the panties from the first time. It's my little memorabilia."

Memorabilia? I had no time for this fetish nonsense; I had already wasted enough on this bastard, and those underwear cost $15. Taco Bell was still laying on the futon and I spotted his pants underneath his foot. I yanked them out from underneath him and dug in his pockets for my shit. Found it!

"Why do you have to be a poor sport?" he whined.

I got out of the room and saw my friends sitting at the table just like they were earlier, all eyes on me. They giggled and the boys nodded with some mmm-hmms.

"Are we good and ready?" I asked

Everyone nodded and we left before Taco Bell emerged from the room. We laughed at his ass the whole way home, and they informed me that his name was Dave. Hopefully he never learned mine; this was one dud that I did not want claiming me.

"WHAT ARE YOU THINKING? ARE YOU SCARED?" TRACY HAD already begun to cry as she sat hunched over in the little chair beside me.

I didn't respond. There was no need to—she already knew. We had spent endless nights talking about it since I got the AIDS test two weeks ago. I read that email over and over until I memorized the words:

DO YOU KNOW THIS MAN?
His name is David and he died two months ago from the AIDS virus. He is twenty-nine years old and lived in the Baltimore County but partied a lot in D.C. Nobody knows how long he

was infected with AIDS, but we do know that he has passed it on to numerous women and possibly some men. Do you know this man? Do you recognize this face? Pass this email along to every man and woman you know in the Baltimore County and south D.C. area so we can break the cycle David has begun.

WE HAD PROTECTED SEX BUT UNPROTECTED ORAL SEX. However, I didn't stick around to see if the green condom broke, but I was pretty sure it wouldn't have. Pretty sure and deathly scared.

The doctor entered the room. "Hi, ladies, which one is . . . uh, Sheila?" His eyes moved in the direction of a sobbing Tracy, and for a second I wished I was there as the support system, but fate had alternate plans. I raised my hand.

"Okay, so you're coming in for some results today? All right, let's see here." He fingered through the papers until he reached the one that I had come for. He lowered his eyes at me and handed me the sheet. "I'll give you a few moments."

Tracy broke out in violent sobs and I sat still with the paper in my hands, a foot away from my face. I knew.

I don't remember much but the muffled noise of Tracy's cries and the soft touch of her hair as it brushed against my cheek. I stayed and filled out the reports, stayed and answered all of their questions and listened to all of their instructions. I never cried in the doctor's office—to tell the truth, I don't even remember blinking. I just remember thinking over and over, *I have HIV.*

LITTLE HEAD

Anthony Paul, 23, New York

FOR AS LONG AS I CAN REMEMBER, THE WILDEST PARTIES have gone down on my birthday. I'd like to believe it's because I'm just that exciting a person, but truth is, I was born on July 4 and the celebration goes on with or without me. This year was going to be different, though. I had no clue what I planned to do, but I was finally turning twenty-one and decided that it was time for the party to be all about me.

Fortunately, my girlfriend, Alicia, shared my sentiments exactly.

I remember her words verbatim: "Book off your whole birthday weekend, we have plans. . . . "

I don't remember what she said after "plans," or if she said anything at all, but it didn't matter—my mind had immediately taken me to my own euphoria. A wave of excitement hit me as my hormones began thinking, *Hotel? . . . birthday . . . sex! . . . long weekend . . . Alicia . . . sex! . . . twenty-one . . . party . . . condoms . . . sex! Her . . . sex! Me . . . sex! Sex, sex, sex!*

Can you blame me? I was about to turn twenty-one, and my girlfriend, who I forgot to mention was a nineteen-year-old model, had just told me about what I thought would be our lustful weekend getaway.

As I said before, I "missed" a lot of that actual conversation with Alicia. We all know the saying "two heads are better than one." Well, for guys, that isn't always the case, especially when the little head does most of the thinking. So it wasn't until the week of my birthday that I actually found out where we were going. The conversation between Alicia and me basically went like this:

"Are you excited about going camping?"

"*Camping* camping?"

"Uh, yeah . . . c-a-m-p-i-n-g—you know, the outdoor activity with nature and tents?"

"Oh, yeah." (I guess.)

I have to give Alicia credit, though: She took it upon herself to organize and prepare the whole "trip" completely by herself.

Sleeping bags? Check. Flashlights? Check. Tent? Obviously. Cooler? Check. Condoms? *For what?* I'm kidding. Double check. We were prepped to the nines and daring anybody to hit us with a camper's survival guide pop quiz.

IT WAS THE DAY OF INDEPENDENCE. I WAS NOW OFFICIALly twenty-one. The city was restless and those angry, electrified flowers we tend to call fireworks were starting to flourish across the sky. We checked into our campsite just as the sun was about to fall asleep.

Our campfire had dwindled down to nothing more than glowing embers and there was a certain *wow, this is so chill* that you never experience while wedged in the madness of city life. Everything was pretty much perfect, besides the fact that Alicia had "accidentally" bought a child-size tent (to be honest, I suspect she just picked up the cheapest one). Without the distraction of . . . well, everything distracting, I truly realized how attracted I was to the girl in the lawn chair across from me. Through the sustained smoke I could see Alicia sitting there in an oversize hooded sweater and dirty track pants. Her hair was in a messy ponytail and her Nike ACG boots looked ridiculous on her feet. But none of this made any difference to me. By this point, everything was an aphrodisiac and she was who I wanted.

Before we completely got into our tiny tent, we removed some clothing. Our tent was so awkwardly small that I had to position myself perfectly diagonal in order to fit inside the tent with her at the same time. I guess amongst the struggle to get into the tent I forgot something very important: Those condoms we were careful to pack never saw any action; instead, they remained neatly packed with our socks and clean underwear. The scene that unfolded was neither sensual nor intimate by traditional standards. In the back of my mind I felt slightly self-conscious about being heard. I remember Alicia's hair smelled like hickory sticks and smoky bacon. But I was so into her, so into it, that eventually I forgot about the rest of the world, focusing only on how happy I was to be with her. We lost track of being considerate and eventually we were loud enough to disturb the campsites on either side of us.

A few weeks after the smell of pine and the ache of a night in an undersize hut had faded, I noticed that Alicia was acting different.

A few times I even heard her say, "I don't feel like myself."

I didn't want to admit it or say it out loud, but I knew exactly what it was. It's a scary reality to face when you know that things will never be the same for you, your partner, or between each other.

More time passed and it was now the middle of August. Alicia and I were waiting in the doctor's office, staring blankly at a poster of an esophagus. The doctor finally returned after what seemed like hours of us studying diagrams of cancerous lungs and diseased livers. Our conversation with the doctor wasn't very exciting.

"Blah, blah, blah and these are the results. Blah, blah, blah congratulations. Blah, blah, blah, this is the projected due date. Blah, blah, blah."

And that was it. Apparently, somewhere along the way we had signed up to be parents.

"Are you mad at me?" Alicia whispered on the slow drive home.

"No, why would I be mad?"

"'Cause everything is so ruined now. . . . "

I didn't realize it at the time, but she wasn't asking for my sake, she was asking because she was hoping that we would share the emotional burden that she was carrying. But we couldn't. I couldn't. And frankly, I didn't want to. I don't think any twenty-one-year-old plans to get their nineteen-year-old girlfriend pregnant with absolutely no plan for the future, but that's precisely where I was at in this stage in my life. From that point on, it was no longer about me. I now had a little person to prepare for and what I wanted became irrelevant.

There are three immediate options any couple faces when put in this position: 1) Keep the child. 2) Give it up for adoption. 3) Have an abortion.

We were both completely against one of the options . . . unfortunately, it wasn't the same one. Abortion was a definite no in my book, and adoption made no sense to Alicia. You would think that meant we were both in obvious agreement about keeping our child, but in situations like these, nothing is obvious and very little makes sense. My lack of sympathizing with her thoughts of abortion probably came off as insensitive or selfish, but in fact it was the complete opposite. To me, it seemed way more selfish not to accept full responsibility for our actions. The child did not ask to be conceived, but it was. We decided that. So why did we think we also had a right to decide if the baby got to live?

Our families were both pretty shocked but, again, had contradictory responses. My family knows that no one will ever be harder on me than I am on myself, so this kind of left them speechless.

Over time, everyone loosened up to the idea, and surprisingly my mom even fit a couple jokes in, saying things like, "I look way too young to be a grandmother" and, "Poor child . . . I hope the baby gets its grandmother's looks."

My dad, however, always states the obvious to an extreme: "You're gonna have to stop buying shoes now. You need to start saving."

And that was pretty much it from my party. Alicia's family, on the other hand, had way too much to say. At the time, Alicia wasn't close with anyone in her family, but they all felt free to give her their miserable advice. Most of her family was adamant about trying to convince us that Alicia just wanted the attention, but that didn't make any sense, especially when Alicia would have preferred not to tell them at all. I was the one who forced her to keep the baby and tell her family. This lack of support from her people played heavily into Alicia's growing insecurities. The day we told her father, I think he actually tried to wed us right there in his living room.

"Proper marriage is what raises a child. . . . "

Of course I strongly disagreed. "No, proper *parenting* is what raises a child."

We didn't quite agree to disagree, because I don't think he even heard a word I said all afternoon.

I TRIED TO FILL THE VOID BETWEEN US, BUT THERE WAS nothing I could do but watch as she slowly became someone I didn't know. The next nine months were the most stressful of my life as I tried my hardest to please everyone: Alicia's family, my family, Alicia, and lastly myself. All while her hormone-fueled confusion boiled into resentment.

It sucked.

Somehow I still managed to keep myself in a positive place, the whole time solely focusing on the fact that any day I would have a daughter.

Everyone adores spring, but now I absolutely love it. In April, spring brought me a seven-pound, six-ounce present. Best gift I'll ever receive, hands down. I could never have imagined how amazing she would be.

Though my sentiments toward fatherhood had improved, my attitude toward the mother soured. Things between Alicia and me eventually went from bad to worse. I felt I had been putting in so much effort and eventually decided the only one that deserved such undivided amounts of attention from me was my daughter. Alicia and I had faded into nothing. You would think that this would make me bitter, but you're wrong. Looking at everything now, I realize it was never about us; we were just setting the stage for someone much more important. I'll admit, sometimes I ask myself if I would do anything different if I had the chance. But before I even have time to think about it, I say the answer aloud: "No, I wouldn't change a thing."

There are days when I look at my daughter confused, like, *Did I really make this?* She has these huge eyes and the prettiest hair. The most beautiful baby I have ever seen. The first time I held her she didn't fuss at all, just held my pinkie real tight and gave me a look that I figured was her way of saying, "Thank you, Dad, for all your troubles."

GOT QUESTIONS ABOUT CHAPTER 3?

SAFE SEX

I've heard the only safe sex is no sex. Is that true?

No. Masturbation, and some other forms of sex (like cybersex, mutual masturbation, clothed, dry sex) do not put you at risk for STIs. When it comes to other kinds of sex, there are condoms, female condoms, spermicide, dental dams (used for performing oral sex on females), gloves, and finger cots.

How do you practice safe sex without killing the mood?

Make it a part of your routine. If you don't act awkward about it, it won't be awkward. Just because it rarely happens in passionate love scenes on TV or in pornos does not make it uncool. I mean, think about it: What's the big deal in putting things on pause while you or your partner prepare to put on something that may save your life and prevent unwanted pregnancy?

If you do not see anything physically weird about your partner's genitals, is it safe?

No, just because your partner does not have visible symptoms, like discoloration or growths, it does not necessarily mean they are not carrying an STI. Some people may experience no symptoms at all upon infection, and if they did have symptoms, they may have cleared without treatment, meaning the person is still a carrier. STIs have no set face, so anybody could be a potential carrier.

HPV

Jaclyn, 18, New York
Adam Smith, 21, Florida

How did you contract HPV?

Jaclyn: I had unprotected sexual intercourse and unprotected oral sex. While I was in the shower, I discovered vaginal warts both inside and on the outside of my vagina.
Adam: Lots and lots of unprotected everything.

Did you tell anyone you know that you got it?

Jaclyn: No, I have never told anyone I know about my STI because of what they would think of me. I agreed to share my story for this book in order to help others, but I don't want to do so at the cost of my respect or relationship with loved ones. I contracted HPV; the symptoms are treatable but treatment does not rid your body of the virus itself. Since the symptoms can come back, I get a sexual-health checkup twice a year to ensure I detect it right away, so there isn't much need to tell others.
Adam: I don't get on a soapbox and preach, "HPV is at hand," but I have told a number of people in order to educate. Yes, my reputation is totally fucked.

Do you tell everyone you get involved with about your infection?

Jaclyn: I have not been sexually active since my infection. Contracting genital warts (HPV) changed the way that I viewed sexuality and my body. I now see sex as something special, and I do not want a lot of people to be able to say that they experienced me completely—both mentally and physically.
Adam: Yes, except for this one girl, but since she fucked a shitload of people, including the guy five minutes before me, I

didn't think it mattered. I was more afraid of what she might give me. Yes, I wore a condom. No, I didn't want to have sex with her. Certain situations call for certain engagements.

HIV

Sheila, 22, Maryland

How did you get HIV?

Sheila: I had protected sex and unprotected oral sex with someone that I knew very little about. I know the condom he used was the cheap colored kind, and I did not stick around to see if he had put it on properly or if it was compromised during sexual intercourse.

What did you do when you found out about your life-threatening illness?

Sheila: I have heard of many different reactions, but personally I was very cold—emotionally and physically. I had brought someone to the clinic with me and her reaction was very strong. I think in a way I let her cry for me. One month after I found out, I sat down and told my mother. This was unbelievably difficult, since she is a single parent and we live together. A lot of my family still does not know, but I do tell everyone who is in close contact with me as soon as possible.

Did you infect any of your close family or friends?

Sheila: Heavens no—or at least I don't think so. There are a lot of misconceptions about HIV contraction; the virus is not as tough as people think. As long as you are aware of your disease and know how to take precautions, there should be no reason for your loved ones to fear loving you.

How do you tell the people you are attracted to?

Sheila: I am actually part of an online HIV dating service. A lot of the people that I date now are either infected or counselors who understand the disease and know how to take all the precautions. I have not been infected for a long time, but if I met someone out of the blue I would probably tell them as soon as the topic of intimacy came up.

How long did the doctors tell you you had to live?

Sheila: It's not like that for HIV victims anymore. For example, Magic Johnson has been living with the disease for decades! If you take your medication, take extra care in keeping healthy, and maintain a positive attitude—sky's the limit.

ABORTION

Lorie Singh, 25, Florida

What happened during your abortion procedure?

Lorie: I almost feel bad saying it, but the actual procedure of having an abortion was not so bad for me. It is one of the most difficult decisions you can make, and I expected to be judged and scrutinized by everyone in the clinic. But it wasn't that way at all. There were no protestors outside with pictures of dead fetuses chanting at me and calling me a monster. Instead, there was a warm staff who understood how difficult this procedure was for me, and they did everything in their power to comfort me and support my decision.

When I was first called into the office, a consultant asked me questions about how I got pregnant, what type of birth control I was on, who the father was and what he was like, what my future plans were, and most importantly, was I sure I wanted to follow through with the procedure. Once that was finished, they gave me some pills to relax me.

Then I was taken into another room for an ultrasound. They brought a picture of my fetus up on the screen and let me choose to look at it or not. At the stage of my experience, my fetus was smaller than a peanut, so I couldn't even see. The technician also asked me if I would like to know if it was twins.

When I was called into the other waiting room, I changed into a hospital gown and waited with about five other girls.

That was an awkward moment. What do you really talk about? What I did was lean on those women for support because several of them had gone through the procedure before or were feeling the same things that I was. It made me more comfortable and reassured me that I wasn't a bad person, and that other women were going through exactly what I was going through.

Now, the actual procedure: A nurse brought me into a room and propped me up on one of those chairs where your legs are spread. Then they inserted an IV into me, and everything went numb and funny. I was aware of what was going on, I just couldn't feel it. Then the doctor came in, and I'm not exactly sure of what he did down there, but I do know it took him about three minutes and it was done.

I was taken into another room at this point, called the recovery room. They let me rest for about fifteen minutes and I was moved into the general waiting room to be picked up. I slept for a few hours and then—I'm not sure if it was a result of the IV wearing off or the shock of no longer being pregnant—when I woke up, I just cried and cried and cried.

Why did you decide to abort your child?

Lorie: I decided to have an abortion because I knew it was an accident and I wasn't ready. He wore a condom but then took it off without me knowing. The next day I took a morning-after pill, which I now know does not always work. I also strongly felt that I did not want to have a child with and a permanent connection with the father of the child. I felt that it was the best decision for me to make.

Did you include your partner in your decision?

Lorie: I did not include my partner in my decision. He didn't even know about it until after it was all said and done. This I regret. I truly felt that the child was as much mine as it was his; thus, the decision should have been as much his as it was mine.

Did you tell anyone else?

Lorie: I did what most young girls would never think about doing in the case of getting pregnant: I told my parents right away. That was the hardest thing about the entire situation. It tore me apart to see my parents look at me differently and become so utterly disappointed with me. The reason I told my parents is because I knew that telling them would make this procedure and decision extremely difficult, which is what I wanted. I could have easily gotten an abortion and no one would have been the wiser. But I didn't want to end up having several abortions. I wanted to make the experience and decision as difficult as possible so that I would always remember the pain it brought, and be more careful so that I would never have to go through it again.

How did you feel after?

Lorie: For me, let's just say it is very hard at points. Though it doesn't haunt me every day of my life, I get sad when I see a little girl who looks like me, or when I see pictures of a fetus, or watch a mother hold her baby for the first time. But what frightens me the most is the thought that I may have ruined my chances of getting pregnant again. Physically, the chances of that happening are slim to none, but it's more mental for me. I almost feel as though I'm not worthy to have another child because I let one go. A lot of different emotions run through my mind, and it's not so much to say that I regret my decision, but what I do know is that had I gone through with it, me and my child would have found a way to make it and survive. And when I held her in my arms and looked at her, I would never have wished that I had done anything different than have her.

How do you cope after a decision that could change your life?

Lorie: I don't know how I cope, I just do. I just keep thinking to myself that I made the best decision that I could make at the time, and reassure myself that I will make better decisions. Now I think differently. I no longer look for the guy who is an all-star basketball player, dancer, rapper, comedian, and all the other things that used to amuse me in a man. I look for a partner. If I give my body to a man, I know that I am running the risk of getting pregnant again, so I want to know that in that event, I will be partnered with someone who will stand by me.

TEENAGE PREGNANCY

Anthony Paul, 23, New York

Why did you decide to keep your baby?

I'm not sure if I ever really looked at it as a decision, because I never saw abortion as an option. I also know how selfish it may seem because I wasn't the one carrying the child, but I don't regret how firm a stance I took.

Did your parents lose faith in you?

My parents were, and have always been, extremely supportive. They might have lost faith in some of my decisions, but they were very good at never letting me know.

Are you still able to have a life?

I don't have the freedom to do as much as I'd like to do throughout the day, because everything I do is scheduled around my daughter. I normally wait till the evening or night (when my parents are home and my daughter is sleeping) before I make plans to go out. Luckily, I have a supportive family who my daughter and I still live with. I also share the responsibilities with my daughter's mother, who I do not live with.

Are you plagued with financial trouble?

A child is an extra expense, but I wouldn't consider it anything unbearable. With decent planning and budgeting, it doesn't seem as bad as people warned me it would be.

CHLAMYDIA

Sarah Lawless, 18, Newfoundland

How did you contract chlamydia?

I contracted chlamydia because I was raped. The individuals who had raped me did not use condoms and therefore made me vulnerable to the disease.

When and how did you realize that you had it?

I had made an appointment with my doctor almost immediately after the rape and after I contacted the police. It was procedure for the doctor to perform a Pap test on me because of the rape, and I had no symptoms prior to the appointment. Chlamydia is one of the most common sexually transmitted diseases, and it is known not to carry any symptoms the majority of the time.

What did the doctors give you in order to cure it?

My doctor suggested that I take the prescribed antibiotic for curing chlamydia. I forget the name of the drug itself, but there were either three or four pills that I took at once, and that was all it took to cure it. The next week I phoned my doctor's office to see if the results from my Pap tests showed that I indeed did have the disease—and the receptionist said yes. But I was already cured. Fortunately, I contracted one of the few curable STIs; the situation I was in made me vulnerable to many.

How has contracting an STI changed your views on protection?

Contracting the disease did not really change my views on wearing protection, as I have always viewed that as extremely important. The contraction only made the risks much more real to me. I do not view the contraction of the disease in a regretful manner, however, because it was not my fault. However, I do always insist on using protection because STIs are very real and can happen to anyone.

CHAPTER 3 CHECKPOINT

MYTH OR REALITY

When it comes to traditional sex education info, you may have heard it all before. But how much have you retained? Get out your pencil and take this quiz to see how sexually savvy you *really* are.

1. Chlamydia is the most common STI. Myth or Reality
2. AIDS is the most underreported STI. Myth or Reality
3. The average cost of raising a baby is $785 per month. Myth or Reality
4. A bladder infection cannot be caused by sexual activity. Myth or Reality
5. HPV is the only known cause of cervical cancer. Myth or Reality
6. Eight out of ten teen fathers don't marry the mother of their child. Myth or Reality
7. Birth control can help prevent certain cancers. Myth or Reality

8. There are no risks involved in having an abortion. Myth or Reality
9. You are safe from STI infections as long as you don't have sexual intercourse. Myth or Reality
10. It's estimated that 25 percent of people who are sexually active under the age of twenty-five will contract an STI at least once. Myth or Reality

For the answers, see pages 288-289.

CHAPTER 4

WHEN NO! LOSES ALL MEANING

INTRODUCTION

"Have you ever seen a rape victim right after it happened? If you look in her eyes, she looks incomplete. It's hard to put into words, but it's almost like there's a piece of that person missing," said Andrea, the editor in chief of a sexuality magazine.

I had the phone pressed to my ear as I listened to her words. I carefully injected "uh-huhs" to stifle my preoccupation with what she was saying. All of a sudden, I was very tired. I remembered having had the same drowsy feeling right after it happened. I remembered taking the two-hour bus ride home and struggling to stop my head from slipping onto a stranger's shoulder.

Andrea's words stayed with me, even though I could hear that she had changed subjects. I hadn't offered her my personal story, but I thought about what I might have looked like in the immediate aftermath. I was seventeen. He had been drinking. After he was through with me, I had no idea where to go or how I would get there. I do remember being in his small bathroom with barely enough room to stand. Avoiding my reflection while I put my clothes back on. I remember that I did not turn on the bathroom light and that I was wearing all black that day: black jeans, black shirt, and black stilettos.

I don't think I ever looked into that mirror because I seem to recall most things (including what purse I wore), but I can't conjure my face. What did my eyes look like? Would I have even recognized myself?

"Are you still waiting on your friend?" Andrea asked, shaking me out of my flashback.

"Yes, and I should get off the phone. We'll talk soon."

She offered her own farewells and I placed my phone in my pocket. I sat still for a beat before adjusting my rearview mirror to the left, away from the street and onto my face. Staring back at me were two wide and empowered eyes and a pair of determined-looking brows. I imagined that many nights ago, underneath the tears and confusion of that bad experience, were these very same eyes.

"THIS BOOK IS TOO NEGATIVE. DESPITE HAVING SOME good information I think the chapter on rape really drags things down," wrote a book agent in one of several rejection letters I received when first shopping this book.

I tossed out the letter and thought, *Silly lady, obviously rape is negative.* The question she should have been asking was whether young people's rape stories were prevalent enough to make up an entire chapter. I could have answered that question blindfolded and standing on my head without a hint of hesitation—yes, yes, and yes. I believe that many people do not realize the high occurrence of date rape in North America. I used to hear stats like over 50 percent of women will be raped in their lifetime and think, *That can't be right.* I thought rape was about masked attackers in parking lots, but the truth is that most rapists have a trusting relationship with their victim. This could explain why so many sexual attacks go unreported.

With that said, I ask you to avoid reading this chapter with a too-bad-for-her attitude. If you take away the instinct to look at these stories as sad cases, you will recognize that every story is set in common environments. Think about how often you and your friends have encountered similar settings to what is described and how easily these stories could become your own. Do whatever you can to control the situations you get yourself into. If a friend is under the influence or making poor choices, make it your responsibility to step up and protect them. Lastly, engage in rape prevention by reinforcing the message that rape is not something to be tolerated. It's not funny to joke about it and sex should only happen in the presence of an enthusiastic yes. For more information about enthusiastic consent, see *Yes Means Yes: Visions of Female Sexual Power and A World Without Rape,* edited by Jaclyn Friedman and Jessica Valenti, a book that seeks to dismantle commonly held views of rape.

My biggest regret about this chapter is that it does not include the voice of a male who experienced rape or sexual abuse. Twice I was contacted by different men who had been a victim of a sexual crime. Both expressed that they were extremely interested in sharing their stories, and neither ended up submitting. After writing several encouraging reminders that went unanswered, I had to give up. I can only speculate why they chose not to share, but a voice like theirs is greatly missed.

Rape, assault, and sexual abuse are issues that every race, gender, and age demographic has to battle. Here are some statistics to help you understand the urgency of this problem:

- Teens aged sixteen to nineteen are four times more likely than the general population to be victims of rape, attempted rape, or sexual assault.
- According to Statistics Canada, only 6 percent of all sexual assaults are reported to the police.
- 84 percent of women who were date raped knew their attacker.
- 90 percent of date rapes occur when either the victim or attacker has been drinking.

- Approximately 28 percent of victims are raped by husbands or boyfriends; 35 percent by acquaintances; and 5 percent by other relatives. (Department of Justice, Violence against Women, Bureau of Justice Statistics, U.S. Dept. of Justice)
- Statistics show one in four Canadian women will be sexually assaulted during her lifetime. (J. Brickman and J. Briere, "Incidence of Rape and Sexual Assault in an Urban Canadian Population.")
- More than 80 percent of rapes that occur on university and college campuses are committed by someone the victim knows, and 50 percent occur on dates. Many of these assaults happen during the first eight weeks of classes. (University of Alberta, "Sexual Assault and the Law in Canada.")
- The effects of sexual assault on a woman's mental health and well-being can be just as serious as physical injuries. Nine out of ten incidents of violence against women have an emotional effect on the victim. The most commonly reported consequences are anger, fear, and becoming more cautious and less trusting. (Statistics Canada, "The Violence Against Women Survey.)
- 2–4 percent of rapes reported are false accusations, which means that 96–98 percent of all rapes reported did happen. (University of Alberta study, "Sexual Assault and the Law in Canada.")

Source: Department of Justice, Office on Violence Against Women

Recognizing that it could happen to you–or that you could be the aggressor, hard as that might be to imagine–is the first step toward prevention. With this in mind, let's proceed to the chapter that is closest to my heart.

HOTEL PARTY

Lauren Matos, 22, New Jersey

THE HOTEL PARTY STARTED
Lots of people, music, and liquor
I was with a guy I was dating, having a good time
He poured me drink after drink
I was loose and carefree
My man felt he should show me how much he cared about me
That's when it went downhill

He knew I was a virgin and was waiting until marriage
He knew that I was going to leave and never see him again
He knew what was about to happen was wrong

He undressed my limp and drunken body
He kissed me all over leaving marks of broken blood vessels
He got on top of me trying to penetrate me
I didn't want for anything to happen

He said five words that tore through me
"But baby, I love you"
It wasn't love . . . it was lust
A quick fix for a horny man
He tried and tried and I kept saying no
I tried to scream but I couldn't
No one realized anything was wrong at all

Eventually he got mad and walked away
I passed out to wake up in the middle of the night
Fear was written on my face
He was on top of me again taking my innocence
I pushed him off me and locked myself in the bathroom
I sat on the floor violated
Ashamed
Scared
I stayed there until morning

I snuck out while he slept
Made my way back to the barracks and showered
I was emotionless
I did not cry, laugh, or smile for days
He took my spirit and trust away
I left a few days later holding on to that night
I had nightmares for months

To this day I am scared when I am alone with a man
Even with my boyfriend whom I love
It took one night to ruin me
Days to make me feel again
Months for me to forgive
And an eternity before I forget

WHY WE DON'T TELL

Stephanie Smith, 23, Michigan

ALTHOUGH IT MAY READ LIKE FICTION, THE EXCERPT YOU are about to read is based on my own personal experience from February of 2003. The character Veronica is a direct reflection of myself. After I was sexually assaulted by someone I trusted as a friend, I had to figure out a way to deal with my various emotions. I found writing was the best way to do so.

Writing has always been therapeutic for me, and writing "Why We Don't Tell" was very cathartic. I was able to confront my feelings about what happened and decide how to handle it. There were many roads I could have taken, but I figured that perhaps by sharing my story I could help other people. Writing this was very emotional, but it was a wiser decision than lashing out at others or myself.

A lot of people are surprised that I included the perspective of my assailant, named Omar. There are several reasons why I decided it was important to include some insight into his mindset and his past. I did not want to make him out to be a monster and take away from the fact that Omar could be any guy, anywhere, anytime. Rapists do not fit one mold. I felt that I should make this apparent.

People are also often surprised at how graphic certain parts of the novel are. I never attempted to glamorize anything. This was not a movie—this was my life. Some of the scenes are play-by-play, word for word, directly from my memory and journal entries I wrote while this situation was unfolding. There are also some individuals who jumped on the fact that alcohol had been a huge factor in the assault, but that is life—statistics show that alcohol plays a role in many date rapes. I cannot take back the past, but I hope that other people will learn from my experiences.

Obviously, there are some things that I made up. There is no way I could possibly know exactly how my assailant handled the situation or how his relationships with his friends changed. The novel also includes a look into not only how Veronica deals with being assaulted, but also how her friends and family feel about the situation.

I wrote this novel to explain exactly what the title says: "Why We Don't Tell." Rape is a very underreported crime, and there are numerous reasons why. Although I strongly encourage rape victims to come forward and receive the treatment they need, I can definitely understand why an intimidating legal system, as well as possible further humiliation, can keep them silent. However in hindsight, I do think that coming forward was the best avenue I could have taken.

THE AFTERMATH

The room was so quiet she could hear the clock ticking. Embarrassed and slightly cold, Veronica used her thumb and forefinger to hold together the thin paper robe she was wearing, hoping to shield her nude body from the breeze coming from the lone window. It was no use; the room itself was just cold. Veronica turned to look out the window. It was snowing, but only enough to lightly coat the streets of the sleeping city. It was dark outside, and Veronica could hear a soft hiss as the wind swept the snowflakes down the street. The scene outside was one of serenity and complete calm, but it was the exact opposite inside both the small examination room and her mind.

Across the room, Sara, the on-call nurse examiner, quietly prepared a small table of instruments, making sure to keep them out of Veronica's view. Although the circumstances were less than admirable—it was close to four thirty in the morning—she handled her patient with extreme tenderness. She was dressed in light blue scrubs, her shoulder-length blond hair held off her face by barrettes.

She turned to Veronica and inquired, "Have you ever had a Pap smear before?"

Veronica shook her head and shivered.

"Oh, are you cold, honey?"

She nodded. She was also nervous; that didn't help.

"Take a deep breath and try to relax, Veronica."

Veronica obeyed. There was nothing she could do to prepare herself for the excruciating pain she was about to endure. Veronica cried out when Sara first inserted the speculum, shaped like a duck bill, into her vagina, and continued to sob as Sara opened the speculum wide enough to where she could see Veronica's injuries. Veronica put her hands on her forehead and bawled, then caught sight of her exposed vagina on the screen. Even from her position, without Sara's medical knowledge, Veronica could see where she was torn. Sara worked as quickly and carefully as she could, photographing the wounds and documenting them, before loosening up the speculum. She took off her rubber gloves and rubbed Veronica's legs comfortingly.

"You're torn in several spots," she said soothingly, "and you're still bleeding. You're bleeding from a hole other than the one from where menstrual flow occurs, so we can obviously see that you've experienced some vaginal trauma."

Veronica tried to dry her tears, but then she remembered what she was there for and began to cry again.

THE BEFORE AND THE BAD

Arbor Dale University had a small number of minority students, and the activities were also few and far between. Veronica herself was involved in several. And whenever there was something in which she could participate, whether she belonged to the particular organization hosting the event, Veronica made an appearance.

Veronica was two semesters away from graduating. She had her life all planned out, and had ever since she first started at Arbor Dale. She would graduate from there with her sociology degree and probably go on to graduate school. Veronica wasn't exactly sure what she wanted to do with her sociology degree just yet, but she knew that it was what interested her the most out of the many academic majors Arbor Dale had to offer.

Saturday night, the annual talent show was being held on campus. It had been a huge success every year, and one of the main events that "everybody who was somebody" attended. A few of Veronica's friends were performing. It was always an entertaining competition. She and Kendra had gone to the mall earlier that day, where each girl had purchased a new shirt specifically for the party following, which was also to be held on campus.

The show was scheduled to begin at seven, but as the girls expected, it didn't. They were expecting no longer than an hour's worth of delays, but the time rapidly went beyond eight o'clock. By then people were getting restless, including Veronica, who had a short fuse anyway.

"What could possibly be taking this long?" she demanded irritably.

Kendra shrugged, her lips pursed tightly. "There's no explanation for this. This is ridiculous. Ten minutes, fifteen minutes late, I can understand that. It's been a damn hour."

Veronica craned her neck and looked around, noticing the impatient looks everyone wore. While Veronica was doing her inventory of the room, she spotted Omar standing at the back entrance with Randall. Veronica had met Omar under somewhat odd circumstances—at a football party, where he had drunkenly exposed himself to one of Veronica's friends, Shawna, and peed right in front of Veronica's eyes.

It soon became apparent that Omar's feelings for Veronica were stronger than her feelings for him. Veronica made no attempts to lead Omar on to believe that they would be anything more than friends. She explained to him that her first emails had just been to razz him a little about his behavior in December, and that their friendship had been a surprise. But that was what it was—friendship. Veronica was not attracted to Omar, and wasn't sure if she was interested in a relationship anyway. She was only twenty-one, and besides, she had never been allowed to date in high school. Now she had the opportunity and was having fun shopping around.

There were several attributes that drew Veronica to Omar as a friend: He was funny, respectful, and easygoing. It didn't matter that Omar wasn't that attractive, or that he wasn't the brightest person she had ever met. Veronica never discriminated when it came to just making friends. As boring as the area was surrounding their campus, most students had the same motto. It was always better to be bored with someone else—or several others—than to be bored alone. Veronica was always up for meeting new buddies.

"Omar and Randall just got here," she reported to Kendra, who also turned around and waved.

The show ran long, since there were seventeen acts, but it was an entertaining collection of performances. Veronica and her friends did not leave disappointed. Several people recited poetry. A young woman who was dressed as a mime did a praise dance. Veronica joined in with the other screaming women in the crowd when a group of guys did a well-coordinated dance routine and bared rock-hard abs and chests. The acts that did not fare well were booed off, and the ones that were better received standing ovations. Even so, there was only one winner—a very talented young man who sang a Stevie Wonder song and played the accompanying music on the piano.

Omar sauntered over then, and he and Veronica exchanged a hug. She looked at the lopsided grin on his face and recognized it as similar to the look he'd had on his face at the party in December when he had peed in front of her.

She knew that look. "What's up with you?"

He shrugged. "Not much," he drawled. "Where are y'all going?"

"We're going back to my place," Kendra responded. "We got some drinks over there chilling on ice."

"So if you want a drink, bring your behind over there," Veronica interjected.

They left then, and went back to Kendra's apartment. Veronica hadn't eaten since earlier that day—and that was only when she wanted to take a pain pill for her aching jaw (her temporomandibular joint syndrome, which she had developed after five years of wearing braces as a teenager, was flaring up). Now she reached into Kendra's freezer and produced the ravioli meal she had brought from home. She stuck it in the microwave. Kendra and Yolanda opted for burritos instead.

The girls sat around the kitchen table eating, drinking their alcoholic beverages, and talking about guys. After she finished her burrito, Kendra called Omar to ask him where he was.

When she got off the phone, Kendra reported to Veronica, "A bunch of the guys are hanging out in 25-A. Randall and them stay over there."

So they went, laughing and talking loudly the whole way. When they got to apartment 25-A, they walked right in—something that was customary; the boys never locked the door if one of them was home and was decent. In the living room, Kendra made herself comfortable on the love seat and Veronica situated herself on the green, three-cushioned couch. The room was beginning to get blurry. She wanted to put her feet up, but remembered this was not her house and figured that might be rude. Her vision grew even fuzzier, and the room began to look like it was part of a dream. It began to sway slowly. Veronica blinked rapidly several times in a futile attempt to clear her vision.

Veronica's head was spinning, and her stomach began to churn a little. It was then she realized that, for once in her life, she had overdone it. She watched as Kendra got up from the couch to talk to Lila, but couldn't bring herself to a sitting position. Her arms and legs felt like lead.

"Look," Veronica slurred, her brown eyes barely open, "y'all go on without me. Nobody else is here but me, right?"

The girls did a quick inventory of the apartment. Omar, Terrence, and Randall were in the kitchen, and Lila went back to ask them what they were doing.

"Veronica doesn't feel good," she explained to Terrence and Randall helplessly. "She needs to get some rest."

"You can leave her there," Omar said casually.

The three girls agreed. Kendra walked out the door first, followed by Yolanda. Lila lingered and cast one last glance at Veronica. She was already sleeping. Lila felt comfortable enough to leave then. She knew Omar lived off campus, and Randall, Terrence, and Gabriel had hung around Veronica before. Lila worried no more about her roommate as the girls walked toward the parking lot.

Club Ecstasy was an overrated spot, and even though half of Arbor Dale was there, Omar was not having much fun. He was tired and uninterested in the small group of young girls who had been throwing themselves at him all night, trying to talk their way into an invitation back to his place. They didn't do anything for him.

His mind wandered to Veronica, as it often did. She was something else. Veronica was the type of person men and women liked immediately. The women who didn't like her were probably just jealous, Omar decided. Jealous of her hourglass figure, her smooth brown skin, her long, soft brown hair, and her dazzling, heart-gripping smile. There was not a single man who, if Veronica ever offered, would not sleep with her.

Omar went and found Terrence. "I'm going back to your place," he said loudly over the music.

Terrence shrugged. "Door's open. But why not just go home?"

Omar grinned mischievously. "I'm gonna see if Veronica's still there."

BACK IN 25-A, VERONICA WAS STILL ON THE COUCH, IN the exact same position she had been in when they left. The entire apartment was silent, and the kitchen and living room were pitch black, except for a small sliver of moonlight that peeked cautiously through the blinds on the patio door. There was no movement from upstairs, even though Randall and Gabriel both were probably up there—and almost certainly with female company. Being careful not to hit his leg on the coffee table, Omar quietly approached the couch where Veronica lay and slowly lowered himself onto the couch beside her.

A voice in the back of his mind warned Omar that there was a good chance that Veronica was not teasing, and that she was drunk. But Omar also knew he had seen Veronica put away seven or eight drinks in one sitting and be completely okay. It baffled him that a woman could do that and he couldn't. His hands ached to touch her, and it appeared that her stomach was visible just for that purpose. Before he could stop himself, he slid his hand carefully across her belly. She still didn't move.

Veronica was now aware that Omar was touching her, and she forced her weary eyelids open. She wanted to remove his hands from her body, but her arms lay limply at her sides. She struggled with all her might to get her muscles to work. They refused. Why the hell couldn't she move?

Omar watched as Veronica's eyes opened, then closed again. Now she was awake! Well, at least partially. Her mouth fell open, but she didn't say anything. All the while Omar was caressing her breasts, but her arms remained on either side of her body. If she wanted to push them away, that would have been the time to do it, Omar decided. He knew then that he had her exactly where he wanted her.

Veronica tried to shake her head, but she did so slowly, so it didn't look like she was shaking her head "no." It looked like she was simply trying to rouse herself awake, or maybe get more comfortable. Veronica was getting nervous. She didn't want Omar to think she wanted to have sex, but for some reason nothing worked. Her jaw had started to hurt again. She couldn't even summon the strength to move her fingers. Veronica didn't know what Omar had in mind, but she knew whatever it was, it had to be stopped.

It would be impossible to get Veronica's shirt off while she was lying down. Omar took a firm hold of her wrists and pulled Veronica up into a sitting position. As he did so, her head rolled back, and he could see by the small slits where her eyes weren't completely closed that her eyes had rolled back too. Whatever she was trying to do, she was damn good at it. Omar wasn't sharp enough to realize that Veronica had temporarily blacked out. All he knew was, he wanted her.

Omar let go of Veronica's wrists, and she fell back into the couch as though she was paralyzed. Even so, she was still straight enough to where he could get her clothes off, even though she had slumped over a bit. Omar used this opportunity to pull her shirt up over her chest and over her head. He liked the way her hair came tumbling down her shoulders, and the shiny black bra she wore felt as smooth as silk. He reached behind her and carefully unhooked the bra, tossing it carelessly to the floor.

The more he took off, the more excited he grew. As his mind worked itself into a frenzy, he completely forgot that this was not just a body he was admiring. There was a person who lived in this body: a person who he called a friend. His memories of how special Veronica made him feel by befriending him quickly escaped his mind as he stared at her body. He was exhilarated.

When Veronica lay completely naked beside him, Omar began to fumble with his own jeans. He hastily threw his jacket to the side. He removed his boots and kicked them out of the way. One of them disappeared under the table. The other one ended up near the wall beside the couch. What the hell—he took off his socks too. Then he stood to take his jeans off. This was it. His mind worked frenetically as he thought of the many things he wanted to do—that he was now going to do. Entirely nude at this point, Omar slid down onto his knees and gently parted Veronica's thighs. Then he entered her with such force that her eyes flew open.

"No!" Veronica gasped weakly, tears forming in her eyes. "Omar, no!" She gritted her teeth, ignoring the discomfort of her jaw, and tried to grab whatever her fingers could reach—which happened to be the cushions on the couch—as she tried to block the intrusion into her body. It was no use. Omar was stronger than she was, and although it seemed some of her strength was coming back each time she woke up from one of the periodic blackouts she was experiencing, she was still in no shape to fight back. Her hands could not form a fist. Her legs could not kick. But she had her voice. Her voice was a good enough weapon. Or it was supposed to be.

Veronica began to cry loudly, as loud as her voice would allow her. After several "nos," she realized Omar had no intention of stopping, and that it didn't seem as though he was paying her any attention anyway. He was looking at her face, but his eyes weren't focused on her. He was somewhere else. He had even started to sweat a little. Veronica continued to plead with him, and tried to brace herself for every one of his thrusts, but her efforts seemed to increase the searing pain going through her body.

Veronica's face was contorted in pain, and when she concluded that Omar was not going to end until he was satisfied, she sank into a blinding period of disbelief. What was happening? This was supposed to be her friend! She had befriended him! She had trusted him! How could she have been so wrong about Omar? What had she done to deserve this?

STOLEN FRUIT

Jae, 20, Michigan

AUTHOR'S PRENOTE:

Even to this day, it's hard to say the words aloud that I am a rape victim. It's been almost a year and I'm still feeling the aftermath. I never saw a psychiatrist and never really talked about how I *felt* with anyone, not even with my own mother. The question was always *what* happened, but never how did I feel when it happened. Needing a way to ease the "secret" pain, I started drinking and then found myself catching an addiction before I was even at the legal age. After many nights of downing pints and waking up still drunk and wondering how I even got home, I knew I needed something else. With that said, the following is a "lighter" sample of what happened and what was going through my head. The more writing I do, the less pints I down and the less pain I have. For all my queens reading this, all I wish for you is that you will never have to go through this. Have fun, but know that no one will watch your back better than you. I had to learn that the hard way. Stay beautiful and keep your wonderful thing pure!

I had something once
Something wonderful and good
I was stingy with it, I admit
Only few to none are worthy of my generosity
Some have gotten close
Hell, some have gotten a taste
But me being selfish and conceited
I never let my good thing slip away
You see, I've had it all my life
Ever since there was a me
Through pain, influence, and joy
My gift always stayed innocent
Not so much, like me
But one day I found someone
Whom I could share my precious gift
It was wonderful and great
I understood what I had missed!
One evening, while with close companions,
My sweet thing was too sweet
And someone unworthy was told they couldn't have it
The stranger wouldn't abort in defeat
Went to the home front to tell his army
And with revenge, late in the night
Like leopards on their hunt
Pounced in the darkness with stealth
And had my fruit for midnight lunch.

HIS DRIP FOR A TEARDROP

Sarah Lawless, 16, Newfoundland

IT SEEMED LIKE I NEVER REALLY HAD IT EASY, ALWAYS getting through rough times, ever since day one. I moved across Canada at a young age, and in the end—after my parents' harsh divorce when I was three—we settled in a very small town in Newfoundland. My two older brothers, Andrew and Matt, were just starting high school and I was starting second grade. I was very industrious and independent and, like my mother, I had a love for the underdog. I was nice to everyone, all shapes and sizes. Innocent, young, beautiful, and pure—my mom said I was her idol.

MY MOTHER REMARRIED, MY FATHER REMARRIED, AND I was too young to notice the change. I eventually stopped seeing my father. My brothers, who were almost men, grew extremely overprotective of me and became the father figures in my life. They would literally make me finish my vegetables before I left the dinner table.

My town had a population of five thousand, so basically I knew everyone. As I entered seventh grade, I became friends with the more popular crowd, the older, eighth-grade girls. When they left for high school, I was still friends with them. The high school had roughly five hundred people (one-tenth of the town), so rumors circulated around the halls like the air. Little did I know that I would be the center of these rumors when I entered high school.

My friends and I got into a huge argument in the summer and I was no longer "popular." My old friends would continuously prank-call me and yell at me on the street. The first few weeks in high school were the worst. These bratty girls were yelling at me in the halls and started ridiculous rumors. Apparently, I went to a field party and gave eight guys oral sex just to get into the party, or I had sex with a twenty-four-year-old. But in reality, I was still a virgin. All these rumors were driving me crazy and I really wish I didn't care, but I did. I would cry almost every night. Things just never seemed to get better.

At this high school, there was a class that every student was required to take in each semester, called an MSIP (Multi Subject Instructional Period). This divided the school day into five short, hour-long periods. All MSIP classes were shared between grades nine, ten, eleven, and twelve. There was this guy in my class, Tony, who was in twelfth grade. In class, I noticed his smiles and his stares at me, but I just dismissed them because I knew that he and his friends were players.

Tony started talking to me on messenger one night in October. He asked me if I was the Sarah Lawless from his MSIP class.

"Yes, I am."

"I thought so. You're cute."

"Ha ha, thanks."

"Word up."

He was very cocky and I could tell that he wanted something more than just talking over the net. Later in the conversation he told me I was "hot as fuck," and that I should call him sometime.

"Okay, sure," I replied, not really meaning what I said.

FOR THE NEXT TWO WEEKS, HE WOULD SEND ME MESSAGes saying, "Call me Friday night" and leave his phone number; he kept begging me to call him. Then I finally gave him my cell phone number and told him that if he wanted to talk to me on the phone, he would have to call me.

So he replied with, "Okay, I'll call you Friday night at nine thirty."

That weekend my mom and her boyfriend left town to go to the States. I was left at home. Friday night came and I found myself trying on different outfits, applying lots of makeup, and straightening my hair to perfection. I caught myself actually anticipating his phone call. I was excited—something about him allured me. He was a bad boy and I had heard the most appalling, slutty stories about him, but I just kept brushing my hair.

Nine thirty rolled around and my cell phone rang. My stomach jumped out of place as the sharp ring startled my thoughts. "Hello?"

"Hey, it's Tony."

We decided to meet at a swing bridge close to his house, near the river, and we were going to watch movies. Now, it just seems so typical what he wanted, but then I was oblivious. As I left my empty house that night and set out into the brisk November night air, I felt lost, completely lost. I told myself, *Not tonight, you are not losing your virginity tonight,* and I honestly wasn't planning to take things that far. I kept thinking to myself, *What are you doing? You don't even know him. TURN AROUND AND GO HOME.* But I ignored my paranoid self and kept walking to the meeting place.

Then, after five or so minutes of walking, I saw him—he was on Rollerblades. How mature. We said our hellos and how are yous and then we walked to his house—well, he rolled. As soon as I walked through his front door, a huge wave of weed stench smothered me. It was gross. He informed me that he and his dad had smoked weed together an hour or so before.

Tony uttered, "Yeah, he's one of those dads."

He immediately led me straight up the stairs to his room after a brief tour. I was glad to get away from the strong stench. He asked me which movie, *Dumb and Dumber* or *Gone in Sixty Seconds.* I was in the mood to laugh—shockingly—so *Dumb and Dumber* it was. He popped the movie into his VCR, and I sat on the end of his bed, hugging a pillow. He sat down at the top of his bed, then shifted to lying down and told me that I could lie down as well if I wanted to. So I did.

While Jim Carrey started making jokes on the screen, I noticed Tony's hand slowly moving up my leg and he started to kiss me. I was suddenly crazy about him, but in my right mind I kept saying, *Not tonight. You're too good for this. What if he ends up just hurting you?* But I avoided these thoughts.

Unsuspecting things led to stupid things and he started to unbuckle his pants. He slid a condom on and I told him it was all right.

In between his moans, I muttered, "I can't."

"What do you mean, you can't? You can't say no now."

I GAVE HIM MY ONLY CHERISHED POSSESSION, ALONG with my fake satisfaction . . . but he was happy.

As he slid his pants on, he told me that he couldn't walk me home because he was tired—he had to get up early for a hockey tournament the next morning, only a few hours away. So he managed to escort me to his front door.

"You're such a gentleman."

He laughed, and so did I. But to me, deep down it really wasn't funny. He wouldn't even kiss me goodnight. He literally held both of my arms, lifted me above his head, and then put me down, thinking I would like it or something. *Wow, that was nice, thanks.* So I slowly dragged my feet home that early November morning, wondering how I could be so naive. For the rest of that weekend, I just sat around the house, watching movies and thinking. My mom always said I was her idol because I was innocent, young, beautiful, and pure. But now I wasn't and I was unsure of what to do, so I decided to keep it from her. At least I would still be her idol.

The next week, he didn't come to MSIP class and I never saw him. I guess he was just a rebel, but I became annoyed with him always being away. I really wanted to see him, at least talk to him. I was afraid I would never talk to him again and he would never care about me because he was one of those kinds of guys: the user, the player. The guy sluts, as I now call them.

THAT NEXT WEDNESDAY HE CALLED AND WANTED TO rendezvous—how could I say no? I didn't want my first time to be with someone who wouldn't want to see me again. So I gave in. I actually started to really like him. I snuck out of my back door in the middle of the night and made love to him, while he only had sex with me. At least this time he did manage to walk me a few blocks from his house—how pathetic. But I laughed—I liked him so much and he said the same to me too. But it was all a lie, a joke.

People started finding out about me and Tony, but not from me; I didn't tell a soul. All the girls would yell, "Woo, go bang Tony," but for some reason I didn't really care anymore, ironically. I thought that once they found out about it, I would start worrying a lot more because it was the truth, but that wasn't the case at all. All these girls already thought I was a slut when I wasn't, so if I actually started having sex it wouldn't change their views about me at all. They would start all the crazy rumors about how I got pregnant or something, and it became humorous to me after a while. So I just kept on going to school and living my life.

FOR A WHILE, IT SEEMED LIKE TONY FORGOT ABOUT ME again, but I never forgot about him. I couldn't stop thinking about him. Every day I would look for him among the five hundred people at school, but he would never be looking my way.

Then, four days before Christmas, I was surprised to see that he called me and wanted to see me. It had been about a month since I had spoken with him, so another night at his house was sounding good to me. He told me he was having a party, so I brought my friend with me. When I arrived at his house, there were about ten guys—that's it, no other girls—no party. That confused me, because most of these guys were around nineteen to twenty years old and had girlfriends. But my friend was very flirty and loved the older guys and didn't show any sign of wanting to leave. So I stayed. I was happy regardless; I got to see Tony again.

After a few beers and a couple hits of a bong, I noticed Tony glancing at my friend and never looking my way. I became so jealous and almost in disbelief that he'd called me over and now I knew he didn't want me. So I threw myself at him, not literally, but I was all over him. I was drunk, I was high on weed, I wasn't in good condition at all. But I knew I wanted him. He took me to his room upstairs and I don't remember much of it, but we had sex. I got what I had wanted, even though it sounds despicable and completely unimaginable to me now.

Then, to my shock, he yelled, "Okay, buddy, your turn!"

His built football friend, Jeff, walked into the room. He was big, intimidating, and he was unbuckling his belt. I was psychologically stunned.

"What's going on?" I knew right then and there, this was not good. I turned to Tony and said, "No. Please no."

"What do you mean, no? Don't be stupid. Don't be like that." His voice was so dominating.

Hearing those words come from his mouth made my insides crumble. I was so overwhelmed that he said that to me, so I fell silent. I was screaming on the inside, but I was too scared to make a peep. Those words kept residing in my head. *What do you mean, no? Don't be stupid. Don't be like that.*

I laid there unable to move, waiting for Jeff to have his way with me as well. I was frightened that if I fought, they would take drastic measures to make me do what they wanted. Jeff held down my legs and positioned himself on my stomach. As he entered me, without a condom, I closed my eyes. I really didn't want to watch him do that to me. But I couldn't help it.

I heard more voices. When I opened my eyes and turned my head to the door, I noticed that different football players, hockey players, and even one of my friends' older brother came into the room to get a piece of my paralyzed body. To them, I was their whore. They were too caught up in releasing their sexual energy to realize I was intoxicated, frightened, and alone. I really didn't want this.

EVERY TIME I OPENED MY EYES AGAIN, I SAW A DIFFERENT guy on top of me—one of them I didn't even know. Another one, Jesse, clamped his hands around my neck as he thrust. I started nudging my head and pushing his hands off. I couldn't breathe, but he kept on insisting. His hands remained there until he was done.

The room was filled with six different guys; they were naked. I remember hearing them say, "It's my turn," or the offending sound of them striking high-fives. I smelt their breath—cheap beer and weed—each and every time they exhaled. Their sweat dripped all over my frail body. Each drop became another tear I would later cry.

Eventually it was over and they all cleared the room. I was left there lying on the dirty mattress.

WHAT THE FUCK JUST HAPPENED?

I could barely answer my own question. I just knew I had to leave. I stumbled to get my pants on, grabbed my drunken friend from the other room, and went home feeling so dirty.

After Christmas break the entire school population knew what happened, except they heard the wrong side. I was named so many things: slut, whore, skank. People said I had gotten "trained" or "gangbanged." But among the collection of malicious words, "rape" was not present.

Everyone at my school, even my friends, thought that I had wanted this to happen to me. When I walked down the halls, people would shove me, shout horrible things at me, tell me to leave and that I was a disgrace. I went to the principal about this behavior, but nothing was done. I couldn't concentrate on classwork, I couldn't sleep, I couldn't smile; continuing at this school was not worth the price. So I stopped going to school and did correspondence. I applied at a school in a close city where no one really knew me.

My mother had found out about that night through my brothers, and she convinced me that going to the authorities was the right thing to do. I had to give a statement, about everything, and it was the worst thing to talk about. Talking about this out loud, in front of police in uniform, video cameras, recorders, and my mom almost bulldozed me into a state of panic. But I knew it was the right thing to do.

MY MOM MADE ME GO TO THE DOCTOR'S AND I DISCOVered I had contracted chlamydia, but thank God it is a curable STI. Now, I am suing the three men and three boys who did this to me. I am still awaiting trial. These guys live in the same town as me; I see them everywhere. I have to face them, their brothers, sisters, moms, dads, and friends. I still have to endure the stares from people when I go to a store and dodge people on the street. I still have to face the night over and over again each time I see one of them drive by. Yet time's effect makes it easier to walk down the street, and to walk through life. People in my small town are starting to realize that I didn't want this—no one would. And I am starting to accept that what happened was not my fault.

A huge part of me wishes that I would have kept my virginity; if I said no that night to Tony, I really don't think this would've happened to me. I feel empty sometimes and I just want to scream at the top of my lungs. Girls all over the place deal with this feeling and it's something that we cannot take back, something that is so precious and is treated so improperly these days. I wish that I could have saved myself for someone who would have treated me right and not bargained me off to his friends for a good time. I hope that all the young girls around the world who have been victimized like this can move on with their life and claim justice. But whether I can really move on—away from these guys who are walking around with my smile in their back pocket—only time will tell.

THEN AND NOW

Toccora, 20, New Jersey

AS I THINK BACK ON MY LIFE, NOTHING SEEMS NORMAL. I mean, who can actually say what normal is? I don't know, but I know my life was far from it. I guess it all started when I was six years old—me being young, and not knowing the difference between right and wrong.

This guy, let's call him JR, was someone I never thought would hurt me, especially with him being my cousin and all. I guess that's why no one really believed me when I finally said something about it, ten years too late. But I'm getting ahead of myself. I'll start from the beginning.

It was a normal spring day. We were on spring break, and being that there was no school and all, we got to hang out with our family that we didn't see as much, since we all lived in different towns. On this particular weekend we were at my aunt's house, visiting her and my two cousins. We were having a great time riding bikes, foot racing, playing games, laughing—you know, being kids. Little did I know that for me, being a kid was gonna end that day.

"Let's get back on the bikes and have a race. Let's see who'll win with two people on the bike!" JR said.

"Okay," we all agreed, because he was older than all of us.

"Toccora, you get on my bike," he told me. I was happy that he picked me to be on his bike. I was the youngest of the group, and he picked me first. "Sit in the front so you don't fall off, because I'm gonna go fast."

I didn't think anything of it, so I did what I was told. The race had started and he was right—we did go fast, so fast that we passed the corner we were supposed to turn at. "You forgot to turn," I yelled back to him.

"I know, I want to show you something," he whispered in my ear.

The way he talked into my ear made me feel really weird, but being six I didn't know why I was feeling that way. We kept riding up the street until we got to some parking lot, about three blocks away from where we were supposed to be. I looked around, trying to figure out what it was he wanted me to see, but I couldn't see anything but old abandoned cars.

"What do you want to show me?" I asked. He didn't say anything, but he grabbed my waist and pulled me into him. My back was still to him, and he was holding me very tightly. "What are you doing?" I was very confused, and still wondering what I was supposed to see.

"Shh, be quiet," he whispered.

We were still on the bike. He picked me up and placed me on top of his groin. He began moving me back and forth on top of him. I got scared, because even though I had no clue what was going on, something in my head was telling me, *This is wrong.* But I didn't say anything. I was frozen, shocked, and lost for words. At age six, never in my wildest dreams would I ever have thought such a thing could be happening to me. This act went on for no more than a minute, I think, but it felt like hours.

"Don't tell anyone. You hear me?" he said, as we were riding back to my aunt's house.

I was still lost for words.

"You hear me!" he yelled.

I quickly agreed, surprised that I actually said something. We arrived at the house, and my cousin, brother, and sister were sitting on the steps with the bikes down by the curb.

"Where were y'all?" asked someone, I don't even remember who.

"We went to the store," JR lied.

"Well, where is what you bought?" the person asked.

"We ate it, duh," the lie continued.

It was getting chilly, so our parents told us to get inside and watch TV and play games. We did as were we told. As we were going upstairs to the second floor, I felt someone behind me. It was JR. He was smiling, and I saw that no one was behind him. I quickly turned around to run up the steps. He stopped me, with my back still to him, and put his fingers between my legs, from front to back. I still remember that feeling I had afterward. The feeling that this was just the beginning of something I didn't want to happen.

The years passed and the abuse got worse. So bad that I just stayed to myself all the time. Never played with other kids because I just didn't feel like a kid anymore. Something was missing—I know now it was my innocence.

I hardly went outside, unless my mom made me, and when we went by my aunt's house, that's when I started lying, saying I was sick or something of that nature. I still was forced to go. You know that feeling you get in your stomach when you get scared, that sharp pain that's cold at the same time? That's what I felt every time the car turned the corner to her house.

"What's wrong?" my mom would ask.

"Nothing, I just want to sit in the car for a while," I'd lie, trying to fight back tears.

"Make sure you lock the door when you get out."

"Mommy . . . " I called out one day.

"Yeah," she said, turning around.

Right at that moment, I thought I could tell her everything. Everything that was going on for years, that I wanted to stop, and I was about to tell her, until . . .

"Hi, Aunt D, what are you and Toccora talking about?" JR said. He popped out of nowhere and I felt myself get sick just at the sight of him.

"Hey, JR. Oh, we'll be right in. Toccora needed to tell me something."

As the words were coming out of my mom's mouth, I was looking at him. He had this indescribable look on his face. He didn't have to say anything—I knew what it meant, and I knew what was going to happen later.

"Mommy, just forget it. I want to go inside now," I ran past him, trying not to look my monster in the face, but it was so hard not to. He still had the look, until my mom came along—then he was all smiles.

Another number of years passed and it got even worse. My body had started to change a lot. I was eleven going on twelve, but looked like I was fifteen going on sixteen. These were the last few months when the abuse was going on. To make a long story short, it stopped because he thought he got me pregnant, thanks to my lie saying that I didn't get my period that month. I never thought that I would be happy about my period being the reason for the abuse to stop, but it was, and I am.

FOUR YEARS LATER, I WAS SIXTEEN YEARS OLD WITH severe depression. I always thought my case was really weird. While the abuse was going on I wasn't that depressed; I still acted like how a kid was supposed to around others. It wasn't until after it stopped that things got out of control. My parents didn't know why. Neither did my friends or teachers. I kept it all balled up inside, and it was literally killing me. My parents thought that it was just being a teenager. That I would eventually grow out of being a loner.

Several months passed and my parents realized it was something deeper. Of course I lied and said nothing was wrong. I felt like they couldn't relate to anything I was going through, so I rebelled even more.

I started drinking at the age of twelve, but at sixteen it became a real problem. I would drink anything I wasn't supposed to. I stole my mom's painkillers that she had from a car accident, along with other pills that I had no idea what they were for. I had poured a few out of each bottle into my wanting hands and I'd drank them down with whatever alcohol I had at the moment. When that didn't deaden the pain, I started cutting myself. That's when I knew it had gotten too far—that I was just a step away from actually killing myself.

I finally told my parents what was going on—not everything, just about the abuse. Nothing about the abuse I had caused myself after it was over. I still haven't. I was put into therapy. It was okay, but it just wasn't helping. The thought of opening up to a total stranger about my personal problems was troublesome for me. I didn't trust anyone, and I mean anyone. Not my mom, sister, brother, or father—especially my father or any male, for that matter. I wouldn't play around with my brother or other male cousins and friends like I used to, because I felt like I was going to give them the wrong message if I was the only girl there. When my sister had my niece, I wouldn't trust my dad or any male with her alone. Even though I knew my dad wouldn't do anything at all like that, I still felt weird about it, and that hurt me just having those thoughts about my dad. I hated JR for making me lose my trust in people.

For a long time I didn't feel comfortable around guys. It was hard not to. I went through six years of sexual abuse and fourteen years of ongoing mental/emotional abuse. It wasn't until I was maybe fourteen that I had my first real boyfriend. It was a bit shaky, I must admit. Every time he would try to kiss me, I'd move away and make up some type of excuse that would explain why I or he had to leave. There were times when he'd sneak up behind me, in school or other places, and he'd put his hands over my eyes, and it would freak me out. Just the thought of someone putting their hands on me, and me not knowing who it was, just brought back a lot of fears that I tried so hard to lose, or hide from.

I knew then that the abuse had affected me in so many ways, from me not being able to trust anyone, family and friends, to not trusting myself. I always felt as though boys only wanted one thing, so I ended up breaking off any relationships.

But things have a funny way of changing when you feel as though all hope is lost. I was living in Virginia for about six months, with my godsister and her husband, Kenny. One day Kenny had a little get-together to watch the fight on TV, and that's where I met Keith. He was the first one there, and it went from there. We talked for hours; even when everyone left the house, we were the only ones still up, talking. The next night, we talked on the phone for almost six hours. I know—what can you talk to the same person about for six hours? Everything! He's a great listener and asked questions that I wouldn't even think of asking someone I just met, but it was good. Coming from a past of secrecy, I have since become a very open person (hence this story), and so is he, which made me trust him.

We became a lot closer, and yes, there are mutual feelings there. Not talking love, just like—a lot. Keith is great. Our relationship, which is just a friendship leaning toward something more, is wonderful. With Keith it was totally different from being with any other guy that I've dated. It's not because he's five years older and more mature, or because he is family oriented and down to earth. I believe I trust him so much because I let him get to know me and some of my story. There is just something about him I can't explain. You know when you meet someone and right off the bat you feel really comfortable with them, and you know that you'd get along great with this person? That's how it was when I met him, and I hope that's how it will continue to be.

He's helped me a lot by just letting me talk about my problems freely and openly with him, without having to worry about him judging me. Talking to him was better than any type of therapy because while I was in therapy, I held back a lot of things, in fear of what my therapist may think of me in the end. So Keith was my own personal therapist, and is still my therapist who's helping me get past what happened to me. I am not sexually active, partly because of what happened to me, but I do know that when the time comes and I feel ready, it will be 100 percent my choice if I choose to give that special part of me to someone. I'll leave you now with some words that I now live by, from a woman who didn't let anything get to her:

"If you judge people, you have no time to love them."

—Mother Teresa

IT SEEMED SO HARMLESS

Adrianna Eisner, 23, British Columbia

IT DIDN'T HAPPEN IN A DARK, DESERTED ALLEY OR IN THE back of a white van with tinted windows. It happened in my cozy dorm room, on the leopard print bedsheets that I had eagerly chosen a few months earlier, when I began my first year of university.

Like most freshmen, I was bright-eyed, bushy-tailed, and flat-out naive. Despite the excitement of all the new things, I managed to maintain some old values: My grades were good, my family ties strong, and I was managing to maintain my long-distance relationship that I wasn't willing to forget. I had made friends at school and in my dorm, but continued to look for new ones—maybe I was hoping to get the "full" university experience. That's how I met him.

"Are you serious? You have no one to help you with those bags?"

I had just finished shopping at the grocery store across from my residence when I heard his voice as I walked out of the store. I didn't hesitate, didn't think twice, as I handed him a bag and gave him a grateful "Thanks!" It seemed so harmless.

He walked me to the door of the building, talking all the while: I was from British Columbia—his mom lived there. I lived downtown—he didn't live far. I was willing to exchange numbers—he was too.

It was a match made in convenience, so we began talking on the phone after our grocery rendezvous. I was still committed to my boyfriend and I made that quite clear. To my surprise and delight, he didn't brush me off and still wanted to be friends. Looking back, I wish I had felt guiltier about talking to this cool new guy, rather than the boyfriend who I loved but had a few problems with. After weeks of talking, I decided it would be okay if we hung out. He had said his favorite basketball player was Allen Iverson. I happened to have a video about him that we could watch, and he invited himself over.

It was spring break at the university and a lot of the people on my floor had gone home. I had decided to stay to get some extra articles done for the school newspaper, and it didn't click in my head how dangerous the get-together had just become. I met him downstairs, feeling a little bit nervous and a bit guilty about taking it from phone conversations to a date. The feeling got worse when I noticed how run-down he looked—for some reason this stuck out in my mind. He was carrying a case of beer in his hand. I raised my eyebrows.

"Beer and basketball go together," he said, reading my expression.

I didn't argue as I signed him in past security. In my room we sat and talked for a while, the regular chitchat when you're face-to-face with someone you realize you hardly know. My boyfriend ran through my thoughts but I ignored the nagging feeling because, after all, he had just told me he wanted a break, and that seemed like more than enough of a reason not to feel guilty about my little rendezvous. After we both got settled on the bed, I pressed play, then I reached across him and turned off the bedside lamp to prevent a glare from bouncing off the TV. He took the opportunity to make his first comment.

"Damn, your ass looks good in those jeans."

I turned bright red as I settled back into the spot next to him. The DVD hadn't been playing for more than fifteen minutes when he handed me my second beer—not yet having finished his first one.

I giggled, "You better catch up."

He smiled, I smiled, and then he leaned over and kissed me. His lips felt rough and I pulled back. With his mouth free once again, he whispered, "You look so good in those jeans, baby."

Baby . . . baby? That's what my boyfriend called me. It made me sick to hear it from him, and suddenly something snapped in my head.

I looked him in the eye and didn't hesitate. "I'm not trying to do that. Let's just watch the video."

He shifted, then sat back in his place, but no more than ten minutes later he kissed me again. My lips felt numb and the kiss lasted no more than ten seconds before I pulled back and said, "Seriously, I can't do this."

He smiled, and it was the kind of smile that gives you a nervous feeling in the pit of your stomach that you know you shouldn't ignore. But that's just what I did—I ignored it. I finished sipping my third beer and felt a rush in my head. His lips were on mine again, more aggressive this time. I pushed back and politely told him to stop, giving him my best *it's cool* smile. But my head banged against the headboard as his forced kisses continued. I heard myself saying, "Stop."

He kept on and my head was on my pillow and my pants were being pulled over my hips as he forced his body on top of mine. That moment is forever engraved in my memory because that's when my body shut down. I wish that I kicked, that I screamed, that I bit and scratched and clawed his eyes. But instead I lay there and felt the painful penetration of a dry latex condom.

I kept saying no, hoping it would stop. And when it didn't, I continued to plead, "Please, just stop. It's okay, just stop."

He was trying to move in and out of me, and the pain was throbbing. I closed my eyes. I shut down. He started hurling insults at me. Calling me names, telling me I deserved it, and I just begged for it to stop. Tears welled up in the corners of my closed eyes and fell silently down my cheeks as my inner thighs throbbed and he kept moving faster and speaking louder, saying meaner things, and then—just like that—it was over. He rolled over and threw the condom in the trash as I went into the washroom. Sitting on the lid of the toilet, I stared in the mirror and felt disgusted. My face looked pale and my eyes were red. I couldn't look at myself. I felt dirty. I stepped into the shower. I didn't care that he was still in my room—I had to wash away the filth. I prayed he would be gone when I came out.

I found him sitting on the edge of the bed, putting the beer bottles back in their case.

"I like to take these back to the store," he said casually.

I stared at him and wondered what was going through his mind. Standing up, he smiled and came toward me. I cringed and pulled back as he stroked my wet hair.

"Come here," he said. My eyes widened as he kissed me on the mouth. I pulled back and told him that I thought it was time for him to leave. He pushed me on the bed and started to pull down my pajama bottoms as I resisted and pulled them back up. His hand was in my pants and I shoved it away, as he pulled the pants down hard.

Holding my hands back, he slipped on a condom as I begged him again, "Come on . . . please stop. Stop now."

He entered me forcefully and I cried out in pain. My nails raked his back and he thrust into me a few times before pulling out. I couldn't wrap my brain around what was happening, as he pulled his jeans over his thighs and grabbed his car keys.

"Come on. Walk me downstairs."

I slipped on my shoes and out of my dorm with him in tow. We didn't say a word while we waited for the elevator. I didn't move an inch once we got inside; I hardly remember breathing.

"Thanks, I had a lot of fun," he said when the door slid open. "My car is parked kind of far, so don't worry about walking me."

Without saying a word, I pressed Door Close and made my way back to my room. For a long time I sat and wondered: *Did I lead him on? Did I make it seem like I wanted it? Should I have kicked him out after the first time he kissed me?*

It's ironic, because when you watch any crime drama you marvel at how stupid rape victims seem when they throw evidence in the trash or bathe evidence off their bodies. I was that stupid girl, except this wasn't a TV show and no one was going to yell, "Cut!" I soaked and scrubbed my body again, this time for more than an hour, wanting to wash the invisible dirt off any part of my flesh that he had touched. As soon as I was done, I threw out the trash, which contained the condom he used. It was about 6:00 AM when I finally sat on my couch, not wanting to touch the bed. After a few hours of falling in and out of sleep, I called a girl from my floor whose cell number I had. I told her what happened and how wrong it felt.

"Oh my god, it was date rape. You need to call someone," she told me.

During the following week, everything felt like one big blur. I spoke to a guidance counselor, who suggested that I call a rape crisis line. I did.

"Are you going to pursue legal action?" asked the counselor over the phone.

I paused, realizing I had never given that question due consideration. I felt lost, scared, and, most importantly, intimidated. I hadn't gone to a hospital, I had thrown away the "evidence"—essentially it was my word against his. After speaking with a rape crisis counselor twice, I decided to take her up on her offer of giving a detailed report, which would be submitted to the police anonymously. They would keep this report on file, and if another girl reported a similar incident, I would be called in. The woman said she would call back the next day to take the statement. When, for whatever reason, she didn't, I felt like giving up. I spoke to a friend's father who was a police officer and gave him some story about my "friend" who had been raped and was confused about what to do. He admitted that taking legal action after a rape case could sometimes drag on and come down to, as I thought, my word against his. That was the final straw. I gave up. My focus shifted from looking for justice to looking for consolation.

I told my now ex-boyfriend about the rape, and his reaction wasn't exactly what I had expected. He didn't blow up, he didn't threaten to kill the guy. Instead he was quiet as he listened. I shared some details of that night with him but held back—something discouraged me from opening up. Telling my mom, with whom I am extremely close, was even more difficult. I remember staring out the window onto the busy street below and finally saying the words.

"Mom, I was raped."

"Who was raped?" she replied almost nonchalantly, as if she expected me to say the name of some person she hardly knew.

"Me."

There were a lot of tears.

As a journalism major, I hoped to find comfort in writing. But one of the worst parts of being raped was that for a while I couldn't figure out how to make the words flow anymore. Something that had always come to me so easily was now more difficult than ever. I became angry, frustrated at him and at myself for allowing him to take my talent away. Not being able to write came along with not being able to study, being scared to leave my dorm, and becoming needy with my ex. The rape was taking a toll on my life. With the end of the school year nearing, I still hadn't written three articles that had to be handed in in order to pass the class. I hadn't even studied for exams. And just when I began to get my footing back, he called just before the end of the school year. I had been studying for a philosophy exam when I saw the number that had become familiar to me from those weeks of talking.

My heart pounded and my breathing became short as I stared at the ringing phone. I didn't answer.

The calls kept coming for about four days, always in the evening when he knew I'd be home from class. Finally I decided to confront him.

"Hey, stranger! What happened to you?" he exclaimed, feigning excitement. I felt my breath shorten as anxiety washed over me.

"Listen," I said, trying to sound stronger than I felt, "what happened between you and I was not consensual, and we both know that."

With that, he hung up. Believe it or not, he actually drove by my residence a few times after that and called the phone once or twice, leaving messages asking me if I wanted to have more fun. I was glad the school year was finally coming to an end and that I would be going home and getting a different phone extension the following year.

During that summer, I also started writing again. At first I wrote random thoughts—anger, happiness, sadness, details of that night. It was my own sort of personal way of expelling the rape from my body. The thing that has taken the most time to heal is my self-esteem. For a long while I felt ugly because of what he had done and the things that he had said. There were also times when I continued to blame myself, thinking that maybe my jeans were too tight or my voice was too flirty. It took me a long time to realize that even if my jeans were painted on and my voice oozed with seduction, *no* really does mean *no* and he should've stopped.

Slowly, I started to feel better about myself—I saw beauty in my green eyes, my pouty lips, and my wide hips. I also saw beauty in my intelligence and in my ability as a writer. Most importantly, I saw the beauty of prayer. It helped to lift me out of some of my darkest moments after the rape. And even though I still have dreams sometimes or thoughts of that night, most of the time I am able to exhale and release the negative energy before it does any more damage to me or the relationships that truly matter.

STOPPING HIM IN HIS TRACKS

Carla, 24, Florida

"YOU KNOW YOU WANT TO BREAK UP WITH HIM" IS ALL I heard him say while I tried to wriggle my arm free. I kept thinking, *Why is this happening? What do I do?* But before I could answer my own question, he kicked his approach up a notch and I knew that there was no more time for questioning.

Wait, step back for a second, and let's start with how I got to that moment. I was at work that weekend and was preparing to go over to my friend Lindsay's house to smoke and drink. And a coworker of mine walked up behind me and tapped my arm lightly. I turned and faced him; his name was Richard.

"Can I bum a ride back to my house?"

I put one hand on my hip and checked the time with the other. I really had to get going to Lindsay's house, but I felt bad for Richard. It sucked not having a car. I should know—I once was a pedestrian myself.

I nodded impatiently, half hoping he would say, "Don't worry about it," but he didn't, so he unloaded himself into my car and off we went. Since I was dropping Richard off at his place, I decided to ask him if I could use his bathroom to change so I could save time.

"Sure," he said, totally casual.

When we got to his spot, I grabbed my clothes from the back seat and ran upstairs with him to his place. He wasted no time with the obligatory house tour, thankfully, because I really didn't feel like doing the whole "nice place" routine. He showed me where the bathroom was and I thanked him, then went inside. He had the type of bathroom that had the two doors that led to different places in the house. I closed and locked one door and then walked over and did the same to the other. Just as I released my hand off of the second knob, I heard it jiggle. My heart skipped a beat.

"Can I help you?" I asked aloud, without hiding the disgust in my tone.

"Uh, no, I was just making sure you closed it okay."

I shook my head and changed as fast as I could. I gathered up my clothes, unlocked the door closest to the front door, and started straight for it. Before I could get close enough to the front door to make a run for it, he grabbed me by the wrist.

"Come look at my PlayStation."

I didn't know what to say or do, so I decided to just act natural and get out of there as peacefully and quickly as I could. I smiled weakly. "Sure, but only for a second." He let go of me and we walked back to his room. I looked at his PlayStation and smiled. "Good for you! Seriously, though, I have to go."

He grabbed my wrist again and whispered those words into my ear: "You know you want to break up with him."

"What?" I immediately remembered that I had been telling Richard earlier that day that my boyfriend and I had gotten into a fight. It was nothing serious, but apparently Richard thought it was. I smiled and shook my wrist free of his hand. "What makes you think that?"

"Because how can you want to be with him and want me?"

I realized then I had been polite for far too long and I needed to take a firmer stance. I looked him dead in the eye and said, "No, I don't want you, and like I said, I have people waiting on me. I have to go."

I turned to leave, then he pushed my shoulders back so hard I fell on his bed. Desperate, I tried to bounce up from the bed as fast as I could but he was already on top of me, pinning me down. I lay on my back, searching the face of someone I no longer knew. His eyes seemed to change, his presence, his being. He looked angry but so was I. It was at that time I decided it was either him or me.

Now, Richard was not a big guy. He was about five-foot-six and maybe 170 pounds. Sure, he had forty pounds on me, but he was nothing compared to my older brother. He started to unzip my jeans, all the while securing my hands with his legs. I took this opportunity to soccer-style kick him in the balls. I felt the weight of his body collapse on me before I pushed him off. I turned around and saw him squirming, but I wasn't done. I slammed him in the face until my hand went numb. He was bloody and a mess.

I screamed at him, *"Don't you ever fucking touch me again without my permission, you fuck!"*

I grabbed my belongings and hauled it outside. I threw my clothes into my car and peeled out without looking back. I wasn't sure what to expect. I was scared on my drive over to Lindsay's house that he was going to call the police on me and I was going to get in trouble.

I decided not to tell anyone except very close friends, and only years afterward, what happened that night. I was scared that I was going to get in trouble, but now that I look back on it, so what if I would have gotten in trouble? I live my life to this day knowing that I stopped his actions dead in his tracks. I live life knowing I beat the crap out of him and there is nothing more embarrassing to a guy than telling his buddies how a girl kicked his ass.

I ended up seeing Richard the next day at work and I completely avoided contact with him. His face was swollen and cut up from the day before. Working with him that day was an unbearable torture of awkwardness. Toward the end of the day, he cornered me in the back of the kitchen and apologized for the day before. I told him it was all right because if he tried it again I would kill him without a moment's hesitation. He looked down at the ground and walked away. I ended up quitting that job about a month later and never heard from or saw Richard again. As I look back on the incident, a part of me feels stronger and more independent knowing that I had the courage to confront the situation and never back down. The other part of me still feels weak for actually telling him it was okay and he was forgiven. It is *never* okay for anyone to attempt to do harm to your body. It is never okay for anyone to cross any boundary that you set with your words or body language. Richard may have acted like he was dumb, blind, and deaf that night, but he sure wasn't immortal, and I just hope he remembers that pain if he ever tries to hurt another living being again.

GOT QUESTIONS ABOUT CHAPTER 4?

DATE RAPE

Sarah Lawless, 18, Newfoundland
Adrianna Eisner, 23, British Columbia

Why would someone you know want to harm you sexually?

Sarah: First of all, it is important to understand that rape is not about sex, it is about power. And in no way is this an excuse for the attacker's behavior. In a deranged way, a perpetrator may also feel as though they have earned sex from someone they know, for whatever reasons, and it leads to the sexual assault. There are many reasons why people sexually assault people they know, but none of them are good enough.

Adrianna: This is a tough question to answer and brings up another good point—the stereotype that rape or sexual harm is always done by someone you don't know. The truth is quite the opposite. Many, many rapes occur with a person that you know. Attackers may do it to feel better about themselves through taking another person's power away, or they may do it because they feel that they deserve it and that you are the one in the wrong for saying no.

Is there any prevention, since it seems so unpredictable?

Sarah: I feel that the only prevention of rape is to be personally aware and cautious of rape and how it can happen. If ever you should find yourself in a situation like I did, it can make you feel so powerless and unsure what to do. It is also paramount to just steer clear of people who you do not feel comfortable around and to listen to your intuition whenever meeting new people.

Adrianna: There are a few ways to protect yourself from rape. The most important thing is not to ignore your instinct. Intuition is a powerful thing and if that little voice says that something is wrong, trust that it is. Another way to prevent rape, even though it may seem unpredictable, is to realize that date rape doesn't mean that you have to be intoxicated and not have control over your body. You can just as easily be raped when you are sober and aware of your surroundings. We shouldn't live in fear, but we also shouldn't throw all caution to the wind. Just be aware.

Note from Shannon: It bears mentioning here that *everyone* can prevent rape by supporting a culture in which rape is not tolerated. The most obvious prevention education must be geared toward the would-be rapist themselves.

Did you report your experience?

Sarah: Yes, I did report it to the authorities. I was thirteen when I was raped, so it was necessary that I report it. I cooperated with the police and court system for the majority of my high school years. In the end, even though the outcome was not as I had hoped, due to the police losing evidence, I still to this day will never regret my decision to seek justice.

Adrianna: I called a rape crisis center in my city; however, when my call wasn't returned I gave up on finding justice and focused on healing. I did not report it to the police.

How did it affect you afterward?

Sarah: My whole life changed after the rape, and there are really no proper words to describe how a trauma like this can affect someone's life. I was so young when this happened to me and I feel very robbed of my innocence, as this whole occurrence caused me to mature very fast. It has affected my personal views and the choices that I make. It has especially affected me when it comes to starting new relationships with friends or opening up to a new sexual relationship. I feel as though I am incapable of trusting someone ever again, and I also feel as though I have secured a huge wall around me and it is extremely difficult and timely to let someone in.

Adrianna: I strongly believe that everything happens for a reason. I am not in any way saying that I deserved what happened to me, but I have grown a lot because of my experience. At first I was very depressed—I had a difficult time functioning on a day-to-day basis. My schoolwork was affected, my grades suffered, and one of the biggest blows was to my relationship. In my story I referred to my boyfriend as my "ex" because we had decided to take a break right before the rape. We eventually got back together and are still together now. However, making him understand why I didn't want to be touched sometimes or why sometimes talking dirty turned me off was difficult. He couldn't get past the fact that he was my "first" and I was treating him this way. It took a lot of conversations to get to a point where he was able to understand.

What advice would you give another date rape victim?

Sarah: It is a huge weight to carry on your shoulders not to talk about it, and even though it is difficult to be open about it, it is so important that you open up to someone. It is crucial to let someone in so you do not feel as though you are fighting this battle on your own, whether it is with a support group, a friend, or a rape crisis counselor. Attending weekly appointments with a counselor helped me through my healing process and I would strongly suggest that for another date rape victim. What happened was wrong and it was not your fault. Claim justice and seek healing, whether it is through the court process or just coming to terms with it yourself. It is a long and tedious process either way. *Life is 10 percent what happens to you, 90 percent how you deal with it.*

Adrianna: I would say speak about it. Getting everything out—the experience, the tears, the anger, the sadness—is a relief. If you have a best friend, a parent, a boyfriend, or anyone you fully trust, talk to that person. Another thing I would say is to find a support group. You can't give up on yourself. Make yourself the number one priority and realize that getting healthy doesn't mean just healing physically, it means healing emotionally as well.

If I am a boy dating a girl who has been raped, should I treat her differently or be more sensitive?

Sarah: I would definitely say that sensitivity is needed if you are dating someone who has been sexually assaulted, but even more so, understanding and support. Let her know that if she ever needs someone to talk to about what happened, she can talk to you and that you are willing to listen and believe her. She needs you to help her heal and experience the good side of life.

Adrianna: If you are dating someone who has been raped, you don't need to treat them differently. But you should be more sensitive. Certain things may upset them that never had before, and you have to realize they are feeling a lot of emotions. At the same time, you shouldn't go out of your way asking if they are all right all the time. In other words, be there for them when they need you, back away when you realize they need space. It's about finding a balance. Help them pick up the pieces but allow them to put those pieces back together in their own time.

SEXUAL ABUSE

Toccora, 23, New Jersey, and Anonymous

What is sexual abuse?

Toccora: That's a good question that I can answer now, but when I was younger I wouldn't have even had the slightest clue of what the question meant. To me sexual abuse is to be taken advantage of sexually against someone's will. Your innocence is often taken, along with trust and the ability to truly open up to people. Also, sexual abuse doesn't have to mean rape; it can also be molestation.

Anonymous: When someone is touched inappropriately without consent. This is probably the most common definition, found in the dictionary, websites, or articles. But consider a child who has their trust betrayed and does not have the ability or understanding to react to this type of behavior. The terminology used if an adult is touched or violated without consent is that they have been raped or sexually harassed. Therefore, to be sexually abused by someone usually means that the victim is a child—someone who is under the age of truly comprehending what is happening to them.

How can you tell if someone has been sexually abused?

Toccora: There are no true signs of knowing if someone was sexually abused, at least to me. Everyone is different when it comes to this kind of abuse. It all depends if you know the person before the abuse happens, and then all of a sudden they're acting different. S/he can withdraw from people, not acting the same and in their own way giving hints about it. But unless the person tells you about it, I truly don't think there is a way you can tell for certain.

Anonymous: Overall, individuals react differently when they have been abused. So what to look for can vary greatly among the population, according to the person's environment, culture, personality, etc. Some of the more common characteristics that are displayed are fear or terror when in certain situations, uncontrollable bouts of screaming and tantrums, or inappropriate sexual acts or descriptions shown by the child which ordinarily would be beyond their comprehension level.

What are the common repercussions of being sexually abused?

Toccora: My entire life changed, from my innocence being taken from me to my trust becoming nonexistent. It was very difficult in my teenage years, even though my abuse was from ages six to twelve. I acted out and isolated myself from others. I also experimented with pills and self-mutilation for several years when I was at my lowest point of depression. Now I have healed and learned to look at myself through a full frame; I no longer focus on my abuse. But of course it still bothers me from time to time.

Anonymous: One of the most common effects to the individual who has been sexually abused is their inability to trust. This may cause them to have problems forming relationships later in life. In some cases they continue the behavior because they think this is the only way that people will like them. For example, in most cases the abuser has a catchphrase, such as "If you do this for ___, you will always be ___ special girl." And in other cases, fear or threats are used to get the child to submit. All of these situations cause that person to grow up mistrusting, especially those who represent the same role as the abuser.

Did you report your experience? Why or why not?

Toccora: Not at first and not by choice. When I was sixteen I confided in a teacher that I viewed as a second mother. You see, I was very depressed and probably suicidal at that point, so she picked up on the signs and asked me what was wrong. One day I just let everything out to her. I didn't know this at the time, but she was obligated by law to tell someone. I was angry with her at first but later grateful, because if it wasn't for her I'd probably be left to deal with the pain alone, and who knows what my life would have been like now.

Anonymous: No! Well, not initially, because as a child you are not aware of what is right or wrong, and also because you wouldn't even know what to report. You don't really understand what has happened to you. You have no prior knowledge of right behavior and wrong behavior; therefore, nothing is to be said. But the biggest deterrents to not telling are the "catchphrases" that you were fed. These play a huge role in your fear; you know that if you speak, something terrible will happen. Therefore, as the child you realize you are alone and on your own, with no one to protect you.

How did your abuse affect your understanding of your sexuality later on?

Toccora: I was more aware of it in a way and viewed sex in a different light. It wasn't like I was a prude or oversexed or anything. I feel like I handled my sex life "normally," actually. I waited until I truly felt comfortable with myself and understood the importance of what it meant to be with someone. Sex was never something I thought I *had* to do in order for guys to like me or fit in. I took it seriously and valued it, and I still do to this day.

Anonymous: In my early teenage years, I realized that I was in control of my own body. I would no longer allow anyone to touch my body without my consent. And I chose not to give consent to anyone—for a long time. When I did give consent and was ready to overcome my feelings of violation, I had numerous episodes of flashbacks, usually triggered by my partner uttering similar catchphrases, or the smell of their breath, bringing forward a disgusting memory. When this happened I would push my partner off or burst into tears. It wasn't until I had counseling that I came to the realization that by acting out this way, I was allowing myself to still be victimized by my abuser. I had to find a way to overcome my anger and anguish. I had to make myself believe that I am a worthy person, worthwhile of someone loving me, not for what I would do, but for who I am.

CHAPTER 4 CHECKPOINT

SEXUAL ABUSE/ASSAULT IS NEVER PROVOKED. AS THE victim, it is not your fault that someone else does not respect human decency and free will. While there is no such thing as rape prevention, since the attack is never justifiable, there are certainly high-risk scenarios and signs that you should make yourself aware of. Check off the scenarios below that you think should be considered high risk.

- ❑ After a late meeting or social event, you don't mind going home solo.
- ❑ At parties, you and your friends have a few drinks and split up to go mingle.
- ❑ It's no big deal if your friend goes off alone with a stranger.
- ❑ It's no big deal if your friend goes off alone with some guy, even if they've been drinking.
- ❑ You've been to a few parties before where there were only a handful of girls and a lot of guys.

- ❑ On first dates you've found yourself in settings where it's just you and your date alone in a private environment.
- ❑ You've gone on a date to someone else's house that you hardly know.
- ❑ You've allowed someone you hardly know to come to your empty house for a date.
- ❑ If a friend isn't feeling well at a party, you tell her to crash in a bedroom alone until you're ready to go.
- ❑ In large groups, there are times when you have no idea where your friends are.
- ❑ You and your friends go out and start drinking without designating a friend to stay sober.
- ❑ You've experimented with new drugs or substances in public places.

Did you miss any boxes? All of the above are circumstances taken directly from stories submitted to *Laid* that resulted in a sexual attack.

As harmless as many of these scenarios may seem, they can be extremely dangerous, especially if you're not aware of the potential danger they could pose for you and your friends. Safety is a community effort.

CHAPTER 5

SAVE YOUR CHERRY . . . OR BANANA

INTRODUCTION

There was a little bit of sun in his eye. Just enough to make his almond eyes sparkle in that movielike way and make his suggestive invitation seem kind of innocent.

"Open your mouth," he said, dragging out the *th* sound.

I craned my neck backward and looked at him suspiciously. "Why, what are you going to put inside it?"

"You'll see, I promise you'll like it," he said, and then rubbed his hand up and down my thigh.

Instinctively, I shifted my attention to my leg. Then, as though he wanted to sneak away before I registered what he had just done, he retracted his hand with lightning speed, tucking it neatly into his own pocket. I laughed inside. It was cute that he was nervous, even though he was a couple of years older.

"Okay," I said, "if it's that important to you." I closed my eyes and parted my lips.

He sat up and I heard him shuffling around with his pants. I heard a zipper being ripped down, but apparently it got caught on something, because it took a few rapid up-and-down movements before he was finally done with it.

"Okay," he announced as his finger touched my chin, "here comes the airplane, or should I say the submarine."

I raised my eyebrows in mock anticipation without closing my jaw.

"So you really trust me this much, huh?" he asked.

I opened my eyes and looked at him. "I trust that you value your life, yes."

"YOU'RE AN INSPIRATION TO VIRGINS EVERYWHERE," THE email read.

This was one of many such messages I received after being featured as a panelist on a nationally aired teen-sex program. I shook my head at people's misconception, knowing that my website, SaveYourCherry.com, had given them a false impression. People naturally assumed that I was promoting abstinence, but really it was just a catchy name meant to draw in teens for the sake of conversation and education. Accidentally, I had become an inspiration to virgins. But a virgin, or even a born-again virgin, I was not.

I felt unworthy of the term "inspiration" because in actuality I was the one in awe of the iron will and self-appreciation it takes to wait for someone you love. Saying no is so much more difficult than letting things just happen. For one, it's hard to stop someone once you're being intimate and let them know you don't want things to progress any further. And I believe that somehow girls have picked up this stupid notion that it is their responsibility to provide sexual gratification if they get a guy horny, even if it is not what they want.

It's also a lot more difficult to relate to someone person to person than it is to relate body to body. When you're touching, kissing, hooking up, it is very easy to get along with someone and feel as though you have a real connection. But it's a cop-out. When I was younger, I used to be so anxious to make out with guys because conversation scared me. I was afraid they would think I was stupid or not cool. I remember being at my boyfriend of one year's house at age fifteen. His mother had decided to stay home from work that afternoon, so with the threat of her coming downstairs looming over our heads, he and I did not have the cushion of kissing or groping to make our time run smoothly. I sat there nodding and laughing like a complete dummy. I tried so hard to think of something witty to say, but apparently my personality had gone on vacation. I was so uncomfortable that I actually snuck in his kitchen and ate a handful of sugar, hoping it would make me hyper.

It takes time to get to know yourself and begin to feel comfortable with who you are in every setting. Give yourself the chance to allow others to get to know you as a person, not just your body.

In an oversexed world, it is very difficult to find a partner who is willing to wait. Many of the girls and young women I've talked to over the years have expressed that although it does hurt to have someone you are attracted to avert all eye contact the moment you pull out your 'V' card, they still do not regret their choice to say no.

After reading several stories in my search for contributions to this chapter, I began to take a good hard look at my own sexual behaviors. In many cases, I took the easy way out by going with someone else's flow, instead of going with my own and listening to my conscience. As I read, I saw that saying no is not just reserved for people who practice abstinence; this choice belongs to every single one of us.

THE HARD WAY

Shannon T. Boodram, 20 at the time of writing, Ontario

THIS IS TOO EASY, I THINK.

"I promise it'll be pleasing," he says.

We only just met.

"I'm going to get you soaking wet."

I'm uncomfortable with this.

"Where do you want me to kiss?"

I know this isn't right.

"I'm glad you're staying the night."

Suddenly my tongue has lost all feeling and I'm finding it all too difficult to get the words that are racing through my mind out of my mouth. I'm not young anymore and I'm miles away from naive, so how did I find myself here, ready to make the mistakes of yesterday?

"Ouch!" He just bit my nipple.

"Don't worry, baby, pain is pleasure."

His eyes are doing a victory dance. There is a knowing glow to them that says, *I'm getting some tonight.* I can feel his body finding its rhythm, preparing for its own victory dance. I can smell the beads of excitement rolling across his forehead, touch the tool of his brimming lust, see that there is going to be a problem when I tell him no.

We met two weeks ago at a nightclub. I know what you're thinking—strike one. I feel the same way about mating and clubbing, but there was something so magnetic about this guy, so we danced. And I'm not just talking about a little bump here and there—it was a seductive slow grind that had my body moving like I was working for my weekly wages. His hands pressed so firmly against my hips, I could swear Dude was trying to press our bodies into one. There is nothing quite like dancing with someone you have that fiery attraction for. Dancing, and I mean good dancing, is like getting all of the closeness and tenderness of sexual intercourse minus the hour or less when all you're thinking is, *When is he going to finish . . .* but that's just my opinion. In the middle of our heated dance, he put his face to the back of my neck and slid his tongue up to the tip of my ear.

"You're sweating. Let's go talk outside and cool off."

The following day he called me and we arranged to meet at the movies the day after that, which was a Tuesday. The date started off fine. We played arcade games, did the whole dinner-and-a-movie bit. When the movie ended we traveled with the crowd into the parking lot, holding hands like we had been dating for years. *I really like this guy,* I thought. As we walked, preparing to separate toward our own cars, he pulled me aside from the sea of people and whispered in my ear, "I want to go someplace where we can kiss."

I love making out. Love the tango, the eroticism, the oneness. But with that said, I'm not really one to kiss just anybody. Kissing is just tongues flopping around in limbo between two people's mouths if there's no electricity. I opened my mouth to say no, but before the words could escape he grabbed my right hand and began sucking my fingers. Licking and lightly kissing the tips. My body began to shoot sparks. Now there was that electricity.

"Let's go back to my place."

All I needed to regain control was for him to say something to overstep his boundaries, and he'd just crossed a major line. Maybe he should have caught me at age seventeen, but at my age there was no way I was going back to anyone's place on the first date. Bad choices create bad habits, which translate into a horrible relationship.

"No thanks. It's getting late and I'm not trying to build you up just to let you down."

We said our goodbyes and I opted out of the first kiss.

On the second date, we took his niece to Chuck E. Cheese, so there was no opportunity for intimacy. On the third, we went to a boardwalk restaurant and stayed until nightfall. After we left we walked a little, talked some more, and kissed a whole lot. He was a really excellent kisser, gentle and patient. But I'll tell you what the difference is between a good kisser and a great kisser: hands. Well, more specifically, hand placement. He rotated his hands from the groove in my hipbone to the small of my back, the lining of my jaw, and the crown of my head. Once in a while he would place both hands under my chin and around my ears and kiss me with his eyes open, let our eyes have their own intimate moment. We never progressed beyond first base (if kissing is even considered first base anymore), but we definitely established that we had some desire to play with.

I felt for him that day and I still feel for him now. So here we lie, on the fourth and potentially final date. This is honestly the first man that I have enjoyed being with in this way for a very long time, but that does not mean I am going to offer my body as a token of my appreciation. I'm not sure how he's going to react, but my tongue has regained consciousness and I better put it to work before it causes another regretful sexual experience.

"This is too easy," I say, sitting up and covering my bare chest with folded arms.

"What's too easy?" he replies, trying to pull my mouth back into his.

"Saying yes."

"So . . . what are you saying?"

"No."

"No to what?"

"No to right now—we only just met."

"We've known each other for over three weeks now."

"Two."

"Two what?"

"Two weeks."

"Whatever, what does time have to do with it anyway? A man and a woman should feel free to express their bodies—there's nothing wrong with that."

"I know there's nothing wrong with it if both people feel comfortable, but I'm not comfortable with this."

"So what are you saying—I make you uncomfortable?"

"No, I'm saying that I know this isn't right. Just because I'm not a virgin doesn't mean that I have no restraint."

He pauses, sits up, and becomes very silent. He runs his hand over his head and covers his eyes. I hook my bra back up, put on my shirt, and stand up to look for my bag.

"Where are you going?" he asks.

"Home."

"You don't need to do that, all right? Just relax." He stands up and places one hand on my shoulder. "Look, want to see if Wendy's is still open so we can grab something to eat?"

"Sure, why not," I say, a little confused at this turnaround. Isn't this supposed to be the part where he tells me to take my frigid ass back to the eighteenth century?

"Okay, my treat." He smiles, then kisses me without tongue, kisses me with open eyes and lets our eyes come to an understanding for us. "You smell good, baby."

"Thank you," I say, still in a slight state of shock.

"One day do I get to see if you taste good, too?"

I shoot him a glance to let him know I'm not pleased with his sexual fixation.

"What? I mean in a life-or-death situation. Get your mind out of the gutter."

I smile and laugh a little. "Maybe one day."

WHEN THESE CLOTHES COME OFF

Mia, 21, California

SITTING ON HIS COUCH, IN HIS APARTMENT, THINKING
Do I really wanna go through with this?
Or did I have too much fun drinking?
I just have a lil' buzz and nothing more
But what's really gonna happen when my clothes hit his bedroom floor?
Could he end up being the soldier I'd been looking for?
Or turn around and tell his friends he got it like that
And label me the whore
I know in the past I chose to wait for that ring and that's all good
But right now he gotta be the finest male species residing in my hood!
I can hear him moving around in the next room, as I sit and contemplate
Will my next decision be life altering? Will saving it be worth the wait?

I want him, I really do
And we have been together for few
So many risks for a couple hours maybe even minutes of pleasure
But then again the pleasure could be stretched to the longest measure
Shit here he comes; I better get my thoughts together . . .
Why he gotta be walking around with no shirt, looking finer than ever
I get a chill when he sits next to me with that sweet-smelling cologne
Damn maybe I should get up, get my keys and go home
So much friction between us could cause a physical disaster
He's putting his arm around me—my heart skips faster
I know this ain't love so it must be that lust
But I know the difference between love and lust
And only one has that lasting element of trust
Do I respect myself?
And do things the way they're supposed to be done right?
Or do I give myself into this temptation for the rest of the night?
Just then he knocks me outta my thoughts looking at me with those deep,
dark brown eyes and says, "Baby girl what movie you wanna watch?" all the
while showing me the different DVDs
He got . . . *movies!*
What the fuck! is my first thought
He sees my face full of confusion, like I just did something and got caught
"Baby you aight?" he says, but I cut him off before he can go on . . .
"Yeah I'm cool, put on whatever" is all I respond
He keeps talking but I'm not even paying any attention
All this time his mind was moving in a different direction

Maybe he too believes in that certain self-respect and didn't want to risk it
I breathe easy at this lucky turn of events, so glad I was there to witness it
Just to think that tomorrow morning, the up-building of us could've been over
I think the silent agreement of taking it slow is something to which we both look forward
I know, soon enough, this relationship could grow past emotional roadblocks
But until then I think my shoes and jacket are the only items that I'll take off

CONVERSATIONS FROM A PRESSURE COOKER

Katherine Kormos, 23, Ontario

"YOU'RE LEAVING ME."

"I'm leaving the city. Not you."

There are things that every high school girl longs for. Cars, jobs, or maybe a good SAT score and an invitation to enroll in a good college. My high school dream was a boyfriend. I imagined that everything in my life would fall into place as soon as I was someone's girlfriend.

I was a student at an all girls' school, so opportunities to meet the boy that would make my life perfect were few and far between. When I did get a chance to talk to boys, I was awkward and tactless. I gained confidence somewhere before I turned sixteen. Sixteen with my braces off and a cute haircut—I figured I was girlfriend material.

I met him in December of that year. We chatted online, over the phone. He called me his angel. It was part of my AOL screen name, because I was innocent, and for some reason he latched on to it. It was February before we finally got out on a date. He was sweet and seemed to be someone who could fall in love with me. He took me swing dancing one night, even though he had no clue how to dance himself. His parents would go out of town, and like any high school boy he would have me come over as fast as his car could get me there.

"How far do you want to go with a guy?"

Evenings at his house were always the same. We talked, watched some TV, and then he would start trying to hint at things. Whenever he kissed me, he was thinking of more. After a few months, he told me he loved me. I now know what he was thinking.

"What do you want to do tonight?"

"I don't know, you?"

"I want to eat you out."

Pressure felt like it was always on me. We barely went out, mostly talked on the phone, and saw each other once or twice a month, and always he would want to do something that would make me feel good in order to convince me that I owed it to him to do the same. It began with that one night, and soon after he started to press. There was always something.

"I've got blueballs here. . . . I took you to dinner. . . . But I love you; why else would I want to make *you* feel good?"

I was his angel, and he didn't realize how innocent I really was. Things became conditional. He would do something for me, but only if I had done something for him. I thought I loved him, and so I would do what I hated most and go down on him, even though I was horribly uncomfortable with it. He would then try to get me to have sex with him. I was innocent, I was sixteen, and didn't want to. I am glad I didn't.

"YOU'RE LEAVING ME."

"I'm leaving the city. Not you."

Twelfth grade brought a new school. It was a boarding school, across the border in my home country of Canada. He spent the last night we had together pressuring me. It was my birthday. He took me to see *The Phantom of the Opera* and gave me a gold necklace: a heart with two angels on it. On the way home we stopped in the schoolyard where he had tried to persuade me many times before. There he told me I was leaving him. I protested with everything I had. I was leaving the city but not him, I loved him, I promised we would stay together and that I would be home for long weekends. Soon I was in tears. I should have looked through them to see what was really in front of me. He dried my tears, told me he loved me, and then asked if he could go down on me. I knew where it would lead—pressure and more fighting—so I said no and he took me home.

"So you don't ever want to have sex with me?"

BOARDING SCHOOL BROUGHT NEW FRIENDS AND WITH IT the coed environment. I fit in immediately. I was in twelfth grade and a new student. The ninth-grade kids all thought I had been there forever and was in grade thirteen. AOL conversations were all I had to keep my relationship alive. Midnight fights with my boyfriend started soon after. He would be drunk and stoned and I would be in tears. Soon I found myself forgetting my boyfriend and spending time with another guy. The other guy had a girlfriend back home, and one Sunday night he came by to tell me he had broken up with her. I told him that I liked him more than the guy back home and I had broken up with him. A lie, yes, but one that needed to be told in order for me to build up the courage to do what I knew I had to. I went home that Thanksgiving and we saw each other for the last time. He wanted to talk in person, even though I told him online that night that I couldn't do it anymore. I told him there was someone else. He flew into a fit there in the car.

"You don't love me?"

I shook my head and uttered a quiet "no."

"So you don't ever want to have sex with me?"

I couldn't believe he asked that. When he heard a "no" escape my mouth, he pressed his foot hard to the gas and the tires screeched. I didn't even have my seat belt on. I was afraid we would crash or he would hurt me. When I got out of the car, I realized that he was angry not because I didn't love him but because I didn't ever want to sleep with him.

It wasn't until too late that I realized the toll that his pressure had taken on my life. I was afraid to do anything to a guy. I would get pleasure from them and then feel guilty that I could never reciprocate. It felt terrible, always tiptoeing around the conversations that I knew would eventually become inevitable.

"I am really uncomfortable with blow jobs," I would say. "I had a boyfriend who was kind of forceful."

Most guys were reassuring about my situation. Only once did I ever get a complaint. I found I was fooling myself a lot, pretending I was okay with giving a blow job when I wasn't. I could never do it for long either. Two or three seconds was all I could handle before I would get scared. It had an effect on every relationship afterward. Eventually, when I fell into a good bond with someone I really did love, that fear went away and I was free to live without the feelings of guilt when I felt good. I was lucky enough that my boyfriend was never physically abusive. His abuse was of a much more hidden genre. To this day I am scared of where things would have ended up if I had ever agreed to have sex with him. It can take a lifetime to get over someone tricking you into doing what you are uncomfortable with. The uncomfortable feelings don't always go away. Mine did—I was lucky—and for that I am grateful.

SOUR APPLES

Holly Vatcher, 22, Ontario

IN DECEMBER 2003 I MET A GUY WHO SEEMED TO BE VERY nice and such a gentleman. We went mini-golfing on our first date and I won, but only because I think he cheated when writing down the scores, because I really suck at golf.

Our second date was at his office Christmas party. I felt so awkward there because I didn't know anyone and I didn't even know him too well. It was at this games complex called Dave & Buster's. He could tell that I wasn't too comfortable around all these people I didn't know, so we went to play games on our own. We played lots of air hockey and some other games too. At the end, he won me a blue and red fuzzy monster. The night was special—filled with hand holding, his arm around my waist, small hugs here and there—and I had a lot of fun. He dropped me off at home around one in the morning. He opened the car door for me too. It was so cute and almost romantic. He thanked me for going with him and said he had a nice time. It ended with a hug and a kiss. He tried for a big sloppy kiss and said sorry when I wasn't going for it.

When we finally did have the big sloppy kiss, it was the best kiss I had ever had, and still is to this day. It made my entire body just melt. I couldn't wait to see him the next time just to feel like that again. I loved kissing this guy. I don't even have words to describe these kisses. His lips were so soft and luscious it gave me butterflies.

My second time at his house, he was upstairs before me because he wanted to make his bed. When I got upstairs he was standing in the doorway, just being cute and not letting me in until I said the "magic word." I pushed him back into his room and closed the door; I needed one of those kisses right then and there. We kissed for a bit, then watched a movie. I fell asleep on his bed and he woke me with one of his magical kisses.

His kisses were very sensual and I couldn't get enough; his hands were so gentle and he made me feel safe. We made out a bit, then he went to undo my belt. I distracted his hands by holding them above my head while we kissed some more. Again he went down to my belt. I was so afraid; I didn't know anything about this guy. He talked of some of his sexual endeavors—God only knows where his dick had been. He was so much bigger than me too. What if he used this power over me and I was trapped under his muscular body?

"No," I blurted out.

"No?" he responded, like he was in shock.

"Not right now." We made out some more, and again he was down at my belt. "Stop, I told you, not right now."

"Well, when, then?"

I pushed him off of me and sat up. "I don't know, but not right now."

"You don't understand how horny I am, though."

"I can see and feel how horny you are, believe me."

"But it's been three months since I've gotten any."

"Well, you're gonna have to wait that much more," I told him straight.

"What are you talking about?"

"I want to go home."

"Are you serious?" he said in a newfound gentle tone. I could tell that he did have a heart and seemed to be respecting my wishes. I nodded yes as I got up to go to the door.

He drove me home and told me that he didn't understand what was going on. So I told him that I was a virgin. He seemed to understand and apologized a few times. I was relieved that he was so sympathetic and thought that this may actually work out.

The next time we were out, that's all he would talk about, how I was still a virgin and how he was gonna pop my cherry. We were in the car and I thought it was rather funny how he couldn't stop talking about it. He told me positions he was gonna do it in: "We could do it in the car and the windows will get all steamy, then I'll take the frost off the windows and put it on your nipples; it's gonna make you so hot. . . . "

"You're a loser," I said, and we both laughed.

"I'm going to make it my mission to deflower you. I never popped a cherry before."

I just drove the car as he talked about my cherry. He was in another world, a dream world. I still laugh about it now, because he was so off in some horny-man world like I wasn't even in the car, sitting right next to him.

A couple days later, he told me that he told his friends about my virginity and they told him what to expect. "It's probably going to hurt a lot. We're going to need a towel so blood won't get on the bed."

I looked him straight in the eye and asked him, "Do you think I'm a fucking moron?"

"No, I just want you to be prepared for when it happens," he said as he made air-humping motions.

He became so obsessed with me being a virgin and how he was gonna "devirginize" me. It was like a game, and I would be his trophy: his first cherry popped. That's when I started being more wary around him.

We spent New Year's apart because we had met only three weeks prior, and we both had plans we couldn't change. I went to a friend's wedding, and he went out with a bunch of his friends in downtown Toronto. I didn't drink much that night; I was with my best friend's family, and I didn't want to look bad.

He called me at midnight and wished me a happy New Year. Aww, I thought.

Around 3:00 AM I was just getting settled in my hotel room in a huge king-size bed, thinking about him, and then he called. He was lost, piss drunk, and walking around Toronto on his own. After I laughed my ass off at him for five minutes, I helped him find his way back to his car. He said that he lost his friends because they were bar hopping and left without him. We were on the phone for about forty-five minutes before he got back to his car on Front Street. During that conversation he asked me what I was doing.

"I'm laying in a king-size bed all alone."

He laughed evilly. "Am I your boyfriend?"

Knowing how drunk he was, I turned the question on him: "Am I your girlfriend?"

"Once we have sex, you can be my girlfriend."

In my head, I knew this was wrong and immoral. I basically just ignored the question and begged him to just call a cab to go home, and I would drive him downtown the next day to get his car. He drove home and called me when he got there so I knew he was safe.

Later that week we got talking again about the whole boyfriend-girlfriend thing. I told him that I would never give in to sex just to have someone say they were my boyfriend. I wanted to have a boyfriend and be in love with him before I gave him my everything.

"I don't know if I could wait for that to happen."

I knew deep down that this would never work out for us, but I still hung on. I hoped that maybe somehow he would change his mind and see that I am worth waiting for. One night when we were heavily making out, he went to take off my pants. I told him to stop and he didn't. We were fighting over my pants. I knew his mother was downstairs and I threatened that I would scream so badly if he didn't stop. He stopped.

He sat up. "Fuck you! You are giving me the worst case of blueballs ever."

"Well, I don't fucking care, go do whatever you have to do in the bathroom."

He couldn't believe that I said that. Then he sat at his computer with a boner to play some online game.

A few days later I was sitting at my computer and then I came across this posting that is in an online community that I'm a part of:

> *I don't know what to do. How can I still love someone who has hurt me so much? I had to see him and his new "girl" this weekend and I thought I was going to die. I just wanted to know why? Why did he tell me he cared so much? Why did he lie? I fucking believed and trusted him enough to fucking lose my virginity to him. And he would just do that to me? Why do guys do that? Someone please help me and tell me how to mend my broken heart and get over him. Because as each moment passes, I feel more and more alone.*

I had totally mixed feelings when I read it. At first I felt so bad for her. I wanted to say something comforting and supportive, but my mind was blank before my personal thoughts came rushing in. This could have been me, I could have been her. Someone might have felt sorry for me but nothing could fix what was taken away. This made me feel good, but in a guilty way. She's the person I'm not. I didn't make the mistake that she did; I don't feel sad about it; I'm not crying over it; I don't have all kinds of questions about it; I'm okay.

That was it for me. I loved those kisses, but the kisses lead to more than I was ready for. And the fact that he was only in it because he had never popped a cherry before made me feel worthless and disgusting. I left that night knowing that I would never see or hear from him again. I wanted to cry but I didn't want him to see how weak I was. I remember that our last kiss tasted like apple juice and now, to this day, the smell of the juice repulses me.

ABOUT ME: TOUCHING ON SEX

Jigabod Walker, 23, Georgia

THE TRUTH IS, I WAS NEVER REALLY *TESTED* ON MY sexuality until college. Before that point I was the too-smart-for-his-own-good (but relatively cute when he takes his glasses off) A-plus student that nobody was really interested in. Don't get me wrong, sex has been with me all my life in one form or another: I saw a porn magazine for the first time in the fifth grade, watched a whole cheerleading squad come up pregnant in middle school, and befriended the neighborhood "go-to girl" in high school. But despite its presence in my life, sex was never really my focus. True, there were times when temptation dangled in my face like a wriggling worm on a hook, but still, my perspective on sex never changed: No sex before marriage. But all my early childhood evasions were nothing compared to the tests I had when it came time for college . . . and freedom.

There was a young lady my first year that I had it *bad* for. I mean, she wasn't the prettiest of the pretty girls; she was easily beautiful but not so much so that it was intimidating. She just had those toe-tingling things that made it too easy to hold my interest: She was exotic, thick below the waist, petite, listened to the same music, liked my favorite groups, had similar beliefs, and was even interested in a career in music like I was. Honestly, she was the first girl I ever saw myself marrying and doing all the things that married people do. . . .

I recall too clearly the time when she and I decided to hold a study session at her dorm on the Friday night before we had a paper due that Monday. The setup was perfect—after all, writing was my forte and I needed an excuse to spend one-on-one time with her. I admit the paper was the last thing on my mind; I just wanted to be romantic with her, tell her how I felt. I didn't know what to expect that night. I figured her roommates would be there the whole time, so I hadn't counted on anything getting too serious, but regardless, I still made sure I was clean in all the right places. Full of anticipation, I took a quick shower and put on my favorite cologne with a nice shirt. My heart was racing thinking about what I would say, how I would act, and how she might react.

It was a relatively cold day but even now, as I reflect, I just remember feeling so warm inside. When I arrived, her roommates were there as I expected them to be, but it turns out that they were on their way to the club. The funny thing about that was her roommates were as exotic and beautiful as she was. So picture this: three beautiful women, changing into club-appropriate clothing (in case you didn't know, that means showing skin), asking me questions like, "How does this look on me?" "Is this too much?" "I probably need more lotion on my legs, huh?" The skin, the tantalizing fragrances, the skimpy dresses . . . quite an experience to have before attempting to be romantic with someone, right?

The young lady and I got started on her paper, and before long she asked me to excuse her while she changed clothes.

The moment she left, I remember one of her roommates (the prettiest one) coming over and telling me, "You should be careful—she's nothing but trouble."

I smiled sideways and nodded. I thought she was joking . . . sort of. Two minutes later the roommates were gone, leaving my study partner and me to ourselves. I sat waiting on the young lady to return to her desk, trying to put the evening's impromptu fashion show out of my mind, when she finally came back out in some nightwear. Not those cheesy negligees in Bond films, something even sexier: some thigh-high boxers and a long T-shirt (my favorite combination, unfortunately). Now, you might say I make too much of things, but I took all this as a warning sign and immediately went on guard. You see, I've never had sex but I know what happens when people get turned on. Their blood leaves their brains to redistribute to "other places," which is why it's often too late to rethink things once people reach that hot point of no return.

She was at her computer; I was a good distance off seated in a chair, admiring her respectfully from afar. Then, without breaking from her keystrokes, she said, "Why don't you come closer; I won't bite."

It's the strangest phenomenon, but when you really like somebody, their voice just sounds sweeter and more convincing every time you hear it. *But* then I went to thinking again—you see, her computer was atop a desk right at the foot of her bed, so basically she invited me onto her bed.

So, with the bit of clarity I still had left, I managed a "Nah, that's all right, I'm fine right here." It sounds easy enough, but don't be fooled—I really, *really* wanted to sit on that bed.

We worked a little longer, but I knew that I was pushing my luck—just because I choose to abstain doesn't mean I always do so willingly. So when I felt her paper was completed enough for her to finish the job, I took license and made an exit. It was dark as heck and bitter frikkin' cold outside, so before I stepped foot into the night she invited me to stay over. Again her voice alone almost convinced me, but I decided I needed to take that walk quickly and alone.

Did it hurt? Heck yeah; for once in my life I really didn't want to do the right thing, and to be honest, when it was said and done it didn't feel like it really paid off. I thought about that night for the longest time, wishing I had gone through with it. It wasn't until a few years later that I had a revelation that made me appreciate doing the right thing that night. I found comfort for that night and countless others like it in knowing that lasting relationships aren't built on fleeting moments of pleasure. Through having true friendships, I have learned what true love is. And I've got news for you: In the grand scheme of love, sex is just a dot. Sex gets its value from true love, not the opposite.

NEAR MISS

Danny Djeljosevic, 21, Florida

LIKE ANY DECENT STORY, THIS ONE STARTS OUT WITH drunken high school girls. They were seniors that went to my alma mater and took a road trip to my college town to apartment hunt for the fall semester. My roommate, Paco, and I stumbled upon them at a friend's place and they decided to follow us home, bored with watching college sophomores playing Guitar Hero and ready to nurse the alcohol addiction they had been developing since the seventh grade.

Once we got to our apartment, we quickly cracked open a bottle of raspberry-flavored rum (which was meant for Paco and his girlfriend, not alcoholic high schoolers—already the night wasn't boding well for us) and watched *Family Guy* on DVD. Alcohol and *Family Guy:* the great uniter of the college-aged! To expedite matters, we halfheartedly played a drinking game that went along with the show. You know the type: "Drink whenever someone gets hit in the groin with a football" and all that.

Among the group was a girl I had a crush on in high school. When I'd admired her from afar years ago, she had black-framed glasses, short brown hair, and resembled Thora Birch in *Ghost World.* I used to stare at her as she passed by in the hallways, which soon led to her looking away uncomfortably throughout our time in high school.

In the years since, she'd evolved into quite the hippie. Instead of looking like someone who listened to the Smiths, she looked like she listened to Phish and got covered in mud at five-day music festivals. She also had long hair now.

The cartoon quickly became mere background to the Dionysian festivities. The bottle ran dry. Someone, naturally, got sick and was administered bread and water as the other girls ate things out of our fridge without permission.

As everyone grew tired, attention returned to the show and I was sitting on one of the couches with the hippie girl lying next to me as everyone else gradually fell asleep. Her feet kept touching my legs, to which I would respond with a little nudge of my own. In a drunken situation, that totally counts as physical flirting—in the world of the sober, it means that your couch is too small.

I had very little experience with girls, aside from pathetic attempts at relationships that never went anywhere (my own fault, really), so there I was, sitting and trying to figure out how to move things along, when suddenly the hippie girl sat up, grabbed my arm, and put it around her. Now this was getting interesting. Moments later, she kissed me on the mouth and before I knew it, she had led me to my room and we were making out on my bed. In between hot kisses, my mind drifted to how random this night was.

In the past, on any other night like tonight, this *never* happened for me. We would have had an all right time and the girls would go home, leaving me to wonder why I never had the experiences others were privileged to have, but here I'd managed to find myself in a steamy situation with a girl I had a crush on in high school. Huh?

But it wasn't quite as "sexy" as it all sounds on paper. Despite the intoxication, I could tell something wasn't quite right. Her movements were noncommittal to the point of feeling obligatory. There wasn't quite the indulgent passion that I had seen in countless films.

I freed my mouth from hers. "Why are you doing this?" *Too blunt,* I thought seconds after I had already said it.

"What do you mean?"

"I mean, why me?" This wasn't my usual self-deprecation and insecurity, though that was surely a factor. I honestly didn't get it. I knew it wasn't a dream; there weren't any moments that I would be forced to describe in a manner resembling "So we were on my bed, but it, like, wasn't really my bed, you know?" Everything about the situation was completely normal, except for the fact that a girl actually wanted to have sex with me.

"You're a decent-looking boy. Why not?"

That's the best she could do? It was like she was intent on hopping into bed with someone for the night, and I just happened to be available. Maybe I missed the part where she looked me up and down and said, "You'll do."

"This is so weird," I said. "I used to have a crush on you in high school."

"That's so cute," she remarked. Condescension aside, I caught a hint of detachment; she could have used the same tone to declare that we were out of bread or that all the dishes were dirty. "Where do you keep the detergent?"

I gave up that line of questioning. Eventually, she was naked on my bed and I found myself quickly undressing in front of her like a person hurriedly searching through a filing cabinet as my clothes dropped to the floor.

Just then, a startling revelation came to me: This was the first woman to ever see my cock, which prompted my next inquiry.

"Should I get the lights?"

She shrugged. "Whatever you want." This girl really had no preference about much of anything, did she? Must have been all the pot. It was a fair assumption, at least. I mean, she was a hippie.

In a moment of needless indecision, I got up, flipped the switch, and then quickly decided to turn the lights back on. Where were my priorities, you ask? Well, people do stupid things when they're drunk, as you'll soon see.

As I crawled on top of her, I noticed a tattoo of a cow on her stomach. It wasn't Clarabelle Cow or the one on the cheese packages at the supermarket. It was an honest-to-God dairy-farm, teats-and-udders, black-and-white cow.

It was then that I realized that I was shaking violently. Real suave, I was.

"Why are you so nervous?" she asked.

To respond to this obtuse question, I chose to spew out the most utterly cliché thing anyone could say, so utterly obvious and stupid that she'd have to physically wipe the words off of her face.

"I've never done this before." No lie: I was about to lose my virginity to a girl I had a crush on years ago in high school.

Thankfully, she didn't get up, dress, and leave at that very moment in a fit of laughter and disgust. Instead, she assured me there was nothing to be nervous about, in that same detached, ennui-laden tone. Oh, thanks. Halfhearted attempts at kind words aside, you'd think the alcohol would have kept the nerves down, but strangely enough, I continued to shiver.

"I should get protection," I announced, breaking the dead air between us.

What ensued was a conversation like the "why me?" inquiry of mere moments earlier. I wanted to put on a condom, as I didn't want diseases, babies, or . . . diseased babies. She, a person who basically amounted to a stranger, kept assuring me I didn't have to and things were "okay," whatever that meant. Still, I insisted, like I learned in high school sex ed.

For nothing more than a moment, my mind wandered from the naked hippie below me back to the high school sex ed videos that warned girls about the naughty boys who whispered between bittersweet kisses, "Baby, I'm too big for condoms." "Don't you trust me?" Or "If you really love me, you'll let me give you syphilis." Perhaps the curriculum should be revised to include women who are completely vague about why the man doesn't need to wear one and may very well just want to be impregnated by a stranger.

Opening my nightstand drawer, I quickly grabbed a condom and tried to stuff it onto my strangely flaccid penis (more on that in a moment).

After a bit of fussing with it, she told me to "stop being lame," and I reluctantly tossed it aside. So much for unwavering willpower. Maybe I would have persevered if I'd remembered the traumatic slideshow of STD-afflicted genitals that had haunted me since the summer of 2000. We returned to the R-rated sexuality for a little, before stopping again. The moment she smirked, I could tell something was wrong. Horribly wrong.

"Well?"

"Uh . . . " Nothing was happening. You know, down there. "Why don't we switch places?"

Okay, me on the bottom, her on top. Nothing. We both tried fiddling with it for a while, but nothing happened. Once again, she stopped and smiled, asking me what was up (no pun intended). The clock read something like 5:37 AM. I let the back of my head fall back to my pillow in frustration.

"I'm sorry."

She was strangely reassuring. She insisted that it was no big deal, and said that maybe next time things would work out. At least she didn't say it happened to a lot of guys, which would have made the whole thing insincere and annoying. So instead of risking potential disease and/or pregnancy, we went to sleep. Of course, as soon as she was next to me rather than on top of me, the erection finally came.

"There it goes," I declared. She ignored me, which was probably for the best, considering the no-condom thing.

The next morning, once we were both awake, she kissed me once, put on her clothes, and returned to her spot on the couch. We didn't talk for the rest of the day, or ever after that. Needless to say, I was confused. Was it a drunken hookup, or was she paying with sex to sleep in a bed for the night? Or perhaps, more terrifying, did she want my sperm to conceive a child of her own? That last one seemed less likely and I had already filled my quota for failed attempts at ego boosts with the Subconsciously Flaccid Penis Theory. I, however, view it as the night my inability to perform saved me from potential catastrophe. Yes, that's it. My mind subconsciously prevented me from getting an erection because it knew the dangers of having sex with a girl who insisted on not using a condom.

No, let's be honest. It was just nervousness—dumb, oddly lucky nervousness.

FRESH FRUIT

Desiree Dorite, 23, California

"YOU KNOW I CARE FOR YOU."

I nod.

"You know I would never do anything to hurt you."

I smile halfheartedly as I pull up my pants.

"You don't need to be so afraid, all right?"

"I'm not scared," I say, breaking my silence, "I just don't think you're ready."

"You don't think *I'm* ready?"

He starts off on this tangent about how experienced he is and how many times he's done it before. I get dressed a little quicker and smile a little wider. I know I've made the right decision. I may have let him touch me a little, but that definitely doesn't mean he's got an automatic green light to park in my garage. I know a lot of my friends ended up losing their virginity just because they felt bad for the guy since they had gotten him hard and all that.

Not me.

It's not my responsibility to make sure that a guy's penis has a great day. If he can't get physical without going all the way, then he should have said that in the first place. . . .

"This is ridiculous—you know that. You're damn near twenty years old; people are going to think you're immature or that there's something wrong with you."

"Sure thing, buddy." I can't believe what a total dick he is being but I have to admit it is slightly entertaining. "I'm going to go home now, so I guess we won't be talking anymore."

"Don't be so sensitive, I'm just looking out for you. I just want to make you feel like a woman, that's all."

I can't help but laugh.

"What, you don't think I could please you?"

"Listen, Gord, as hard as it may be for you to conceive this, some people aren't all about sex. It's just not in my plans or priorities right now." I wink and kiss him on the cheek. "I had fun, and no hard feelings, so if you ever want to hang out sometime give me a call. Or I'll just see you around school—whatever suits you best."

He sits on the edge of his couch dumbfounded as I walk out of the living room and then out the front door. As I leave Gord's house and stroll down his driveway toward my little Civic, his neighbor, who is playing basketball, stops and nods.

"How are you doing, little miss?"

"On a day like this, I can't complain."

"I bet the sun shines wherever you go."

"You have a nice day."

"It would be even better if you gave me your number."

I pause for a second—what the hell.

"Hope you have a good memory to go along with that smooth talk." I give him my number, then drive off.

I'm nineteen, a freshman in college, and having the time of my life. I've had my heart broken and done some breaking of my own, but I've never given anyone the benefit of my totality. Not because I'm waiting for marriage, not because something's wrong with me, but because it's my choice and I'm waiting for my standards to be met. I went home that day and wrote "Fresh Fruit."

There is a garden that bears fruit every month
Fruit so sweet
Fruit so enchanting
Fruit so whole
That it has the ability to create life
The best part of all is this garden lies within my inner belly
Uninhabited and undisturbed
I am responsible for its health, its care, and its seeds
Many have tried to enter the grounds
To witness the fruit that it bears for the one
Or perhaps to steal a slice, like a thief who preys on the night
For these reasons I know I must remain adamant on its behalf
NO TRESPASSERS ALLOWED
Some have come close to the gates
But none with enough exceptionality
None worth the power of my virtue
For I remember the lesson that many of us have forgot
I know the price of eating forbidden fruit
So I wait patiently, all the while knowing
Knowing that this fruit is not for the picking
It is for the chosen

GOT QUESTIONS ABOUT CHAPTER 5?

ABSTINENCE

Holly, 22, Ontario, and Danny Djeljosevic, 21, Florida

Does abstinence mean that you don't care about sex?

Holly: No. I do care about sex. I'm just waiting until I find the right person that I want to have my first time with. I don't want it to be with just anyone, I want it to be with someone I really love and that really loves me. I want to make sure that my first time will be memorable and not regrettable.

Danny: I'm not intentionally abstinent, but I imagine the abstinent care so much about sex that they're waiting for the right time to do it. Unless they're doing it for religious purposes.

Are you lonely?

Holly: When I was single, yes, I was lonely sometimes, but not because I didn't have sex. I just wanted someone to care for me as much as I cared for them. I think the hardest part is when I don't hear back from a guy after I tell him that I'm waiting for love. I feel like it's all my fault that he doesn't want to wait for me. But then I think, *Do I really want to be with someone who doesn't want to respect my choices?* I am now in a relationship with no sex involved, and I'm not lonely at all—I'm actually very happy.

Danny: Oh, extremely. Thanks for rubbing it in . . . jerk! Joking. No, just because I'm not having sex, that doesn't mean I'm not expressing my sexuality in other ways by dating, kissing, and getting to know members of the opposite sex that might end up being the one. . . .

Do your religious beliefs stop you from having sex?

Holly: For me, it's not a religious thing at all. It's a personal choice. Many people have beliefs that stop them from being sexually active and I think that's totally cool. It's all about comfort and being consistent with the kind of person you want to be.

How do you deal when you're horny?

Holly: Ha ha! Get out the vibrator! You need to know how to pleasure yourself before anyone else can do it for you; you need to know what you like and don't like or just find other things to occupy yourself. Just like when you're trying to diet and avoid sweets, you need to find good alternatives so you can do what's best for yourself while still enjoying life.

Do guys that know you're a virgin find that sexy or sad?

Holly: This is a hard question. I have had various reactions. I wrote "Sour Apples," where one guy took me on as a game. He was very excited about popping my cherry, which pushed me away. Other guys will say it's cool but I never hear from them again. My current relationship is still new, but he is not pushing me into anything. He knew well in advance how I stood on things.

How do you tell your boyfriend no when you're in the moment?

Holly: Simple: Say no. My story talks a little about how I said no. Something I also do is redirect his hands, but the best way is to be up front and just say no. Communication is big in any sort of relationship. Talk about what you are comfortable with and what you are not.

What is the biggest misconception that people have about guys who are virgins?

Danny: The biggest misconception is probably that they're totally undesirable lepers of society.

***By chance, are you really into* Star Wars?**

Danny: I've never dressed as a Storm Trooper, but I do read lots of comic books. Guess what, kids? Stereotypes are true!

SAYING NO EVEN THOUGH YOU'VE SAID YES TO SOMEONE ELSE

How do you tell someone you don't want to have sex even if you've already had sex?

Honesty is the best policy. Tell the truth, explain your reasoning, look the person in the eye, and say, "Look, just because I'm not a virgin, that doesn't mean I'm having sex with you." It's your body and you do not owe anybody a free pass for it. Be confident in your response and recognize that how they handle your feelings is his/her problem, not yours.

After you've had sex, how do you go without it after that?

Actually, it really isn't that big of a deal for me to go without being sexually active with someone else. I'm always a sexual being, whether I'm having sex or not, but above all else I'm a rational human. I know what it's like to be intimate with someone for the sake of being intimate, and to be honest, it sucks. If I'm not in a place where all the elements that I need (my terms, satisfactory protection, strong bond with my partner, emotional security, and good timing) are in place, I won't be able to enjoy the experience anyway.

CHAPTER 5 CHECKPOINT

HOMEWORK OR FACEBOOKING

Life is all about prioritizing. Arrange the following elements below, making 1 the most important on your list of priorities and 10 the least important.

1.
2.
3.
4.
5.
6.
7.
8.
9.
10.

a) Family
b) Friends

c) Reputation
d) Education
e) Religion
f) A boyfriend/girlfriend
g) Sex
h) Fun/leisure time
i) Health/safety
j) Job/career path

The purpose of prioritizing is to make sure you're putting your focus on the areas that are truly important to you. For example, you might place safety above having fun. If this is the case, you might want to think about whether you would avoid dangerous activities, like car racing, even if you think it might be cool to try something new. Having sex is no different. It's a major decision, and before you decide to partake in it, just make sure that it doesn't place at risk the things that you place in higher importance.

WRAPPING IT UP

WRAPPING IT UP

TEN THINGS I WISH I'D KNOWN EARLIER

I REMEMBER THE DAYS WHEN I LAY ON MY BACK, EXHALING much louder than necessary, rubbing my clammy hands over someone's back that was—for the moment—mine to touch. Every so often I would softly bite down on my partner's shoulder as if I had to wrap my mouth around something just to stop myself from screaming bloody murder. I would whisper fragmented sentences in short, hot syllables, then bring my mouth to his ear for the closer as I let the words "I love you" escape in one clean break.

It was a routine, a role—and unfortunately, most of us are able to play it all too well. Every girl and most men have probably faked an orgasm or faked enjoyment at some point during his/her sexual history. Stroke your partner's ego, and they'll reward you with the love/money/respect/acceptance you've been looking for. But have you ever thought about it this way: If you're feeding someone else BS, isn't your partner fully entitled to dish you back the same? The best way to get what you want is to pursue it with purpose and projection, don't be sneaky, and definitely don't be submissive.

Excuse me for being a little forward, but it's all backward to me. At this point in my life, I wouldn't fake it for my partner's benefit. I wouldn't fake an orgasm, fake being okay with a subpar relationship, fake like I didn't know about protection, fake like I'm happy when I'm actually bored, or fake as if I'm the servitude type who would do any of the above. I think "fake" is the perfect way to describe my sexuality from when I was fifteen probably up until I was twenty. Lying consumed my sexuality, from the way I dressed to the sounds I made to the orgasms I manufactured to the stories I told others. I thought if I made up my sexuality that I would find real love and real happiness in the end. As I learn more and listen to others, I find it harder and harder to understand that seventeen-year-old misguided fruitcake I once was. That's why I am able to write about her so honestly, without flinching, because I know that person is no longer a representation of who I am today.

Today I can't stomach phoniness being associated with sexuality. Every time I see something that I know is untrue about sex in the media, I feel like that doctor who watches *ER* with clenched fists, shouting at the TV, "That's not the way it really is!" Honesty is the single most important attribute of a positive sexual lifestyle. That is why it was so important that all the contributors in *Laid* be completely honest with you and with themselves in their published pieces. I hate all those stupid over-the-top sex tales that people openly share with their cocksure grins and unsteady eyes. Having worked on this book for the better course of four years, and in my growing role as a sexpert to young people, I've had an amazing opportunity to think and talk honestly about sex far more than most people get a chance to. I am a product of the vicarious sexual education approach that I created.

I owe every bit of my sexual confidence to what I have learned while working on this book. I think I have learned the most from the positive submissions to *Laid.* I love the stories about people who have totally honest and wonderfully fulfilling sexual experiences. There is a lot to take in from people who have gotten it right, especially since there are so few opportunities to get honest accounts of great sex. And if you're thinking, *Really, Shannon? But pornos are so easy to find,* then you need to head back to page one!

There are so many experiences I would like to share with every young person I know, and so many more conversations I wish I had the opportunity to engage in—but each person has their own life to live and their own conclusions to draw! So instead of a ten-page extro, I've decided to recap what I've learned in a good old Top 10 list:

1. Sex is not just put it in, take it out. There are books, classes, and religions dedicated to learning the art form of making love, so why not pass on the fifteen-minute rendezvous and seek out a person who will make it the beautiful experience it can be?

2. Most people love talking about sex—until you start talking about it realistically. If you try and have a real conversation in which you discuss factual information, real emotions, and specific instructions, lots of people get very uncomfortable. So take it slowly, but inform yourself. Don't let other people's discomfort stop you from delving into everything there is to know about sex and your sexuality.

3. Everyone thinks they're good at sex without even really knowing anything about it. Being an effective sexual partner has more to do with understanding your partner's unique human anatomy and emotional needs than it will ever have to do with porn techniques or the hot new moves discussed in men's magazines. Many people choose to forgo lessons on the basics, but how can you build if you have no foundation? Educate yourself on the clitoris, the prostate gland, and other erogenous zones that are often ignored, like the back and even the scalp.

4. STIs are very real and very common, and so are babies. Learn all that you can about practicing safe sex. Believe me, the information you learn about the responsibilities that couple with sexual behavior will come in handy more than once. You don't want to risk the consequences on account of your ignorance.

5. Demand the truth about sex from your teachers and make sure they take adequate time to talk about myths versus reality. When I was in sixth grade we did a full unit on dinosaurs, but we had only two half-hour sessions on sexual education. Since then I've never had to escape a raptor, but I have been confronted by plenty of penises.

6. Most cases of rape do not happen in underground parking lots or after some goon has slyly slipped a pill in your drink—most cases of rape happen in familiar settings among familiar people. Don't give anyone the benefit of the doubt. If you're going to be in a private setting on a date, make sure you've considered all of the potential dangers and how you intend to address them.

7. Be confident and deliberate, especially when it comes to your personal life. Relationships and sex are supposed to be positive additions. They are the things you participate in just for you—a treat for how hard you work to fulfill your other responsibilities. If a relationship brings you more stress than joy, it is defeating its own purpose. As much as I'd like to have someone in my life, I'm not going to stay in a relationship if the price to do so is the sacrifice of my own happiness.

8. There are no guarantees that having sex with someone will make them: love you, hate you, respect you, like you, want you, loathe you, marry you, dream of you, chase you, or chase you away. So, since you don't know what kind of effect sex will have on your partner's behavior, is there any logical reason to

give someone the gift of your body other than because you wanted to do it for you?

9. The more you know, the less likely you are to run out there and be friendly with the whole town. A lot of people associate sexual knowledge with sexual promiscuity; on the contrary, the more you know, the more selective you will be. If your parents catch you reading a sex ed book and they gasp, let them know that they don't need to worry about you—you have it under control.

10. I'm not even sure where or how I learned to "fake it," but it was something I did without hesitation, like it was a natural part of sex. Maybe I did it for the same reason people dab at their dry eyes while the whole theater is crying around them. I guess I felt ashamed that I didn't feel compelled to moan like a madwoman. I accepted that it was okay to fake it, but now I realize that's crap. First off, if you're with someone who you can't be honest with about your needs, then you shouldn't waste your time with that person; secondly, your sexuality was not given to you so you could please others. Think about it: sex-*you*-ality. So go ahead—it's all right to put yourself first.

I wish you a lifetime of healthy and *wow, that was amazing* sexual relationships.

—Shannon Teresa Boodram

CONTRIBUTOR WRAP-UP

CONTRIBUTOR WRAP-UP

SIXTEEN THINGS THE CONTRIBUTORS WANT YOU TO KNOW

TRUE COMPANIONSHIP ACROSS MANY LEVELS—spiritual, emotional, and physical—is much more satisfying than just an intense physical connection. If you were driving ahead of a friend and got pulled over by the police for speeding, you'd call your friend and warn them the first chance you got, right? Our sentiments exactly! Sixteen of the contributors responded to my request for last words on the topics they wrote about, and here's the wisdom they have to offer:

Jamie Reid, "State of Confusion"

Embrace your sexuality. If you find you like something a little different than the norm, it's okay to explore—but always know the consequences. Protect yourself at all times. There are too many STDs out there! I don't care what he/she has to say about the feeling. IF THEY CAN'T WRAP UP, THEN SAY NO!

Laurence Anthony, "The Lido Deck"

Have fun. Sex should be fun and it's not some formality where business contracts are signed. Have a joke, laugh, enjoy yourself. But be respectful. Respect is important in sex whether you're dating or just having sex. Sex is actually a sacred thing and people are opening up when they're having sex with you. Remember that.

Desiree Dorite, "Fresh Fruit"

You do not have to have sex if you don't want to. I know that seems super obvious, but you'd be surprised how many people don't grasp this concept—so don't be one of those people. Nobody has the right to get mad because you're not working on their schedule of when the right time is.

Lauren Matos, "Hotel Party"

You have the right to say no! And if the other person doesn't listen, you have the right to bust their lip! If you are ever sexually assaulted, tell someone. Don't be ashamed. Don't blame yourself.

Danny Djeljosevic, "Near Miss"

If you don't talk about sex the day after it happens, it may seem like it never happened—except, you know, the ensuing emotional turmoil. If after being intimate with someone the other person gets dressed and decides to sleep on the couch, talk about it! Avoid being someone else's regret at all costs.

Adam Smith, "Checkmate"

Sex without feeling is just a short-lived attempt to feel better. Sometimes it works and sometimes it's best to ignore the temptation of that quick emotional fix. Also, nobody is safe until you have their test results. Never assume it's okay *not* to use protection, even if it's someone you think you know well.

Crystal Coburn, "Popping"

Being horny is not something to be ashamed of. Sex is not overrated, and it'll be as good as you make it—although sometimes waiting for the other person to get it right will take too long. I've learned to take control of my own sexual happiness.

Gabrielle Unda, "In Between Roots and Wings"

Become an expert on your own sexuality. Take the time to get to know yourself, including what feels good and what you're comfortable with. If you're not sure, ask questions! Find an older, knowledgeable person that you trust to talk to about sex. Your friends might not be able to offer you the support or information you need.

Sarah Lawless, "His Drip for a Teardrop"

Sex has a soundtrack. When it comes to all the seemingly hilarious noises associated with intercourse, a girl is better off laughing it off rather than sweating it or being embarrassed. Confidence in between the sheets is the most striking thing one could ever bring to the bedroom: eye contact, eye contact, eye contact! Honesty is another biggie, so don't give your partner false hope by "faking it."

T.C., "Nothing but You"

Sexual intercourse is not enough! Foreplay is definitely necessary, especially for women. If both individuals in a relationship haven't mastered the art of fellatio, kissing, and caressing the body from head to toe, they are missing out. Sexual pleasure is so much more than the intercourse itself. If you don't have the sort of relationship with your partner where you can be open about your needs, then you should not be having sex with them. It's a waste of time!

Alyssa Varin, "Brooklyn Nights"

Sex is complicated. Don't expect to have an emotionally devoid sexual experience and feel good about it afterward. Sex with exes and friends is dangerous territory. Navigate it carefully if you dare.

Charles Keeranan, "Backseat Baseball"

Guys, think with the head on your shoulders when making important decisions about love/sex—not with your other head. Sex changes everything, and I mean EVERYTHING.

Amethyst, "Wonder Woman"

Your partner's sexual personality should be compatible with yours for sex to be enjoyable. For example, a woman with an intense, dominating sexual style might be too intimidating to a guy with more demure sexual tastes. Make sure you want the same thing out of the sexual experience as your partner does. As long as you do, it's totally possible to have great sex with hookups or casual sex buddies. Be honest with what you're looking for—ulterior motives where sex is concerned are very, very dangerous.

Anthony Paul, "Little Head"

Having a baby is a big responsibility, but it is not a dream crusher. There are many people who are more motivated to reach their goals after having a child, but knowing that you're responsible for someone for at least eighteen years is no joke. People who think it's glamorous to have a baby at a young age need to think again.

Adrianna Eisner, "It Seemed So Harmless"

Talking during sex can be just as rewarding as the act itself. Hearing the words "I love you" or "you're amazing" can help you explode. You've got to be in a place where you feel free to act on impulse, which is why trust is so key. So guys, having the girl you love and the girl you screw is not cool. It doesn't make you a player—it makes you selfish.

Michael Villo, "She's Pigeon-Toed and Wears a Scarf"

You're young. It's a given that you're going to screw up a shitload—relationships included. If you're going to take that step and have sex, don't do it just to please someone else. Do it because you're ready. Do it because you want to.

CHECK YOURSELF

AS YOUR LAST BIT OF BUSINESS IN *LAID,* TAKE SOME TIME and create your own Top 10 list. You're welcome to copy and paste phrases from any of the stories or sections that you've read. However, it will mean so much more if you put it in your own words.

After reading this book, you are just as well equipped to be a sexpert as I am. It has been proven that people retain the most information when they teach others. Can you say "win-win"? I hope you go on and share your own Top 10 list with the people in your life that you want to positively impact, just as I have done with you.

1. ______________________________
2. ______________________________
3. ______________________________
4. ______________________________
5. ______________________________
6. ______________________________
7. ______________________________
8. ______________________________
9. ______________________________
10. ______________________________

EXCELLENT SEX ED RESOURCES

THERE IS NO SINGLE WORKSHOP, WEBSITE, CONVERSAtion, or book that provides all of the information you will ever want—or need—to know about sex; your sexual education is truly a lifelong commitment. *Laid* may be one of the first steps you've taken toward self-sexual education, but it certainly should not be your last.

SEX ED SITES

coolnurse.com (accurate & comprehensive info)
goaskalice.com (best Q & A)
LaidTheBook.com (the book's website)
plannedparenthood.org (USA find your sexual health clinic)
rainn.org (rape, abuse, and incest national network USA)
scarleteen.com (my fav sex ed site)
sexetc.org (a website for teens by teens)
sexualityandu.ca (interactive sexual education)
spiderbytes.ca (basic sex ed info)
wavaw.ca (women against violence against women Canada)

SEXUAL ED BOOKS

100 Questions You'd Never Ask Your Parents, by Elisabeth Henderson and Nancy Armstrong, Uppman Publishing, 2007.

All the Way: Sex for the First Time, by Kim Martyn, Sumach Press, 2004.

A Queer Geography: Journeys Toward a Sexual Self, by Frank Browning, Farrar, Straus and Giroux, 1998.

Real Girl Real World: A Guide to Finding Your True Self, by Heather M. Gray and Samantha Phillips, Seal Press, 2005.

S.E.X.: The All-You-Need-To-Know Progressive Sexuality Guide to Get You Through High School and College, by Heather Corinna. Da Capo, 2007.

Sex Matters for Women: A Complete Guide to Taking Care of Your Sexual Self, by Sallie Foley, Sally A. Kope, and Dennis P. Sugrue, The Guilford Press, 2002.

Talk Sex: Answers to Questions You Can't Ask Your Parents, by Sue Johanson, Penguin, 1989.

The "Go Ask Alice" Book of Answers: A Guide to Good Physical, Sexual, and Emotional Health, by Columbia University Health Education Program, Holt, 1998.

The Secret Language of Girls, by Josey Vogels, Thomas Allen & Son, 2002.

Yes Means Yes: Visions of Female Sexual Power and A World Without Rape, edited by Jaclyn Friedman and Jessica Valenti, Seal Press, 2008.

ANSWERS TO CHAPTER 3 CHECKPOINT

1. Myth. HPV is the most common STI in the US. Chlamydia is the most commonly *diagnosed* STI among teens. Many people live with HPV without knowing it.
2. Myth. HPV is the most underreported.
3. Reality. According to the Campaign for Our Children, Inc.
4. Reality. Bladder infections cannot technically be transmitted through sexual intercourse. However, the friction generated during intercourse can introduce bacteria to the urinary tract or bladder, which can result in an infection. In order to avoid bladder infections from sexual activity, always urinate and clean your genitals after intercourse or heavy petting.
5. Reality. There are over one hundred strains of HPV, some of which have been linked to cervical cancer.
6. Reality. These average absent fathers pay less than $800 annually for child support. According to Brein, M.T, and Willis, R.J. "Costs and Consequential for Fathers"

in R. Maynard, Ed. *Kids Having Kids.* The Urban Institute Press, 1997.

7. Reality. Birth control may help prevent ovarian cancer and cancer of the uterine lining.
8. Myth. As with any surgery, abortion carries some risks. Abortion is, however, around ten times less risky than childbirth.
9. Myth. STIs can be transmitted through oral sex, frottage (rubbing two sets of genitals directly together) or manual sex (fingering/hand jobs). Some are transmitted through bodily fluids, but some can be transmitted without sharing any fluids at all. That is why it is important that safe sex is practiced throughout the entire sexual experience and not just at the last minute.
10. Reality. Check.

MEET THE EDITOR

© Maya Washington

SHANNON TERESA BOODRAM IS A YOUNG JOURNALIST and a lifelong learner. She began her role as a sexual educator when she was nineteen, when she appeared on a Canadian National network as a contestant, wearing a SaveYourCherry.com T-shirt. Since then, she has gone on to host a seven-part sex ed podcast series produced by Imperial Music Studios, she was an expert panelist on MuchMusic *MuchTalks: Teen Sex* alongside Sue Johanson, and she has spoken to various youth groups and newspapers on her brand of sexual education.

Shannon is a graduate of Centennial College in print journalism and has gone on to work as a TV host for *High School Rush* on Rogers TV and as a freelance writer for publications like CBC.ca, *Metro News,* and *Cream World* magazine. She has interviewed and written features on Natasha Bedingfield, Robin Thicke, Robin Antin (manager of the Pussycat Dolls), Simple Plan, Girlicious, and Deborah Cox, to name a few.

She runs a women's networking site (www.shannonteresa.com); a blog with her best friend, Andrea Lewis (www.thosegirlsarewild.com); and her own photography business. She has volunteered with Big Brothers Big Sisters, as a coach of youth basketball, as an intern with MTV Canada, and as a mentor for an inner-city youth organization.

She considers herself a writer first and has had a lifelong relationship with words. You are holding her proudest accomplishment in your hands right now. To continue the discussion on sex and sexuality with me, please visit *Laid* at www.laidthebook.com

MEET THE CONTRIBUTORS

Amethyst

I have lived in Seattle since birth. I will be graduating from the University of Washington with a degree in physiology and another in sexuality and gender studies. I plan to attend medical school, and in fifteen years I want to be known as the visionary gynecologist who is changing the landscape of women's health. As for this book, I wrote because I wanted people to remember that it's possible to have safe, orgasmic, highly enjoyable casual sex without any strings attached, while still maintaining a solid sense of self and self-esteem. Thanks to my pop tart friend who taught me what it was to feel from the depths of my heart and my body.

Andrea

My name is Andrea and I grew up in Quebec before moving to Ontario, where I now live. I am currently out of school, traveling, meeting new people, and learning about myself. Self-exploration has always been a big part of my life—hence my story. I decided to contribute to *Laid* because I hope no one does that . . . lay something on someone else and take control. My story is dedicated to Good For Her and all other sexually empowering establishments.

Laurence Anthony

My name is Laurence Anthony and I'm a writer, poet, actor, producer, and graduate of Ryerson University. I founded Hot-Seat Enterprises Inc., an entertainment production company, and I also write and perform poetry in Toronto and in New York. I wanted to write for this book because I wanted to contribute a positive work of art about love and sex. I've admired Shannon's work for a while, and her honesty when writing about relationships while empowering youth matched my own. I strongly dedicate my piece to my mother, my grandparents, Hummingbird, and love itself.

Carla

I currently reside in Fort Lauderdale, Florida, and I'm about to finish school with a BA in English and public communication and a minor in European history at Florida Atlantic University. I will be pursuing my master's in communication in the fall of 2010. I thank everyone who took the time to read my story, and my advice to readers is, never put yourself in a situation that you would normally question.

Crystal Coburn

I just graduated from York University with an honors BA in kinesiology, but I've always been a writer, even before I knew I was one. Right now I'm writing for the student newspaper at George Brown College. I also lend my hand to freelancing opportunities that have something more than money to offer me. When I was asked to write for this book, I wasn't just caught off guard, I was excited. Sex is not something I speak or write about so candidly, so by contributing to this book I was able to examine my self-awareness. Overall I hope the readers will come away with a clearer understanding of themselves and what they're comfortable doing. This story is for Aaron, whose selflessness has taught me more about myself than I ever thought I could learn.

Danny Djeljosevic

Danny Djeljosevic is a blogger, minor internet personality, and freelance writer of comic books, screenplays, prose, party banners, and whatever the hell else you're willing to pay him for. A University of Florida graduate, he currently lives in San Diego, California, and runs a blog at www.dfordjeljosevic.blogspot.com. When approached to write for the book, he had only one story in mind for it. He knew it was perfect because it had everything an anthology about young sex should have: contraceptives, alcohol, and bad decisions. All the necessary bits without, y'know, the SEX.

Desiree Dorite

I am currently pursuing a career in marketing at a community college. I have been a journal writer since before *Gossip Girl* made it cool, and to me, writing for this book was just an extension of one of my journals. I hope that people read my story and change their view on people who wait—we're not all squares or ugly. We can be just as desirable as anyone else; we just choose not to let people have us. My story is dedicated to my younger cousin AP: I want you to be able to turn around and write the exact same thing when you're my age!

Michelle D'Souza

I have been in New York long enough to practically forget that the rest of the world exists! I am a university student studying geography and I hope to graduate and become a high school teacher. I contributed to this book because when Shannon contacted me, I just knew I was meant to share my story in order to help someone else. Protect yourself if you're going to do anything sexually! I had to throw that in there one more time.

Adrianna Eisner

I immigrated to Surrey, British Columbia, at age six. I always knew I wanted to be a journalist and graduated from Toronto's

Ryerson University. I'm currently the editor-in-chief of a magazine. Writing for *Laid* was my way to let go of being raped and find peace of mind. I needed this book more than it needed me. I hope my story teaches that intuition is the most important voice you will ever hear. I'm blessed with a strong support system. My mom is my rock and I know she'll always be there. My best friend, Samaya, who *always* answers my calls. And finally Bighead: Your love and support make me realize my worth.

Jae

The person I was at that time I wrote "Stolen Fruit" is very different from who I am today. I've regained self-confidence and self-love. I've even taken up a hobby of modeling, so I must be feelin myself! I have my family, my health, my happiness, my future husband—and it's getting better every day. If you can relate to my poem or if you just feel compelled to do so, please email me at JaeLynnPlus@yahoo.com. I dedicate my story to the people in my life who push me forward and I dedicate my poem to the Detroit Police Department for, ugh, well, never mind!

Jay

I am a graduate of Coppin State University. I am currently an elementary school teacher and I'm going to the University of Maryland in 2010 to study educational counseling. I decided to contribute to this book because there are some young ladies out there who grew up in a good home, just like me, but are still naive to sexual relationships. I want to give them an eye-opening experience: my younger sister, Jessica; my three goddaughters, Janne, Savannah, and Chaliah; and my niece, Laila Grace.

Justin

I am a very focused and goal-oriented. God has brought me a long way and will continue to. I graduated from Lock Haven

University and I am now heading into the field of public relations and marketing.

Charles Keeranan

I was born in the Philippines and lived in Thailand, Indonesia, and Japan before moving to California. I'm currently a graduating senior at California State University of Northridge, majoring in English. I am the editor of a student-run literary anthology, *The Bandersnatch.* This year, I'm writing/directing a play in April and graduating in May. I would like to thank my family and friends because without them I would be nothing.

Katherine Kormos

I grew up in Pittsburgh, Pennsylvania, before returning to my hometown to study theater and English at the University of Toronto. I now work for North America's largest cruise travel agency and perform with the Oakville Drama Series. Having two younger sisters, I realized that the more often you share your stories, the greater the likelihood that they will reach someone. I would never have had the courage to share my story without my partner in crime, Chris.

Sarah Lawless

I am an eighteen-year-old living and going to university in downtown Toronto for a business degree. My goal was to get out of my small town and move on to bigger and better things in a huge city, and that's exactly what I've done. I chose to write a piece in this book because I saw Shannon Boodram on MuchMusic, and I was going through such a hard time and I just really needed a creative way to channel all the crazy emotions I was feeling at the time. I also really want to shed light on date rape and all the negative stereotypes that are associated with it. I want to let other women and young girls know that they are not alone in this.

Lauren Matos

I am originally from New Jersey, but I now live in Texas. I am majoring in psychology at the University of Texas in San Antonio, with a dream to work with young adults who suffer from mental illness. When I was asked to be a part of this book, this project was called *Save Your Cherry,* and at nineteen years old I had done just that (I'm still going strong!). I initially wanted to write about abstinence, but I decided to share my story about a terrifying night with an ex-boyfriend. It's a sad truth, but it happens all too often. I owe everything I know about anything to my mother—she taught me that my body is *my* body. Love you, Mommy!

Mia

I'm a Polynesian woman from Southern California. I am a full-time student, getting my general education done before focusing on my intended major. Family is a big part of my life, along with music and writing poetry. I chose to write in this book to share my poetry and a true experience of my own that other young women may have possibly been through. I hope readers will find it entertaining but also find that it gives a different view of things. I dedicate my poem/story to all who read it and can relate to it.

Nikol Notiq

My name is Alesia Turner (a.k.a. Nikol Notiq). I hail from the Midwestern state of Missouri—Saint Louis, to be exact. I'm attending college, and I'm a writer, poet, and (let's not forget) graphic designer. My mind is in a frenzy, but I can handle all of that. Harris-Stowe State University is a small university but the love is strong there—everybody knows everybody. My dreams ARE bigger than the state of Missouri; I'm telling you, I'm destined to be someone. I chose to be a part of this book because I thought it would be a great experience for me to reach out to others. "Sex with You" is about all the emotions you have when you are in the moment, loving this guy for whatever it is, and you just lose control. I would love to have someone tell me they love my poetry; that would mean the world to me.

Anthony Paul

I am a father first and everything else second. I tried the college thing but it was not for me; my passion is in music, so that is my current pursuit. I wanted to be a part of this book because I know there are many misconceptions about teenage and young adult pregnancy.

Jamie Reid

I was born and raised in North Carolina, and my first love has always been writing. I want for my words to speak to someone who is in my shoes right now so they can know that someone else has been there and done that. I wanted to get involved in this project because I had been fighting an ongoing battle with myself and wanted to share my story. I felt there was no one for me to really talk to without being judged. There are many to thank, and so little space. I want to thank my mother, my "mini-me," and last but not least my three best friends, M.W., D.T., and S.J.

Jaclyn Sanchez

I live in New York, frequent Europe, and hope to die somewhere in Spain. I am a soul traveler and a poet of all sorts. Writing for this book was different because I've never really written a short story. Reading Shannon's story online inspired me to tell a story that I probably should have kept to myself, but I thought, *Hey, if her story inspired me, chances are my story may inspire someone else.* I dedicate my piece to everyone who can't relate, because I'm glad that you don't have to!

Lorie Singh

I have a BA in radio and television arts, but I currently work at an office. My passion is music and my family—which will be extended by the time this book is published, as I am expecting. I decided to write for this book because when I heard about it, I thought, *If I had a kid, I would want him/her to read it.* Now that I'm about to have a kid, I thought I should tell my story in a book that I'm going to have him/her read when he/she is old enough.

Adam Smith

May 1, 1987, spawns a miracle child in San Francisco. I was predicted to be an April Fool's baby, but I guess the joke's on me. I've lived in Arizona, made friends, got in fights, fell in love, found my niche, and then moved to Florida. Florida is where you come to die, and I did many times over. Welcome to the Sunshine State. I wrote for this book because I thought my story needed to be told. Hopefully you've read it and you see why.

Stephanie Smith

I have spent the better part of my life in Ypsilanti, Michigan. I have been writing for as long as I could hold a pencil. I chose to write "Why We Don't Tell" after being raped at my former university by an athlete. I was infuriated by how I was treated by the legal system and the school I had attended for the last four years. I knew full well I was not the first woman to go through such an ordeal and unfortunately would not be the last. I do not expect to become a millionaire off my writing, but if it touches just one person, or stops one person from going down a path of self-destruction after a similar event, I will feel as though I have accomplished my goal. Thanks to all the people who supported me after the assault, most importantly my parents, my sister, Matt, and Jayden.

T.C.

I am a professional track and field athlete, and I decided to write for this book to enlighten women who have been robbed of great sexual experiences. I feel that it is important for women to share their good experiences to show women who have had bad experiences that good ones do exist. I wanted to be a part of this book because your personal experiences are what people get the most out of, not the fallacies and fantasies that are portrayed in movies. My piece is dedicated to the females who are still searching for their self-worth and haven't yet realized how sacred they are and, most importantly, how sacred their body is. I truly hope this book enlightens many individuals out there, including males.

Toccora

I was born and raised in Jersey. I chose to write for this book because when Shannon came to me about it, I was going through a lot in my life and this was a great way for me to vent and open up like I never have before. I dedicate my story to myself. I'm so proud of myself for opening up so much. I've *never* done this before, and I'm grateful to Shannon for bringing this blessing into my life.

Gabrielle Unda

I'm currently a university student, studying child- and youth care. I'm doing an internship placement at a world-renowned hospital, supporting teens struggling with substance abuse– and eating disorder–related challenges. When I wrote this story, I wanted to let other young people know that even if your experiences haven't been positive up to this point, it is still possible to be happy and to find healthy relationships. I wish each of you the courage and honesty to trust yourselves and to create your own life path filled with many wonderful experiences.

Alyssa Varin

Born and raised in New Jersey, I'm a twenty-one-year-old Rutgers University student and I'm majoring in women and gender studies. I also intern for Callen-Lorde Community Health Center, a GLBT health center in New York City. I have a passion for writing, photography, and music. I chose to be a part of this book because I thought my experience and position could provide a different perspective on sex and sexuality. When I was younger, I struggled to find resources on queer issues. I'd like to thank Jessica Valenti (of Feministing.com) for being an awesome professor. I'd also like to thank my mother for always being my biggest fan.

Holly Vatcher

I have been working with children and teens with special needs since 2003. I currently work for a school board and do respite work in the evenings and on weekends. I found out about this book by watching the national TV station MuchMusic when Shannon was on. I visited her site, and as a longtime blogger, I already had something I could submit for her book. Many people looked away when I told them I was a virgin, so I wanted to share this story with everyone to let them know it's okay to say no. So I dedicate this story to everyone that may be struggling in the same way as I did. Someone is out there for you, and you *are* worth the wait.

Michael Villo

I'm a twenty-year-old trying to figure out what to do with himself. I'm taking a much needed break from college in order to explore, to write, and to paint, until I'm ready to settle down and study. To get published is one thing, but to have it be something so personal, so honest, makes it pretty difficult to just put out there. I thought, *I can regret the awful things I've done or I can share the lessons learned.* My piece is dedicated to the people I love. You know who you are!

Lakia Williams

I am an aspiring actress, writer, and director. I have a BA in theater arts from Southern University. I'm interested in sex ed because there really weren't any role models or sources available to me; although we had health in high school, we really didn't get that much insight on sex. And if I knew back then what I know now, I would still be a virgin. So I'm here today to tell my story and help our teens make better choices in life. I hope you females and males out there really take the time to read each story and feel it. By reading our stories, you see firsthand. I would like to dedicate my story to those in the world that are still virgins—stay that way until marriage.

Matthew Williams

I'm Matthew, a.k.a. Jigabod Walker, and I'm a freelance writer/musician and educator hailing from Augusta, Georgia. I have a BA in history and a minor in sociology, and I currently teach at Hephzibah High School. My interests include social activism, promoting love, songwriting, producing, and Jesus Christ. I dedicate my piece to all young people to encourage celibacy until marriage and to help make a clear distinction between true love and youthful lusts.

The following contributors couldn't be reached for biographical statements:
Derek, Emma Johnson, Olympia, Stacy Rees, and Sheila

ACKNOWLEDGMENTS

I'VE SPENT MY WHOLE LITERARY LIFE READING ACKNOWLEDGMENTS at the backs of books, so you've got to give me a moment to flip out over how surreal this is—WOOO!

Okay, now down to business! My understanding is that this is the place where I can be totally honest and unbearably grateful (although I can't seem to shake my fab Seal Press editor's advice, *"Don't make it one of those drawn out Oscar speeches"*).

So before I get to the big speech I'm going to start with the big confession: Dear reader, I am terrified! When I was searching for contributors for *Laid* I promised people they would not be sharing their secrets in vain and if they wrote the things society told us to keep to ourselves they could really help someone else. I am super-protective of everyone who trusted me with their stories and I pray that in return each reader learned something rather than judged someone.

The fact that you've read this far has to be a good sign, so my first thanks goes to my readers for taking the time to, well, read! Second, I have to shift the spotlight to my amazing coauthors—all thirty-seven of ya! Special thanks to Toccora,

Renee, Emily, Lauren, and Jamie—the most supportive strangers I've ever met.

Okay, now for my big, short Oscar speech. Lauren Elizabeth Boodram, I love you! My big sister, my big huge rock who stood by me from start to finish. Can you imagine what this book would have been like without your support? Let's be real, it would be nonexistent! Second, mom and dad, thank you for being proud of me. Dad, thanks for being the first person to read the first draft. After he read my story he told me, "I was reading it thinking, wow, this is shocking, but Shannon's a good storyteller." Mom, you weren't so onboard at first, but the conversations we've had about sex because of this book reaffirm my belief in how much good it can do for others. I hope every reader gets the chance to have such honest conversations with his/her parents/mentors.

Arnold Goswewich, my agent, I don't know if I ever told you this, but I half-heartedly gave up on the idea that this book would ever be published—but you didn't. Thanks to Alana, my four-years-younger cousin who unknowingly gave me the idea to begin this project. Thanks to my best friends, Andrea Lewis, Paul Jefferies, and Tabia Charles. Thanks for never getting tired of me talking about this book and for supporting me!

Finally, Seal Press, my dream factory, and Brooke Warner, my editor, and everybody who submitted a piece that I did not use—thank you for teaching me!

SELECTED TITLES FROM SEAL PRESS

For more than thirty years, Seal Press has published groundbreaking books. By women. For women. Visit our website at www.sealpress.com. Check out the Seal Press blog at www.sealpress.com/blog.

Full Frontal Feminism: A Young Woman's Guide to Why Feminism Matters, by Jessica Valenti. $15.95, 1-58005-201-0. A sassy and in-your-face look at contemporary feminism for women of all ages.

In Love and In Danger: A Teen's Guide to Breaking Free of Abusive Relationships, by Barrie Levy, MSW. $12.95, 1-58005-187-1. Updated with expanded resources, this revised edition continues to speak directly to young adults about dating violence.

Invisible Girls: The Truth about Sexual Abuse, by Dr. Patti Feuereisen with Caroline Pincus. $16.95, 1-58005-301-7. An important book for teenage girls, young women, and those who care about them, that gives hope and encouragement to sexual abuse survivors by letting them know that they're not alone and that there are many roads to healing.

Listen Up: Voices from the Next Feminist Generation, edited by Barbara Findlen. $16.95, 1-58005-054-9. A collection of essays featuring the voices of today's young feminists on racism, sexuality, identity, AIDS, revolution, abortion, and much more.

The Purity Myth: How America's Obsession with Virginity Is Hurting Young Women, by Jessica Valenti. $24.95, 1-58005-253-3. With her usual balance of intelligence and wit, Valenti presents a powerful argument that girls and women, even in this day and age, are overly valued for their sexuality—and that this needs to stop.

Valencia, by Michelle Tea. $14.95, 1-58005-238-X. A fast-paced account of one girl's search for love and high times in the dyke world of San Francisco. By turns poetic and frantic, Valencia is a visceral ride through the queer girl underground of the Mission.